Best
of the
Children's
Market

A Collection of Over 80 Articles
and Stories Published by
Leading Children's Magazines

INSTITUTE *of*
CHILDREN'S
LITERATURE

PUBLISHED BY THE INSTITUTE OF CHILDREN'S LITERATURE

Editors
Pamela Glass Kelly
Mary Spelman

Contributing Editors
Brett Warren
Pat Conway

Copy Editor
Cheryl de la Guéronnière

Production
Marni McNiff

Cover Design
Joanna Horvath

Contents

Good News for Writers!

The Best is designed to serve as a window on what children's magazine editors are buying and contemporary youngsters are reading. In showcasing 84 stories and articles from 49 different magazines, this collection represents virtually every type of periodical published for young readers and illustrates the considerable range of subject matter and approaches possible in the field. If you aren't familiar with today's juvenile magazines and their opportunities for writers, you're in for a happy surprise.

Are you thinking of writing a simple bedtime story for young children? A tale of adventure for middle-grade readers? A problem story for teenagers? You'll see examples of each in these pages. If you're interested in fact as well as fiction, you'll find how-to pieces (recipes, crafts, science experiments), colorful depictions of historical events and personalities, articles about animals and archaeology, self-help and sports, physiology and photography.

Where did all this material come from? Where did the writers get their ideas? A special feature of this anthology is the "From the Author" column that accompanies almost every story and article. Here the writers describe their diverse backgrounds and experience and share with you the techniques they used to create, develop, and market their successful manuscripts. They have been extraordinarily generous with their comments; we think you'll find their words a source of inspiration as well as a treasure trove of practical advice.

How the contents are organized

Obviously, there's an enormous difference between what a 6-year-old can read—and enjoy reading—and what will appeal to a 16-year-old. Traditionally, children's publishers have broken their audience down into three main age groups: youngest readers/listeners (ages 3-7); intermediate readers (ages 8-12); and teenage readers. For ease of organization, this book follows those broad divisions.

At the same time, you'll notice considerable variation in reading level and subject choice within each section, as well as some overlapping between sections. For example, some of the selections included in "Youngest Readers" are clearly designed as read-aloud material for preschool children (ages 3-5), while others target beginning readers (primary graders, ages 6-9). Stories and articles aimed at older intermediates may appeal to young teens as well (an audience categorized in the trade as adolescent readers, ages 10-14), while the teen section ranges from adolescent material to sophisticated, near-adult reading.

You'll also notice that many children's publications are designed to appeal to a considerable range of readership age and ability. *Highlights for Children*, for example, is published for ages 2-12, which means you'll see it represented here in both the youngest and intermediate sections.

The name of the magazine where each selection appeared is followed by its readership span. Another useful notation is the word count of each piece—in itself a guide to its intended readership. As you'll learn, magazine editors set definite word lengths tied to readership age levels for the stories and articles they publish.

If all this sounds confusing, don't worry! As you page through the anthology, you'll soon get a feel for what's involved in writing for each major age group, from types of subject matter and approach to vocabulary, style, and appropriate length.

As you'll see, each age-level section is further divided into fiction and nonfiction selections. If you've thought only in terms of writing fictional stories, the factual articles included here will come as an eye-opener. Articles, too, tell stories—about almost everything under the sun. They're fun to write and fun to read. They can also be your ticket to publication, since children's magazines publish roughly twice as much nonfiction as fiction in a given year. Here's a brief rundown of what you can expect to find in the pages ahead:

Youngest readers. Fiction for this age level is characterized by clear focus, lively pace, and liberal use of dialogue. Some of the stories are pure fun, while others deal with real-life problems; still others appeal to the young child's enjoyment of magic and adventure. Nonfiction taps into children's endless curiosity about the unfolding world around them, whether close to home (How many times a minute does my heart beat? What is soap made of?) or far away (How do penguins tell each other apart? What would it have been like to grow up in ancient Egypt?). Activity projects abound—recipes, games, simple science experiments.

Intermediate readers. The range here is a broad one in terms of approach, subject matter, and reading level (vocabulary, sentence structure, complexity of ideas, length). In fiction, almost anything goes—humor, adventure, sports, problem stories, science fiction, stories with historical settings. Nonfiction is equally diverse, as indicated by the variety of markets represented in this category—not only general interest magazines like *Boys' Quest, U*S* Kids,* and *Cricket*, but special interest publications like *Cobblestone, Muse,* and *Odyssey*.

Teenage readers. The stories included in this section reflect the spectrum of contemporary teen experience, with its testing of identity and its difficult moral choices. Note that religious periodicals account for a substantial portion of the teen fiction market. Nonfiction, the staple of most teen magazines, tends to focus on social and personal issues, along with profiles of people in sports and the arts. At the upper end of the spectrum in both fiction and nonfiction, the writing approaches adult subtlety and complexity.

How to find an individual selection or market

At the end of the anthology, you'll find three indexes. The first gives an alphabetical list of titles. The second lists authors in alphabetical order, and the third lists the magazines in which the stories and articles appeared.

We think you'll find this collection entertaining as well as instructive. Use it as a tool to learn how other writers have met editorial standards and to explore new directions for your own writing. Use it, too, for pleasure—to renew acquaintance with the child you once were.

The Editors

Mary Ellen Had a Sheep

By Karen Troncale

Mary Ellen woke up and found a sheep crying in her bedroom.

"Why are you crying?" she asked.

"You dropped your book of nursery rhymes last night," said the sheep. "And I fell off my page."

"I'm sorry," said Mary Ellen.

"Now I can't find the page where I belong," said the sheep.

"Don't worry," said Mary Ellen. "I'll help you find it."

Mary Ellen picked up the book and sat down next to the sheep. She began to turn the pages.

"Do you belong here?" she asked. She read, "Baa, baa, black sheep, have you any wool?"

"No, no, no," interrupted the sheep. "My wool is white."

"Oh yes, you're right," said Mary Ellen. She turned several more pages. Then she read, "Mary had a little lamb."

"I'm not a lamb, I'm a full-grown sheep. And I don't think I'll ever get back!" He began to cry again.

"There, there," said Mary Ellen. She patted his head. "If you don't get back, I'll take care of you."

"But I don't belong here!" The sheep cried even louder.

"Don't cry," said Mary Ellen. "We're not finished with the book yet." She quickly turned the rest of the pages. But she didn't see any more rhymes about sheep.

"Are you sure you fell out of this book?" she asked.

"Of course, I'm sure," said the sheep. "It's the only book you dropped."

"I'll go through the book again," said Mary Ellen. She turned the pages slowly, one by one. Suddenly she cried out, "This must be the page!" She read, "Little Boy Blue, come blow your horn, the sheep's in the meadow, the cow's in the corn."

"That's it!" shouted the sheep. He jumped up in joy. When he came down, he landed right back in the book of nursery rhymes.

Mary Ellen looked down at the sheep on the page.

"Good-bye," she said. "It was nice meeting you." Then she closed the book and put it back on the shelf.

Ladybug
2–6 years
335 words

From the Author

I wrote this story for a *Children's Writer* contest. I began with a "bare bones" story: writing one main sentence for each paragraph and developing the story from there. When the story didn't place in the contest, I sent it to *Ladybug*. Having read several copies and their guidelines, I felt the story would be a good match for their publication. They accepted it with minor changes.

I've written for *Boys' Life, Wild Outdoor World, Clubhouse, Jr., Guide,* and adult magazines too.

My advice to new writers is: *read, read, read.* Read the magazines you want to write for. Send for guidelines and follow them exactly. Enter contests—it's great practice, and winning something (even if it's not first place) is a great ego boost. Join or start a writers' group—the input you'll receive is priceless.

The Bridge of Liars

By Bonnie Highsmith Taylor

Franz and Grandfather were walking to town. A rabbit ran across the road.

"What a big rabbit!" said Grandfather.

"Why, that was nothing," said Franz. "Once I saw a rabbit as big as a cow."

"Really?" said Grandfather. "How interesting. And have you heard that the bridge we are coming to breaks down when someone who doesn't tell the truth crosses over it?"

"Uh—perhaps the rabbit was only as big as a goat," said Franz.

"Perhaps," said Grandfather.

"Or maybe it was only as big as a dog," Franz said.

"Maybe," said Grandfather.

They came to the bridge. Franz stopped.

"Now I remember," he said. "It was only as big as a—"

"A rabbit?" asked Grandfather.

"Yes," said Franz. "A rabbit."

Highlights for Children
2–12 years
122 words

Late for Lunch

By Betty G. Birney

Dora Mouse was in a hurry to get to Skunk's house. *I do not want to be late for lunch,* thought Dora.

Dora heard someone call out, "Help!" She looked behind a toadstool. There was a fuzzy caterpillar. All his legs were caught in a spider's web.

"Can you help me?" asked the caterpillar.

"Yes, I can," said Dora. She carefully untangled the web and let the caterpillar out.

"Thank you," said the caterpillar.

"You are welcome," said Dora, "but I must hurry on. I do not want to be late for lunch."

As Dora passed a hollow log, she heard a voice call out, "Help!" Dora looked inside the hollow log and found a chubby chipmunk.

"I am stuck," said the chipmunk. "Can you help me?"

"Yes, I can," said Dora. She gave the chipmunk a big push, and he popped out of the hollow log.

"I would stay to talk," said Dora, "but I must hurry on. I do not want to be late for lunch."

As Dora passed by the brook, she heard a voice call out, "Help!" Dora saw a large moth lying by the water.

"My wings are wet and I cannot fly," said the moth. "Can you help me?"

"Yes, I can," said Dora. She fanned the moth's wings until they dried and he could fly again.

"Thank you," said the moth.

"You are welcome," said Dora, "but I must hurry on. I do not want to be late for lunch."

When Dora arrived at Skunk's house, she asked, "Am I late for lunch?"

"Yes, you are," said Skunk. "But you are not late for the party."

"What party?" asked Dora. Just then, Dora's friends came out of Skunk's kitchen. The caterpillar, the chipmunk, and the moth were there, along with rabbits and owls and weasels from the forest. They gave Dora a bouquet of flowers and shouted, "Surprise!"

Dora was surprised. "Why are my friends giving ME a party?" she asked.

Skunk smiled. "Because you always take the time to help a friend. And you are hardly ever late for lunch!".

Humpty Dumpty's Magazine
4–6 years
349 words

From the Author

I had been thinking about the theme of being on time: a character is late *but* for a very good reason. Helping others is always a good topic for preschoolers.

I had been writing animal characters for a television series, and I was right at home in the woods, so I selected a mouse as protagonist to show that even a tiny creature can have a powerful effect on others.

A clear beginning, middle, and end will make any story work. The beginning: Dora doesn't want to be late. The middle: three things happen that threaten to make her late. The end: Dora is rewarded for her helpful nature with a surprise party. The same formula works for books or films.

Over the past 15 years, I've written books, stories, software, and live-action and animated television series. I always revise (20, even 30 times) before submitting a manuscript.

Zack and the Cornstalk

By Joanne Coughlin

1 There once was a boy named Zack who lived on a corn farm. His mom ordered him out to pick corn, so off he went to the field where 60 rows of tall corn grew. In one hour he'd picked all the corn from 10 rows. What fraction of the corn-field had Zack picked?

2. Zack made 40 bundles of corncobs and placed them on the ground side by side. Crows flew off with eight of the bundles. What fraction of the bundles did the crows get?

3. By mid-afternoon, Zack had become bored. He began to climb one of the tallest cornstalks just to see what he could see from up there. He climbed 1/10 of the way up, then paused. He went on an-other 2/10, took a deep breath, and finally went 2/10 more of the way up when he noticed a huge, glorious castle in the air. What fraction of the stalk had Zack climbed when he noticed the castle?

4. Zack climbed off the stalk and entered the castle. He wandered into one great room, then another and another. He had explored 40 of the 50 great rooms of the castle when suddenly, he met the giant! What fraction of the castle had Zack explored before he met the giant?

5. The giant was a friendly one. He sat surrounded by sack after sack of gold coins. After Zack and the giant chatted for a few hours, Zack said it was get-ting late and that he had to return home to his mom. The friendly giant insisted that Zack take 70 of his 700 sacks of gold coins with him as a gift. What fraction of the sacks of coins did the giant give to happy, lucky Zack?

Good Apple Newspaper
7–10 years
288 words

From the Author

As a teacher of every grade level for the past 26 years, I've had a strong desire to share origi-nal ideas that I've used effectively in my class-room with other educators.

"Zack and the Cornstalk" came about because I had been teaching fractions to third graders and needed to make this math concept relevant yet entertaining. I decided to write a series called Fractioned Fairy Tales to allow my students to solve word problems involving fractions in a stimulating way that involved humor. "Goldi-socks and the Four Scared Bears" and "The Three Big Pigs" were just two of several more articles that followed "Zack and the Cornstalk." My en-tire series was published. I was thrilled!

Turning my lessons into entertaining articles helps me think through and present my lessons more effectively. Sitting down at the computer and revising my work as I go along is the easiest way for me to write. When I'm ready to print out a page, it is just the way I want it to read.

Fifteen years ago, I completed a course at the Institute of Children's Literature and had my first article published shortly thereafter. I have been writing, mostly for educators' magazines, ever since. Writing has made me feel I've achieved something meaningful to share with others.

The Night Before Thanksgiving

By Virginia L. Kroll

I was so excited. Monday would be Thanksgiving Day, and all my relatives were coming to Grandma's. I got to come a whole two days early to help Grandma get everything ready.

"You're a good help," she said, "and great company too."

"So are you, Grandma," I said. That made her laugh.

We baked four pies—two apple and two pumpkin. We put them out on the wide porch railing to cool off. It was dark. The streetlights cast a golden glow on Grandma's porch. The steam rose out of the pies like filmy ribbons floating on the air.

"The smell of that steam is making me hungry, Grandma," I said.

"Cinnamon and spices do know how to tease a tummy," she said. Then she gave me a snack of oatmeal sprinkled with sugar and cinnamon.

She sunk her hands into the dish suds to tackle the mess and said, "When you're finished eating, you can check on the pies."

"You're asking God to bless him 'cause he stole, Grandma? Are you saying stealing is all right?"

I added my spoon and bowl to the sink and opened the door. I froze. One pie was already missing. Two hands were grabbing another as I stood there gaping.

It was a moment before I could get myself back to the kitchen. "Grandma," I whispered, "a man stole the pies."

"What?" Grandma gasped, wiping her hands on her apron as she ran out to look.

She clucked her tongue. "Did you get a look at him?"

"Not close," I admitted. "It's dark."

"Well, God bless him," Grandma said, picking up the remaining pies.

"He needs all the blessings he can get if he's hungry enough to steal somebody's Thanksgiving dessert."

I opened the door and followed her in.

"God bless him?" I said. "He robbed our pies, Grandma. Now there won't be enough dessert for all of us. Why would you say, 'God bless him'?"

"We won't go hungry for want of two pies, child," Grandma said. "We can always open that box of cookies I've got stored. Maybe that poor fellow is starving. God bless him."

"You're asking God to bless him 'cause he stole, Grandma? Are you saying stealing is all right?"

"Stealing's wrong," Grandma said. "So is hunger. He needs all the blessings he can get if he's hungry enough to steal somebody's Thanksgiving dessert."

"Grandma?" I asked. "What if he took the pies just 'cause they were there?"

"Then God bless him all the more," Grandma answered. "Anyone who steals just to steal needs double the blessing."

I shrugged and said, "I don't always understand you, Grandma, but I sure always love you." Then I whispered, "God bless him" too.

She pulled me close and hugged me tightly. Her apron smelled just like the pies. I breathed deeply, thinking about Thanksgiving Day. I couldn't wait. It would be wonderful—cookies and all!

October 12 is Canadian Thanksgiving.

Story Friends
4–9 years
458 words

From the Author

There is never enough room in our refrigerator for all the Thanksgiving food. So, on the night before, we always put some of it on our enclosed front porch. I got the idea for this story when my daughter Katya, then four years old, asked, "What if a robber came in and stole all the pies?"

We had a conversation similar to the one between the child and the grandma in "The Night Before Thanksgiving." It followed naturally that I should write it in first person, from Katya's point of view. Because I geared the story toward her age group, and because Katya virtually gave me the story, the word count (under 500) simply happened.

"The Night Before Thanksgiving" was first published in *Primary Treasures* (November 1991) and later in *Story Friends* (October 1998). In both cases, I chose the markets because I love the messages they impart, and I enjoy working with their wonderful editors.

I have been a published writer for 15 years. I have written more than 30 children's books and 1,600 magazine articles. People say I'm prolific, but I think I'm lucky. As a children's writer, I've been blessed with the most valuable resources imaginable: three daughters, three sons, and one grandchild. I've based dozens of stories on actual events and quotes, just like the one from Katya one night before Thanksgiving. Raw gems come "out of the mouths of babes," as the saying goes. If you put them in worthy settings and polish them a bit, their sparkle will capture the attention of readers for years to come.

The Blue Demon
A Chinese Tale

Retold by William Groeneweg

In the days of the Great Emperor of China, a merchant had to travel many miles to sell his goods in a city by the sea.

When he arrived, a terrible storm struck. The rain pounded down on his head and clothes. The merchant ran to an inn; but it was full. He ran to a second inn; it was full, too. The merchant was wet, and very cold by now.

At the third inn the innkeeper said, "I have a room, but it's haunted. If a guest goes in, he soon runs out screaming. No one ever stays in that room all night long."

"I'm cold and dripping wet. I have to have a room," said the merchant. "I'll take it."

"Very well," said the innkeeper. "It's up to you. But pay in advance!"

After the merchant paid his money, the innkeeper led him down a long corridor. He stopped at a crimson door and unlocked it. He pushed the door open, then stepped back.

The merchant, wanting to pray before entering the room, knelt down and tapped his head three times on the floor. After this he peeked into the room. "The room looks clean and neat. I want a good breakfast tomorrow."

"You're a very silly servant," said the merchant. "If you don't get to work, I'll leave you no tip."

"If you're still here in the morning, I'll fix you a *grand* breakfast," said the innkeeper. "Goodnight."

The merchant got ready for bed. But first he took his crickets from his sleeve. He kept them there in a tiny cage. He set the cage on the table by his bed. Most merchants kept pet crickets for luck and for their music.

"I have some treats for you," said the merchant. And he smiled. "I've gathered your favorite—grub worms." He fed his crickets, then got undressed, got into bed, and fell asleep.

Late in the night the crickets began to chirp. The merchant woke up. There at the foot of his bed was a huge blue demon—with red eyes, pointed nails, and sharp teeth.

Instantly the demon turned into a squawking chicken. "Bagwok, bagwok, bagwok!"

Though the merchant was frightened, he quickly said, "You're late. Fold up my clothes and begin the dusting at once."

"What?" roared the demon.

"You're a very silly servant," said the merchant. "If you don't get to work, I'll leave you no tip."

"But I am a demon!"

"A servant."

"Demon!" shouted the demon so loud that the room shook and tiles fell from the ceiling.

"If you really are a demon, prove it," said the merchant.

"How?"

"Well," said the merchant, "change into another shape. That's what most demons do."

"Watch this," said the demon. At once he turned into a roaring lion. Though the merchant was frightened, he pretended to be calm.

"Yes, that's very good; but it's easy to turn into something big. How about something smaller, like a chicken?"

Instantly the demon turned into a squawking chicken. "Bagwok, bagwok, bagwok!"

"Quite good," said the merchant. "But can you turn into something *really* small? That's a trick! How about a grub worm?"

"Just watch!" The demon twisted and shrank into a little grub worm.

Quickly the merchant sprang out of bed, grabbed the grub worm, and fed it to his crickets.

How surprised the innkeeper was to see the merchant the next morning. He cooked up a wonderful breakfast. "Eat this, and take this bag of gold, too. With the demon gone, I can rent out that room again."

The merchant saw that he made more money and ate better killing demons than he ever had as a merchant. So from that day on, he went through China destroying demons.

That is why in China to this day there are few demons but many crickets.

Acorn
3–10 years
606 words

From the Author

"The Blue Demon" began in a store in Chinatown, where I saw cricket cages made to fit in a merchant's sleeve. This fascinated me and led me to the public library, where I read for hours about ancient Chinese life. The story began to take shape.

The story gradually developed orally, as I told it to classes of students from grades two through six as part of a literature program. After several tellings, I had it in a form I—and the kids—liked.

I sent the story to several magazines I'd sold to before, but no luck. The marketplace section of *Children's Writer* listed *Acorn* as needing stories like mine. I mailed it off in November, and in January I received an edited copy of the manuscript and a letter from the editor that said, "If you approve, phone me—we go to press this week."

I read the manuscript, and I found that the changes she had made vastly improved my story. I phoned and suggested replacing one word. It went to press that day. It was the fastest response I've ever had.

The Boomerang Smile

By Sara Murray-Plumer

Morgan woke up grumpy.

"I don't want to go to school," she said to her mother. Morgan dragged her feet over to her dresser and pulled open the drawer. She pulled out a black shirt and picked up a dirty pair of jeans off the floor. That outfit matched her mood.

"I'll tell you what," Morgan's mother said. "I'll give you one of my smiles."

Morgan's mother wiped the smile off her face and put it on Morgan's lips. Then she traded Morgan's dirty jeans for a clean pair and her black shirt for a pink one.

"You look like you could use my smile," Morgan said, slipping her smile off her face and gently placing it into Shirley's hand.

Morgan pulled on the pink shirt and adjusted her new smile. She kissed her mom and headed out to catch her bus.

The bright yellow bus pulled up in front of her house. Morgan bounced up the steps.

"Hi, Shirley!" Morgan greeted her bus driver with a smile.

Shirley frowned. "Take a seat."

"You look like you could use my smile," Morgan said, slipping her smile off her face and gently placing it into Shirley's hand.

The smile crept around the corners of Shirley's mouth, then burst into a big grin. "Thanks, Morgan," Shirley said.

At Shirley's last stop, she picked up Kyle Beverly. Kyle stomped up the bus steps. Shirley had seen his frown from a block away. She loosened her smile, and as she greeted Kyle, she let it jump right off her lips and onto his.

As the kids filed out of the bus, Tommy Johnson tripped on the sidewalk and fell. He looked down at the rip in his jeans. He felt like crying.

Kyle reached down to help Tommy up. As he did, the smile slid off his face, down his arm, and onto Tommy's face.

"Thanks, Kyle," said Tommy. Together they went into the building. Tommy headed to Mrs. Willabee's first-grade class.

Mrs. Willabee was having a bad morning. She was running late. She got to class just as the bell rang. Plopping her books on the desk, she mumbled, "Good morning, class." But she did not believe it was a good morning.

Ms. Phillips gave her smile and a small glass of soda to Megan, who had a stomachache.

As she removed her coat, she brushed against the stack of books. *Bang. Boom!* The whole stack went crashing to the floor. Mrs. Willabee sighed.

Tommy hopped out of his seat and began to pick up the books. He handed them in a neat pile to his teacher. He also gave her his smile.

Mrs. Willabee put the smile on. By lunchtime, everyone in the class was smiling.

Mrs. Willabee headed to the lunchroom. Principal Powell rushed around the corner and ran right into her.

"Sorry," he said gruffly.

"It's all right," said Mrs. Willabee, grinning. Her smile sneaked into the pocket of Principal Powell's jacket. Maybe he would use it later.

Principal Powell stormed into his office and slammed the door. After an hour, Ms. Phillips, the school secretary, thought it might be safe to deliver his mail. She knocked gently, and she slowly opened the door.

Principal Powell was tapping a pencil happily on his desk. Ms. Phillips quietly laid his mail on the corner of his desk. As she left his office, she took a part of his smile with her.

Ms. Phillips gave her smile and a small glass of soda to Megan, who had a stomachache. Since she was feeling better, Megan went back to her class and passed her smile to her best friend, Courtney. Courtney shared her smile with Susan, Troy, Ann, and Carol at recess. They carried it back to their own classes. By the end of the day, the smile had spread through the whole school.

That night Morgan got ready for bed. "Good night, Mom!" she yelled.

"There's no need to shout," said Morgan's mom. She was tired from her busy day.

"Sorry, Mom," said Morgan. She gave her mom a big hug. "And thanks."

"Thanks?" her mother asked. "For what?"

"For everything," Morgan said. Then she returned the smile to her mother with a kiss.

Pockets
6–12 years
663 words

From the Author

One enduring theme in many of my stories is that one person's efforts can make a difference. "The Boomerang Smile" demonstrates how one little girl's kindness affects her entire school.

I initially envisioned this story as a picture book. Eventually, I revised it with *Pockets* in mind. *Pockets* likes picture-oriented stories that portray a Christian lifestyle but aren't "preachy."

After I wrote the first draft, I received positive feedback during professional critiques and from my writers' group. I revised the story so many times I lost count. It was rejected 14 times before *Pockets* accepted it. With each rejection came a critical review of my manuscript and more improvements. I didn't give up on this story, which I really believed in, and it paid off.

Dialogue is one aspect of my writing that I constantly struggle to improve. I've made a conscious effort to really listen to the way people talk. I read my dialogue out loud to make sure it sounds realistic.

My writing has appeared in *Spider*, *Pockets*, and *U*S* Kids*. My book, *A Hero and a Halo*, sold more than 600 copies and raised money for the local Humane Society. I work full-time in public relations, and am also a regional advisor for the Indiana Society of Children's Book Writers and Illustrators.

The Best Word of All

By Dawn Lamuth-Higgins

Miranda drew a big bone with a black crayon. She pushed a loose curl behind her ear. *I'll draw myself looking at the bone and then I'll draw a dinosaur*, she decided.

Ms. Valino walked to the front of the class. "You are doing good work on the drawings of what you want to be when you grow up. I'd like to hear what you have chosen. Let's go around the room. We'll start with you, Darrin," she said.

"I want to be a police officer so I can ride a motorcycle," Darrin answered. He held up his picture.

Sara sat next to him. "I drew a picture of a doctor. But, I won't be the kind of doctor who gives shots," she said.

Robby answered next. "I want to be a movie star. They make a lot of money."

> *"It's probably just some big word that Miranda made up. She likes to sound smart and use big words."*

It was Miranda's turn. She wanted to study dinosaurs when she grew up. She knew that a person who did this was called a paleontologist. She held up her picture so that the class could see. "I want to be a paleontologist," she said.

"What's that?" asked Sara.

Darrin interrupted before Miranda could explain. "It's probably just some big word that Miranda made up. She likes to sound smart and use big words," he said.

The other kids laughed.

Miranda felt her face getting hot. "I did not make it up. It *is* the real name for someone who studies dinosaurs. I was just using the best word I knew," she said.

Ms. Valino held up her hand like a policeman stopping traffic. "Okay, class. Let's get control of ourselves. Yes, it is a real word. And it's a good idea to use the best words that we know. It's also time to clean up for today. By the way, we have a new stu-

> *"That's a good drawing of an apatosaurus skeleton. My favorite dinosaur is the triceratops."*

dent starting tomorrow. His name is James. Please make him feel welcome," she said.

The class rushed to put their supplies away. Miranda got ready to leave slowly. She didn't want to walk home with Darrin today, even though he lived across the street from her.

The next day, Miranda arrived at school early. She pulled out her unfinished picture. She drew a dinosaur skeleton like the one she saw at the museum.

Miranda looked up to find someone looking over her shoulder.

"Hi. I'm James, the new kid. That's a good drawing of an apatosaurus skeleton. My favorite dinosaur is the triceratops," he said.

"It's just a picture of someone who studies dinosaurs," Miranda said and pointed to the person in the drawing. She was careful not to use a big word.

"Oh, you mean a paleontologist," James said.

"Yes, that's right," said Miranda, surprised. "I'm

finished with this drawing. Why don't I show you around?"

"Great," said James.

Miranda smiled. She was thinking of the best word of all—FRIEND.

Story Friends
4–9 years
476 words

From the Author

Growing up, I was surrounded by adults. I listened to their vocabulary and loved to learn as many new words as I could. When I went to school, some kids made fun of me because they couldn't understand the words I chose.

The idea for "The Best Word of All" came from a story my husband told about meeting a three-year-old boy who said his father was a paleontologist. This little boy, who knew such a big word, reminded me of myself when I was little. The story came together from there.

This was the first story I wrote for very young readers. I wanted to write something for children who were beginning to read by themselves, so after I wrote the story I edited it twice: once to eliminate every single unneeded word to keep the word count down, and again to make sure I had used simple, easy-to-read words whenever I could. After this careful paring, I was amazed that I could tell this story in only 476 words.

I've had to be persistent in my desire to write for children. Although I've been working at writing all different types of children's stories for more than five years, I first found success in freelance writing for adult readers in newspaper features and parenting markets. "The Best Word of All" was a thrill for me because it was the first children's story that I've had published.

My volunteer work coordinating the Western Pennsylvania Society of Children's Book Writers and Illustrators conference paid off when I was trying to decide where to submit my story. I submitted it to *Story Friends* because I met the previous editor of the magazine at our SCBWI conference and knew that the magazine targeted the same age group I was thinking about when I wrote it.

Aunt Millie's Handbag

By Eileen Spinelli

One morning Aunt Millie arrived to take Ashley to the city.

Ashley had never been to the city. In fact, she had never been very far from the farm, so she was a bit nervous when they got on the bus.

"Don't worry," said Aunt Millie, patting her handbag. "We'll be fine."

Soon the bus was turning off Ashley's little country road onto a big highway. Then it stopped.

"Flat tire," announced the bus driver. He removed the old tire and took out the spare. "Oh no!" he cried. "This one's flat, too."

Aunt Millie climbed off the bus. She smiled at the driver. "Don't worry," she said, patting her handbag. With that she pulled out an air pump she used for her bicycle.

Whoosh—whoosh—whoosh. She filled both tires.

The bus driver grinned. "We're back in business!" he said, and off they went.

"My vacuum cleaner is in here somewhere," said Aunt Millie.

By the time Ashley and Aunt Millie reached the city, they were feeling hungry.

"May we go to a restaurant?" asked Ashley.

"I have an idea," replied Aunt Millie. "Let's have a restaurant come to us."

To Ashley's amazement, down the street came a hot-dog vendor pushing a cart.

"Two hot dogs with mustard, please," said Aunt Millie.

"Sorry," said the vendor. "I'm all out of mustard."

"Well, now, let me see," said Aunt Millie, digging into her handbag. "Aha!" Out came a large jar of mustard. Aunt Millie traded the mustard to the vendor for two lemonades.

Then Aunt Millie marched to the fountain in the park. "This is my favorite place to eat lunch!" she exclaimed.

But the fountain was dry.

"Must be a plumbing problem," said Aunt Millie. She rummaged around in her handbag until she found a wrench. She went right to work.

Soon the water was shooting into the air—and so was Aunt Millie.

Out of Aunt Millie's handbag came a hammer and nails.

Damp but smiling, Aunt Millie pointed to a nearby bench. "Let's sit here," she said.

But no sooner did they sit then the bench collapsed. Hot dogs and lemonade toppled to the ground.

Out of Aunt Millie's handbag came a hammer and nails. After she had repaired the bench, a second plunge into her bag produced two new hot dogs with mustard.

"The ones from home never taste as good as the ones you buy on the street," she sighed.

When they finished lunch they went to a bank so that Aunt Millie could cash a check.

There was a long line at the bank. Suddenly, the man at the head of the line sneezed, and money went flying into the air.

"Wow!" exclaimed Ashley. "It's a dollar-bill blizzard!"

"My vacuum cleaner is in here somewhere," said Aunt Millie. In a jiffy, she vacuumed up all the money and returned it to the bank teller.

The bank president was so grateful he gave Aunt MIllie a handshake and a blue pen with the bank's name on it. He gave Ashley a peppermint taffy. A photographer from the *City News* took several pictures.

After Aunt Millie and Ashley had waved good-bye, Aunt Millie said, "We must hurry to the Music Academy. The Great Spagatini is going to sing today."

"I don't think so," said Ashley when they arrived. She pointed to a sign that read: CONCERT CANCELLED.

"I don't suppose you have a bus in there."

"Well," huffed Aunt Millie. "Let's see what this is all about." She led Ashley through the side door of the theater.

"The Great Spagatini has a sore throat," the conductor announced.

Aunt Millie laughed. "Not to worry," she said. She searched in her handbag...."Squeeze this lemon," she told Ashley.

"Pour this honey," she told the conductor.

"Open wide!" she told The Great Spagatini.

Soon the singer was on stage in fine voice, and Aunt Millie and Ashley had front-row seats.

When the concert was over, the sun had set. Aunt Millie checked the cuckoo clock in her handbag. "Oh dear, I'm afraid we've missed the last bus home," she said.

Ashley's eyes fell to Aunt Millie's handbag. She sighed. "No," she said, "I don't suppose you have a bus in there."

Aunt Millie giggled. "Of course I don't have a bus in there, silly. I have something much better. But we have to go back to the park—away from the buildings and wires and trees."

When they got to an open space in the park, Aunt Millie dug into her handbag one last time.

She tugged and tugged...and pulled and pulled....

"I'm going to need help," she gasped.

Ashley helped.

Together they pulled...and pulled...and pulled... and pulled...until the handbag turned completely inside out into a hot-air balloon!

Aunt Millie fired up the propane tanks, and the balloon began to rise. "All aboard!" she called.

"All aboard!" called Ashley.

Soon they were high above the city, heading for home.

Highlights for Children
2–12 years
799 words

From the Author

In the second grade, my teacher, Miss Campbell, read my composition aloud as an example of the worst one handed in. I've been writing ever since. I've published 12 books (including *Lizzie Logan Wears Purple Sunglasses*, *Naptime/Laptime*, and *Boy, Can He Dance*), and I have 13 more under contract to come out during the next several years.

The idea for "Aunt Millie's Handbag" came to me because my mother carries a similar handbag. No hot-air balloons in hers—but practically anything else one might need. Bra strap break? Mom's purse has safety pins. Bad breath? Mom's got mints. Hungry? Crackers. Headache? Aspirin. Hands cold? Extra gloves. Diner out of doggie bags? Mom's got plastic baggies.

The list goes on and on: pens, Bandaids, cotton balls, Q-tips, nail clippers, Peds, stamps, bingo markers, tissues, prayer cards, yarn, a whistle, a comb, a picture of Frank Sinatra.

It wasn't difficult to go from the reality of my mother's purse to the fantasy of Aunt Millie's handbag. I did it by playing with the idea.

I seldom think about readership age. I just tell the story, hoping it will be good enough to appeal on some level to all ages.

How do I make my dialogue sound authentic? I listen. I listen to my memories, my grandchildren, the kids in the neighborhood. I listen at the supermarket, the video store, the Dairy Queen and McDonald's. I just listen.

Although I did revise "Aunt Millie's Handbag" quite a few times, it was not to get my story under 800 words. If it *is* under 800 words it's because that's how many words it took to tell the story.

I chose *Highlights* because I knew *Highlights* likes fiction, especially fantasy and humor.

Prairie Light

By Marcia Freeman

Grass. Sky. Sonja stared across the empty prairie. Where was Papa? The flattened grass of his wagon tracks stretched out to the edge of the sky. Sonja stood motionless, a hand raised to shield her eyes from the setting sun.

Moonlight. Mama braided Sonja's hair and tucked her into the trundle bed.

"When will Papa be home?" asked Sonja.

"Soon, Sonja, soon."

A cricket chirped. Sonja crept from her bed. From the shadows of the sod house, she strained to see down the moonlit wagon tracks. No wagon. No Papa.

"Come back to bed, Sonja," Mama called softly.

Morning. Papa had not returned. Sonja went to the well for water and pumped the handle to fill the buckets. Her eyes swept the smooth unbroken line of the horizon. She stared down the wagon tracks until spilling water drew her back.

Sonja woke to a strange thump, thump, thumping overhead.

Sonja climbed to the roof of the sod house. The sky was like Mama's blue china bowl turned upside down over the prairie. Sonja turned slowly, slowly. Nothing stirred under the bowl of the sky. No sign of Papa anywhere.

Mama stood beside Sonja in the fading afternoon sunlight. They watched and waited. A hawk hovered above them. Shadows crept across the wagon tracks as the sun slid into the horizon.

Suddenly Sonja turned her head. "I hear something," she whispered. She pointed south, away from Papa's wagon tracks.

"Be still," Mama said. "Listen."

They heard the faint jangling of harnesses and creaking of wagon wheels. It grew louder. Soon they could see the horses and wagon. Now they could see Papa waving to them. Sonja ran through the grass to meet him.

Like a beacon, Mama's dandelions glowed from their rooftop.

Papa climbed down wearily from the wagon. "I lost my track. I followed someone else's by mistake," he said. "I've been making big circles to find mine again, and I couldn't see the house. Our roof looks just like the prairie."

Sonja and Mama helped Papa unload the winter supplies. Bags of flour, beans, and sugar. New boots for Papa and Sonja. A bundle of wool yarn for Mama.

At supper Papa unpacked his special bag. He gave Sonja a twist of candy and a bright blue ribbon. He handed Mama a thick paper packet. She smiled when she saw the writing on the packet. She read Aunt Anika's letter aloud.

Mama braided Sonja's hair. She tucked her into the trundle bed. "Papa's home now," Mama whispered. "Sleep well, Sonja." Sonja snuggled into her quilt.

Sonja woke to a strange thump, thump, thumping overhead. She ran from the house and climbed to the roof. Mama knelt there, a small shovel and a folded paper packet in her hands.

"What is it, Mama?" asked Sonja.

"Dandelion seeds from Aunt Anika," said Mama.
"Why are you planting them here?" Sonja asked.
"You'll see," Mama promised.

In the spring, Sonja went to town with Papa for supplies. They followed their wagon tracks homeward. Sonja leaned forward in the seat as the wagon crossed a small rise. A fiery yellow light blazed in the endless green prairie. Like a beacon, Mama's dandelions glowed from their rooftop.

"We're home, Papa!" cried Sonja. "We're home!"

Ladybug
2–6 years
508 words

From the Author

I was trained in science and began to study writing as an elementary school teacher after discovering I didn't know what to teach my students about writing. Now I teach writing all over the country, to teachers and to children.

Many of my books are photo-illustrated science and geography books for primary students. The idea for "Prairie Light," came from listening to my great-grandfather's stories from his childhood on the Dakota prairies in the late 1800s.

The final scene inspired the title and the story itself. I often write toward an ending I envision when I first get an idea. I wrote in a deliberately terse style to mirror the stark conditions of prairie life. This took a lot of work—I revised some sentences more than ten times to get them just right.

When I compared the sky to "Mama's blue china bowl," I built a strong analogy by using "turn" and "stir," words that are associated with bowls. *That* idea came from my amazement when I stood on a central Florida prairie—for the first time I saw the sky as a complete hemisphere—not at all like the sky in my home mountains of Vermont.

I strove to use as much alliteration and as many strong verbs as I could. These are the things that appeal to kids and provide good models for their writing. I read my work aloud both as I compose and after I think I'm finished. I listen for the rhythm and sound of sentences, and I determine whether they are easy to read. If I stumble over the wording, so will my readers.

Something Terrible

By Lisa Harkrader

"Mother," whispered Oliver, "something terrible is living under my bed."

"Did you see it?" asked Mother.

"No. I had my eyes closed."

"Did you hear it?"

"No," said Oliver. "I think it knew I was listening, so it stayed quiet. But I thought I smelled it once. And sometimes, if I keep very still, my bed jiggles just a little."

"Sounds serious," said Mother. "We should investigate."

"What if it does something terrible?"

"We'll defend ourselves," said Mother. She reached in the closet and pulled out a broom.

Mother poked under Oliver's bed with the broom. She jabbed at a mound of dirty socks. She prodded a pile of dusty books. She nudged Oliver's chewed-up stuffed rabbit.

"A-ha! Just as I thought." Mother sat back and pointed.

Oliver couldn't look. "What is it?" he asked.

"A dust wuzzy," said Mother. "Don't worry. This one seems tame."

Oliver peeked under the edge of his bedspread. He could see a small gray ball of fluff shivering in the corner.

"He looks awfully thin," Oliver told Mother. "I can see right through his middle. What should I feed him?"

Oliver leaned closer. "He looks scared."

"I'm sure he is," said Mother. "Half of him is stuck under your crayon box."

"I better clean that stuff out so he doesn't hurt himself," said Oliver.

"Good idea," said Mother.

Oliver scooped his dirty clothes from under the bed and put them in the hamper. He gathered up his toys and books and stacked them on his dresser. He rescued his favorite dinosaur from a heap of old gum wrappers, then threw the gum wrappers in the trash.

"There's a very nice family of dust wuzzies living in the vacuum cleaner."

"There," he told the dust wuzzy. "All clean. Now you don't have anything to be afraid of."

The dust wuzzy skittered back and forth along the wall. He seemed happier, but Oliver was still worried.

"He looks awfully thin," Oliver told Mother. "I can see right through his middle. What should I feed him?"

Mother rubbed her chin. "They're usually quite fond of lint," she said. "But don't feed him too much."

Oliver nodded. Mother had just washed his favorite red sweatshirt. Oliver pulled a big ball of sweatshirt lint from the dryer. Each morning he fed a bit to the dust wuzzy. The dust wuzzy grew fatter and turned a healthy pink. Still Oliver worried.

"He shakes whenever I lift the bedspread to talk to him," said Oliver.

"Maybe he's lonely," said Mother. "Dust wuzzies like to stick together. This one is all by himself."

"Where can I get another one?"

"Well," said Mother. She chewed on her lip and thought about it for a moment. "There's a very nice family of dust wuzzies living in the vacuum cleaner. I'm sure they'd welcome a new dust wuzzy."

"How will we get him in there?"

"We'll suck him up," said Mother.

"Won't that hurt?" asked Oliver.

"Of course not. He'll think it's fun."

So Mother plugged in the vacuum cleaner, and Oliver sucked the dust wuzzy up through the nozzle.

Oliver nodded. He knew what he had to do.

"Do you think he's all right?" asked Oliver.

"I'm sure he is." Mother turned the vacuum off. "There's plenty of lint for him to eat, and he has lots of company."

Oliver put his ear against the vacuum. "What do you think they're doing?"

"It's hard to tell," said Mother. "They probably know we're listening, so they're staying quiet. But you don't have to worry about that dust wuzzy anymore. It's the next one you have to watch for."

"The next one?"

"Oh, yes," said Mother. "There's bound to be another one. And probably one after that."

Oliver nodded. He knew what he had to do. Every morning when he woke up, he peeked under his bed. Once in a while, but not very often, he'd find a small dust wuzzy shivering in the corner.

Oliver would feed the dust wuzzy a bit of fluffy lint, then suck him up into the vacuum cleaner.

Story Friends
4–9 years
633 words

From the Author

For almost a year I've been a full-time writer and freelance graphic designer. I got the idea for "Something Terrible" when I worked for a graphics company. Huge dust bunnies sprouted up behind the computers, and I started naming them.

I knew I had to write a story about a boy and his pet dust bunny. I always interview my main characters to get a firm grip on their voices. I ask them questions like: *What are you most afraid of? What's your biggest secret?* Then I let the character answer in his or her own first-person voice. Once I hear that voice, I've got the story.

Oliver and his mother started talking to each other while I was in the shower. I ran into my office wrapped in a towel so I could write everything down before they stopped talking. I got most of the story down in that one sitting, which hardly ever happens to me.

I'd read a copy of *Story Friends,* and I thought the characters, action, and gentle humor of my story really fit that magazine. Happily, the editor agreed. I can't emphasize enough how important it is to study your target magazines. For example, *Story Friends* is a Mennonite publication, but its stories are not overtly religious or preachy.

The editor did change one word in my story to make it more fitting for a religious audience. When I submitted it, Oliver called his pet a "dust demon." When the story was published, the "demon" had turned into a "wuzzy." And honestly, I like "wuzzy" better.

"Something Terrible" is a something-under-the-bed story, a theme that might seem like it's been done to death. I've learned, though, that editors don't mind a common theme if a writer gives it a fresh and surprising twist.

I've published stories about the new baby, the cranky old woman next door, and the weird new kid at school. The key to making these familiar themes fresh is to make the characters fresh. If they're living, breathing people in your head, they'll end up doing new and surprising things on the page.

Windows of Gold

By Marianne Mitchell

Nestled in the hills above a valley, there once lived a poor farmer and his daughter, Emma. Each morning, as Emma lugged her milk pail and stool out to their old cow, she looked across to the other hillside and sighed. For each morning she saw the same beautiful sight. There, far across the valley, golden windows winked back at her.

"Who lives in such beauty?" Emma wondered. "Who can be so rich that even their windows are made of gold?"

"Why do some people have so much and we have so little?"

As Emma went about her milking, she thought about life "over there." Surely those people didn't have to get up early and do farm chores. They probably had dozens of servants cleaning the floors and polishing the windows. Every meal must be a banquet, not the simple stews and plain bread Emma and her father had to eat. Life in such a place must be spent having grand parties. It surely wouldn't be spent digging and hoeing, trying to grow potatoes in stony fields.

One day Emma's father said, "You look sad. What is the matter?"

"I wish we were rich," Emma answered. "Why do some people have so much and we have so little?"

"I have you and you have me. I think that makes us quite rich."

Emma sighed. "Have you ever been across the valley, Father?"

"No, I am happy here. Aren't you?"

"But I want to see the palace with golden windows. I want to find out who lives over there," Emma begged.

Emma's father thought for a moment. "All right," he said. "But you must promise to be satisfied with what you learn."

Early the next day, Emma and her father hiked down the rocky hills and into the valley. By noon they had started the steep climb up the other side. Now and then they passed a small cottage, but their eyes were fixed on the hills above.

By late afternoon they arrived at a cluster of houses. All had thatched roofs and mud walls, just like their own. The fields around them were lumpy with stones, just like their own.

Emma saw a girl leading a cow out of a barn.

"Good afternoon!" Emma called out. "We are looking for the palace. Is it far from here?"

The girl gasped, her hands flying to her mouth. "You come from over there?" she asked.

The girl stared at them, confused. "A palace? Around here?"

"Yes. The one with golden windows," said Emma. "I know it has to be close. You see, we live over there, across the valley. Every morning I can see the golden windows from my yard."

The girl gasped, her hands flying to her mouth. "You come from over there?" she asked.

"I have always wondered what your life must be like. Each afternoon I come out and marvel at your golden windows."

Emma laughed. "We don't have golden windows."

"Yes, you do! Look!" The girl she pointed across the valley toward Emma's house.

Emma and her father turned and looked. In the glow of the afternoon sun, the windows of all the little houses on their side of the valley glittered like gold.

"I hope you can stay for dinner," said the girl. "It's not much—just a simple stew and plain bread."

Emma squeezed her father's hand, letting him know she was happy with what she had learned.

"Thank you," she told the girl. "That sounds perfect."

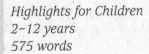

Highlights for Children
2–12 years
575 words

When I was a child, our pastor liked using stories to make his points, and I remembered one about a house that looked like it was made of gold because of the sun's reflection on the windows. That story stuck in my head for decades.

Later, I decided to retell it, thinking it was a folktale. I spent months trying to track it down. I never found it, but I learned that many folktales were based on the theme "the grass is always greener on the other side." With only a memory to go by, I made up my own story using a third-person folktale voice. By focusing on the basic elements of the story, I used only as many words as I needed. I was glad it was under 600 words, because shorter stories are easier to market.

I sent my story to a few religious magazines, and they rejected it. Then I remembered that the deadline for the *Highlights* fiction contest was nearing. The category that year was a toughie: "stories that break the mold." I had no idea what that meant!

I'd written a lot for *Highlights*. I'd entered their annual contest three times—and lost. I knew my story would suit 8- to 12-year-old readers. Why not send it?

Three months later, I got a call from *Highlights* telling me I had won. I was stunned! Each of the three winners got $1,000. Wow!

My writing career began as a student of the Institute of Children's Literature. The two courses I took taught me the discipline of "writing tight" and researching the markets. That training has paid off nicely.

My advice to anyone who wants to write for magazines is to read lots of issues. Learn each magazine's style. Subscribe if you can. Send for guidelines and theme lists. And remember, just because a story gets rejected doesn't mean it isn't "golden."

A Fishy Story

By Linell Wohlers

Val kicked the soccer ball to an invisible teammate and then raced over to kick it back. *It is no fun trying to be a soccer team all by myself,* she thought.

Mom and Dad said the new house they were renting was a good deal. But Val thought that moving to a neighborhood that had no children was not a good deal.

When the landlord said, "No pets," Val asked about Angelo.

"Fish are OK," he told her, "but no dogs or cats."

Although she would rather have a dog, Val was glad she could keep Angelo. He was a feisty goldfish who splashed and begged at the edge of his bowl every time she came near. His bubbling noises were so loud that he had to be taken out of Val's room at night so she could sleep. Lately she had tried getting him to jump over her finger like a trained seal she had seen at the zoo. But Angelo thought her finger was food and tried to bite it instead of jumping over it. Angelo was funny, but Val had to admit that no one was impressed by goldfish.

Dogs, on the other hand, were liked by just about everyone. A dog would fetch toys and attract new friends. A dog could even bark at the grumpy man next door who scolded her for kicking her soccer ball. It was not her fault that Mr. Steinmiller's garage had a broken window. Why was he always so crabby?

Mr. Steinmiller's pickup truck pulled into the driveway. Val quickly sat on the soccer ball, hoping he would not notice it. "Hello," she waved politely.

"Humph," he grunted, not looking her way. He slammed the door shut and hurried toward his house. The key was in the lock when he suddenly asked, "How many of you live there?"

Val was so surprised, she rolled off the ball with a thump. "Mom and Dad and me," she said, scrambling up. "And Angelo."

Mr. Steinmiller grunted again, probably noticing the soccer ball. "The last renters had six," he said. "That is too many. How old is Angelo?"

"I don't know," said Val. "We have only had him for a little while."

"Angelo is not a bother," Val insisted. "All he did was bite me once."

Mr. Steinmiller nodded. "Just a baby, then."

"I guess so," said Val. "Anyway, he makes a lot of noise at night and keeps me awake."

"It will get worse," Mr. Steinmiller warned. "He will get bigger and bigger."

Val frowned. "Angelo is not that bad. Besides, he can do tricks."

"Tricks? What kind of tricks?" asked Mr. Steinmiller.

"Well," Val hesitated, "he blows bubbles in his bowl."

"A messy eater," Mr. Steinmiller mumbled, going back to his lock. "They are all a bother, if you ask me."

"Angelo is not a bother," Val insisted. "All he did was bite me once."

"You see?" said Mr. Steinmiller. "He will probably grow up to terrorize the neighborhood just like the others."

Val almost laughed. What did Mr. Steinmiller think Angelo was? A killer whale?

Youngest Readers' Fiction

"Angelo never terrorizes anybody," she said. "He just swims all day."

Mr. Steinmiller stopped. "Your baby brother can swim?"

Val and Mr. Steinmiller stared at each other.

"Who said anything about a baby brother?" asked Val. "Angelo is my goldfish!"

Mr. Steinmiller blinked. Then his mouth twitched. Suddenly, he burst out laughing harder than Val had ever seen any grumpy old man laugh.

"In that case," he said, catching his breath, "go ask your mom if you can come meet my family."

Mr. Steinmiller's family, it turned out, was a big shiny aquarium full of fish.

"They are even fancier than Angelo," said Val, staring at the colorful, darting fish.

"Tropical fish are fussier than Angelo, too," said Mr. Steinmiller. "They need just the right temperature and food."

"Maybe a dog would be easier to take care of," said Val.

"Not for me," said Mr. Steinmiller, laughing. "Fish are the best pets. Of course, I have never had one bite me! I knew there was something *fishy* about your story."

"Hey—can you help me train Angelo?" asked Val. "And maybe I can help you fix your broken window."

Mr. Steinmiller looked surprised. "Maybe we will be good neighbors after all," he said, smiling.

"Even if we *do* tell fishy stories," Val giggled.

Children's Playmate
6–8 years
717 words

From the Author

I did some freelance writing for children's magazines when my children were young and we lived in a remote farmhouse. I sold more than 30 stories during that time. Then we moved to a more urban setting, where I became employed as an occupational therapist in the public schools.

After moving from the farm, we found it harder to have "real pets" that were interesting. "A Fishy Story" is based on a feisty goldfish we had. My husband joked about training this goldfish to jump over his finger.

At the time I was also thinking about relationships between old and young people. After moving to a new neighborhood, my children were crushed to discover that many old people were suspicious of children. I wanted to create an open door between generations with this story.

There's humorous potential in communicating with children. Like Val, first graders may not instantly grasp the fact that Mr. Steinmiller doesn't realize Angelo is a fish, but they're delighted to see how mixed-up he's been when he admits to thinking Angelo was her baby brother. I had to think about all the characteristics a fish and a baby brother could share in order to carry off this humorous misunderstanding. Angelo's distinctive personality and Mr. Steinmiller's grumpy, suspicious nature helped intensify the interaction.

The third-person point of view worked well for this mostly conversational story. I didn't pinpoint *Children's Playmate* when writing the story— Children's Better Health Institute always decided which magazine was the best fit for my stories. However, most of my stories sold to *Children's Playmate*. I've learned to make stories "tighter," and that's helped me sell to this market.

Zindy Lou and the Dark Place

By Judy Cox

Everybody said Zindy Lou was a brave girl. When she was stung by a bee and didn't yell, Grandma said, "What a brave girl!" When Dr. Patti gave her a shot and she didn't fuss, Dr. Patti said, "My, what a brave girl!" And when she went skating on her new blue roller skates, fell down three times, got a bloody knee, and didn't even cry, Daddy picked her up and said, "You're a brave kid, Zindy Lou."

There never was a dark so dark since the world began.

But no matter how brave Zindy Lou was, one thing really scared her: dark places. There was a dark place under the basement stairs. Zindy Lou always ran past it as fast as she could, pounding up the stairs without looking. Her bedroom was dark if Daddy forgot to turn on the night-light. And the inside of her closet was dark. Zindy Lou kept the closet door shut tightly so she couldn't see the dark inside.

But the worst dark place of all—the very, very, absolute worst—was the girls' rest room at school. There never was a dark so dark since the world began. It was darker than the place under the stairs. It was darker than the closet. It was darker than outer space.

Once when Zindy Lou was in there, a big girl turned off the light. The big girl couldn't see Zindy Lou in her stall, because her short legs didn't hang down below the door. Zindy Lou was alone in the terrible dark of the girls' rest room. She was too scared to flush the toilet. She was too scared to wash her hands. She felt her way along the wall until she found the door handle, and then she pulled with all her might and escaped into the sunny hall.

Zindy Lou never wanted to go in that rest room again.

All through kindergarten she waited to go until she got home at noon. "I don't have to," she said when Mrs. Jones saw her jiggling and squirming. As soon as the school bus dropped her off in front of her house, she ran inside to the bathroom, not even stopping to kiss Daddy.

But this year Zindy Lou would be a first grader, and Marissa, the big girl next-door, said first graders *had* to go to the rest room by themselves. "You have to raise your hand and ask the teacher, and then you have to get a hall pass, and then you have to go by yourself so you don't waste time. And when you're

What if some big girl turned off the lights again?

done, you have to remember not to spill the soap and turn the water off so you don't waste it and turn the lights off so you don't waste electricity." Marissa was an expert on the girls' rest room.

Zindy Lou didn't want to go to the rest room by herself. What if some big girl turned off the light again? But she knew she couldn't wait all day to go to the bathroom at home. She'd have an accident. So she set her mind to solve the problem.

The first day of school, she used the rest room during recess. Her friend Jade went with her. "Stand by the light and make sure nobody turns it off until I'm ready," she told Jade. That worked pretty well.

But the next day Jade wasn't in school. So Zindy Lou dragged a chair from the classroom to prop the door open. Then she could still see if the lights went out.

But the big rest room door was too heavy. It slowly slid shut, pushing the chair into the hall. Zindy Lou would have to think up another solution.

"Zindy Lou," said her teacher at the end of the day, "tomorrow is your sharing day. You may bring something to show the class."

Zindy Lou knew just what to bring: her rock collection! When she got home, she dug through the toy box in her room, looking for the egg carton containing her rocks. She found a green crayon she'd thought was lost. She found her princess doll's missing crown. She found the china teapot lid from her tea set. And down at the very bottom of the toy box, she found the answer to her dark problem. She put it in her backpack so she wouldn't forget to bring it to school.

The next day at sharing time she held up a shiny silver flashlight. "I got it for my birthday," she said. She showed everyone how to turn it on. They all wanted a turn.

Now Zindy Lou brings the flashlight to school with her every day. She keeps it in her backpack so she won't forget.

And whenever Zindy Lou needs to use the rest room, she raises her hand and asks politely, "May I use the rest room, please?" Then she takes the hall pass—and her flashlight—and uses the rest room all by herself. Just like a brave girl.

Spider
6–9 years
827 words

From the Author

When my son was four years old, he skinned his knee and told me, "I didn't cry, did I? I'm a brave boy, aren't I?" That was the beginning of "Zindy Lou and the Dark Place."

I came up with the name from the song "Cindy Lou." I knew Zindy Lou was a brave girl, so I tried to decide what would frighten her. When I was young, I was afraid of dark closets and of someone turning the light out in the bathroom, so I used these elements in my story.

Because this is a problem young children have, I made my character a first grader. This also gave me a readership age. When writing for children this age, it's fun to use repetition. I repeated the phrase "brave girl" several times. I also varied sentence length. I used the "rule of threes" by repeating lists of actions and metaphors. Zindy Lou solves her problem after three tries.

Although I typically revise a story 10 to 15 times, "Zindy Lou" was one of those lucky pieces that seem to spring forth fully fledged. I wrote the story and cut about 100 words to meet magazine guidelines. I submitted to *Spider* after reading several issues. It was my first sale to *Spider*, and I was thrilled. They only asked for small changes.

I've been writing since I was 11 years old but began to publish about eight years ago. I am now the author of more than 30 short stories, articles, essays, and poems, as well as three picture books and a chapter book—but when I wrote "Zindy Lou and the Dark Place," I had not published any fiction. I am currently a kindergarten teacher.

BRRRR!

By Bonnie Compton Hanson

Playing in the snow can be fun: building snow forts, throwing snowballs, making snow angels, skiing, sledding, snowboarding, ice-skating or ice fishing.

But what if you lived in ice and snow year-round with no house or shelter of any kind to go to when you got too cold? With no hot cocoa to warm you up? What if you slept right out on the ice?

"No, thanks!" you say.

The emperor penguin of the South Pole feels at home in the snow and ice.

During blizzards, penguins have to huddle together by the hundreds or even thousands to keep from freezing to death.

With penguins looking so much alike, you might think that they have a hard time telling each other apart. But every penguin has his or her own individual "song" or call. Even in a blinding snowstorm, penguin couples can recognize and find each other.

Every year, each penguin couple lays one egg. They can't build nests in trees or bushes. The snow and ice would freeze the egg if it were laid on the ground. So the parents take turns holding the egg on their feet, inside a warm pouch of the parents' skin and feathers. This pouch is also home for the penguin chick when it hatches.

Penguins feed on fish from the open water around Antarctica. Sometimes in the winter, when so much water freezes over, open water is as many as 50 miles from land. To get there, the grown-up penguins "row" across the ice on their bellies, using their flipper-like wings as "oars" and their sharply clawed feet as "motors."

While they are gone, all the young chicks huddle together for protection in huge "nursery schools." When the parents return with food, they have to figure out which of all those identical gray, fluffy babies belongs to them!

We needn't worry. Remember, every penguin has a completely different sound. Every baby penguin knows its own parents' voices. So as the grown-ups go through the crowd calling out, each joyous baby rushes off to welcome its parents back and to share some of that delicious fish!

Story Friends
4–9 years
203 words

From the Author

I've always loved penguins. When I decided to write about them, I researched encyclopedias and nature books and collected pictures from old magazines. My research material lent itself to many focuses, such as penguins' fun times and eating habits. But what impressed me was the marvelous ability of parents and young to seek and find each other, even when it seems impossible. I opened my article by tying in what most children already know about snow activities and leading them into a world where snow is not a novelty but a constant fact of life.

Many children's markets love nature studies, especially those with a point or "moral," but with a top limit of 450 words or so. I targeted markets using market guides, guidelines, and sample copies. Then I submitted the article directly with a cover letter—many children's periodicals editors prefer that. But always check specific guidelines: they are your *life*lines, and no guidelines means you'll be sitting on the *side*lines.

Snackin' Snowmen

By Peggy Robbins Janousky

Here's a healthful winter snack that's lots of fun to make! Ask an adult to help you. (This recipe makes 5 to 7 snowmen.)

You Will Need:

½ cup crunchy peanut butter
½ cup honey
½ cup dried fruit, chopped
½ teaspoon vanilla
½ teaspoon cinnamon
2 cups crispy rice cereal
Shredded coconut
Raisins
Wax paper

Directions:

1. Wash hands. Mix the peanut butter, honey, dried fruit, vanilla, and cinnamon together in a medium-sized bowl.

2. Add the rice cereal and stir until completely mixed. Using wet hands, roll the mixture into golfball-sized balls.

3. Pour the shredded coconut into a small bowl. This is your "snow." Roll the peanut butter balls in the coconut until completely covered. Place them on waxed paper.

4. To form a snowman, stack three balls on top of one another. (Use a little peanut butter for glue if needed.)

5. Push two raisins into the top snowball for "eyes." Cut a raisin lengthwise to use for a

mouth. Your snowman is ready for snackin'!

Children's Playmate
6–8 years
159 words

From the Author

As a teacher and parent of two young boys, I am constantly reminded of how difficult it is to present material to small children. Many things need to be taken into account: attention span, ease of use, and age appropriateness. The best poem, story, or craft is meaningless if it is presented to the wrong audience. In addition to all this, I need to take into account the needs of the magazine I've targeted. If this sounds like an awful lot of work for one recipe, you're right. On the other hand, magazines often need recipes, puzzles, and crafts. Loosely translated, it's a great way to break in.

Always test your recipe before you submit. If you don't know any kids in the appropriate age group, ask a friend or librarian for help. Make sure the ingredients are simple and easy to find. No parent wants to drag a preschooler around to three supermarkets just to find the right food.

Always send for magazine guidelines and read several copies of a magazine before you submit. Remember that they purchase material six to nine months prior to publication.

Each magazine has a special niche. *Children's Playmate* is a wellness magazine, so I made sure my recipe contained only healthful ingredients.

Don't quit. Everyone gets rejected sometimes.

I Only Have Beats for You

By Tamara Angier

Hey, you out there! This is your heart talking. I'm down here—inside your chest. You can't see me, but you can feel me working. Put your hand on your chest. Can you feel me beating? That *thump-thump* you feel is me. I beat about seventy times a minute. That's more than 100,000 times a day! I've been with you your whole life, and I'm the only heart you have. I have a very important job to do.

Did you know that I'm a muscle about the size of your fist? You have other muscles in your body, too. The muscles in your legs help you walk. The muscles in your face help you smile. All of your muscles depend on me, and you, to keep them healthy and working well.

I pump blood all through your body. Each part of your body needs fresh, healthy blood. Take a deep breath so that your chest swells up like a balloon. When you breathe in fresh air, I squeeze myself together and pump blood into your lungs. The blood gets refreshed from the air you breathed in. Then I pump the blood through your body.

It takes less than one minute for the blood to travel around your whole body and return to me. When it comes back, I pump the used blood to your lungs for fresh air. Then it starts traveling all over again. This process is called *circulation*.

In order for me to be healthy, I need your help. You need to exercise. I pump about five liters of blood each minute, so I need to be strong! Does exercising sound boring to you? I bet running, swimming, walking, inline skating, dancing, and biking don't sound boring! When you do some of these things, you make me work harder and pump faster.

For a good workout, choose something that you would have fun doing. Start by stretching, or warming up your muscles. This helps them get ready to work. Then exercise for about twenty minutes. Finish by cooling down and doing more stretches. This helps muscles relax. I need a good workout about every other day to get fit and stay fit. But wait! Make sure your fun exercise is OK with your parents and your doctor before you start.

If you live to be seventy-four years old, I will beat about 2.7 billion times during your life! I can't ride a bike or put on inline skates, but you can! When  we work together as a team, we make a healthier you.

Humpty Dumpty's Magazine
4–6 years
382 words

From the Author

"I Only Have Beats for You" started as an assignment for a writing course I took through the Institute of Children's Literature. It was my first attempt at nonfiction. Many editors wanted health-related material; one was *Humpty Dumpty's Magazine,* a magazine I enjoyed as a child. I used the library to gather information on the heart's function and how exercise affects it. Then I condensed my extensive notes by talking to a child about the information I'd found.

Writing from the point of view of the heart enabled me to involve readers immediately by using the word "you." It was challenging to explain how the heart works in a manner children could understand, and to find ways children could apply this material to their own lives.

Let's Celebrate

By Darlene Buechel

10...9...8...7...6...5...4...3...2...1...a giant ball drops down a huge pole in Times Square in New York City. Fireworks light the midnight sky as thousands of people in funny pointed hats blow horns and hug and kiss. Shouts of "Happy New Year" fill the brisk air as January 1 ushers in a brand new year.

Yes, you probably know how most Americans ring in the new year, but did you ever wonder how people around the world celebrate?

If you live in Belgium, you will get your new year's exercise walking out to the barn to talk to your cow.

If you are in Spain on New Year's Eve, you will be popping grapes. When the clock strikes 12, you will eat 12 grapes—one for each month of the year. Each grape is supposed to bring good luck for that month.

Kids in Switzerland have a messy custom which is supposed to bring good luck. They pour a drop of cream on the floor. The Swiss have to watch where they step, or they may start the new year with the bad luck of a broken leg.

If you live in Belgium, you will get your new year's exercise walking out to the barn to talk to your cow. Belgian farmers believe it's good luck to talk to their animals early on New Year's Day.

If you live in Greece, you will clean your walking shoes and leave them out on New Year's Eve. If you are good, St. Basil will come and fill the shoes with presents. At midnight you will get to welcome the new year by opening your presents.

The people of Vietnam give presents but not to each other. They give gifts to their gods because they believe that gods live in their homes and protect their families. Before the Vietnam New Year, which is called Tet, the families give presents to their gods. Then when Tet arrives (sometime between Jan. 21 and Feb. 19—the exact date changes from year to year) the people set off firecrackers and send the gods off to heaven with a bang.

In Japan the new year is also welcomed in with loud noise. On New Year's Eve most people stay up to hear a big gong ring 108 times. Then, at the moment of the new year, the people start to laugh. Lots of laughter on New Year's is supposed to bring luck in the new year.

If you want to guarantee a lucky new year in France, you will probably pass the syrup. Pancakes are eaten on New Year's Day in France to bring happiness and health for another year.

Puerto Rican children ring in the new year by throwing pails of water out their windows at midnight.

If you want to stay healthy in Puerto Rico, you must stay away from open windows on New Year's Eve. Puerto Rican children ring in the new year by throwing pails of water out their windows at midnight. This custom is done to get rid of any evil spirits in their homes.

Isn't it amazing how many different ways people around the world celebrate the birth of a new year? This New Year's Eve, whether you ring in the new year with hats and horns, grapes, gongs, or pails of

water, may you have a new year filled with health and happiness.

Boys' Quest
6–13 years
215 words

From the Author

I am a graduate of the Institute of Children's Literature, and while studying the *Children's Magazine Market,* I saw that many magazines were in need of catchy nonfiction articles. I also wrote "Let's Celebrate" because I thought it might be fun to try writing nonfiction.

While browsing through the children's section of the local library, I saw many books about holidays, but little about New Year's. I checked out several books and compiled information about the fun and unusual ways the new year is celebrated throughout the world.

I wrote the article, let it stew, gave it a final polish, then sent it to my first choice, *Hopscotch, The Magazine for Girls.* I chose *Hopscotch* because it had the right age range (6–13 years), needed nonfiction pieces under 500 words, and is 100% written by non-staff writers—they publish 100 freelance submissions yearly.

I sent the entire manuscript with a cover letter, and about a month later I received a postcard saying *Hopscotch* already had similar material, but *Boys' Quest* would be interested in publishing my article in an upcoming issue. I quickly let them know that would be great, and on July 21, 1997, I received payment from *Boys' Quest.* I know the exact date of the check because a copy of it is framed by my computer!

I was not required to do any revisions, but I would have been willing to revise if necessary. Getting my article published has given me confidence as a writer.

An Eye for Ants

By Gretchen Noyes-Hull

"Most people have a bug period. I never grew out of mine."

Dr. Edward O. Wilson, scientist and teacher, has spent his life peeking into the nests of ants. He's curious about the job of each ant in the colony. He wants to uncover the secrets of ant colonies' success.

As a child, Edward was often alone. His mother and father separated. He had to move many times. In 11 years he went to 14 different schools! Wherever he lived, snakes, fishes, and insects became his friends. For a time, he even kept a colony of harvester ants in a jar under his bed.

An ant colony can have as many as 20 million members.

The summer he was seven, Edward hurt his right eye in a fishing accident. As he says: "The attention of my surviving eye turned to the ground." It wasn't long before Edward decided to become an entomologist—a scientist who studies insects.

Ants live almost everywhere—from tropical climates to beyond the Arctic Circle, from dry deserts to shady rain forests, from city sidewalks to wild woodlands, and from deep in the ground to the tops of the tallest trees. They live in colonies. An ant colony can have as many as 20 million members.

There is only one queen ant in a colony. It's the queen's task to lay the eggs. Out of the eggs grow worker ants and sometimes a new queen. Every ant in a colony has a job. The main goal of all of the worker ants is to take care of the queen and her offspring. This they do in some amazing ways.

For 40 years, Dr. Wilson has traveled around the world looking for new kinds of ants. Sometimes he brings entire colonies back to his laboratory in order to observe them more closely. He wants to learn about each ant's job within its colony. He wants to know how each ant's job contributes to the future survival of its species.

You can do an experiment to test the odor signals of ants.

Dr. Wilson's discoveries help us understand why many animal species develop social organization. In a social organization, each member of the group has specific jobs. Each job is important to the entire species' success.

Whenever possible, Dr. Wilson still returns to the place where he first watched ants. He notes the changes in ant species that have occurred over the past 60 years. And today he still relies on the observations and collections of specimens that he made when he was a young boy.

An Ant Experiment to Try

Worker ants must build, feed, and guard their colony. To do this they need to communicate with each other. Like most living things, ants depend on chemical odors (known as pheromones) to send messages such as, "I found food over here...this ant looks dead—take him out...alert! there's a stranger in here." Over the years, Dr. Wilson has carried out hundreds of experiments to find the meanings of these odor signals. Although he's made important discoveries, many mysteries remain.

You can do an experiment to test the odor signals of ants. Put several drops of sugar water on a piece of paper. Place the paper near some ants. Watch as one ant discovers the food. Other ants will soon follow the first ant's odor trail. Turn the paper sideways. The ants will still follow the scent of the odor trail, although the sugar water is now in a different place.

Amazing Ant Facts

There are almost 10,000 known species of ants and many more remaining to be discovered. At any one time, 10 million billion (that's 10,000,000,000,000,000) ants are alive. (The world's population of humans is only about 5.8 billion!)

Some queen ants live a long time. One lived in a laboratory colony for 29 years. But the worker ants that bring the queen's food usually live only for a week or so.

Most ants are scavengers. They find food outside the nest. But some kinds of ants actually "farm" their food. Some "farming" ants grow fungus on underground leaf farms. Others "milk" drops of sugar, called "honeydew," from aphids.

Many species of ants kidnap "slaves." They capture ants from neighboring colonies. The "slaves" do some of the work of the colony.

Some worker ants act like storage containers. They fill themselves up with food like a balloon. If food becomes scarce, they regurgitate it for the rest of the colony. (*Regurgitate* is the scientific way to say "throw up.")

AppleSeeds
8–10 years
716 words

From the Author

I was a scientist long before I was a writer—I have advanced degrees in zoology and oceanography—but even when I was little I spent most of my time in the woods or with my head in a tide pool. I was lucky to be able to follow up my natural interests with school and research, but I've found that I really enjoy the way children see the world. Teaching and writing science for children helps me to see the world in different ways.

"An Eye for Ants" was written for *AppleSeeds'* charter issue, titled "Learning with Animals." The editor approached me. I had recently read Dr. Wilson's autobiography and realized that his descriptions of his childhood interests in insects and the natural world would be interesting to children. He's written many other books about his research, which really began when he was in elementary school. For the article, I never talked directly to Dr. Wilson, but relied on what he had written, including his well-known book, *Ants*.

It is very difficult to write a short article about something that interests you! (The publisher told me how long the article needed to be.) So in addition to the article, I submitted a number of facts that I wanted to share. These were used as the sidebar; this is a good way to get around word limits!

I was pleased with my title. It came from a true story and expressed the idea that scientists hold onto their childhood curiosity.

I recently visited a third-grade class that had read my article. We spent a long time together talking about ants. It was wonderful to find that, just like Dr. Wilson, so many of them had observed and were intrigued by the very special behaviors of these insects.

Youngest Readers' Nonfiction

Dead or Alive?

By Victoria Earle

Have you ever wondered whether your hair is dead or alive? Carefully pull one hair out of your head (and keep it). I expect you could feel it leave your scalp. Perhaps it even hurt a little. Each hair has a bulb, called a follicle, buried in a hole in your skin. Nerves surround the follicle. They send a message to your brain as your hair is being pulled out. That's why you can feel it leave your scalp.

Hold the end of the hair that you pulled out in one hand, and pull the hair between the finger and thumb of the other hand. You should be able to feel a little bump at the end of the hair that was rooted in your head. You can feel the bulb. You may be able to see that it's white. The rest of your hair is called the shaft.

You can grow very long hair, but your cat or dog can't.

As well as nerves, there are blood vessels around the bulb. These bring the food that allows the hair to grow. Hair can grow as fast as 3/4 inch each month. Human hair grows all the time. You can grow very long hair, but your cat or dog can't. Each of their hairs stops growing after a certain length of time.

Hairs don't stay forever. Perhaps you know a dog that sheds or a cat that leaves fur everywhere, especially in the spring!

Did you know that we shed too? We shed all the time! Our old hairs, which could be more than three years old, are replaced with new ones. The old ones fall out. I expect you have found some of these old hairs in your brush or comb. There should be lots to find. You can lose up to 100 old hairs each day. But there's no need to worry because there are about 150,000 left in your head!

Did you know that there are hairs in your ears which help stop you from falling over?

We have hair for lots of reasons. Hair helps keep us warm. This is more important for animals than it is for us because we can wear clothes. But you may have noticed that when you get cold, the hairs on your arms and legs stand up on end. Your skin looks lumpy. This is caused by little muscles pulling the hair upright. The upright hairs trap the air warmed by your body. This works much better for furry animals than it does for us. They have more hair!

Hair also helps to protect delicate parts of our bodies. Eyelashes help stop dust from getting into our eyes. Of course, quills do a good job of protecting the whole of the porcupine.

We have sensitive hairs in our ears. These hairs are in a fluid, deep inside. Vibrations, caused by sound, make the hairs move. The nerves surrounding the hairs give the brain information about the sound. There are about two million of these hairs in each of your ears! But that's not all of them. Did you know that there are hairs in your ears which help stop you from falling over? The nerves around these hairs tell your brain the position of your body. They help you balance. Although sensory hairs have lots of nerves surrounding the root, hairs don't have nerves inside. That's why it doesn't hurt to have your hair cut.

What do you think? Is hair dead or alive? Well, it's a bit of a trick question because it is dead and alive. Hair is alive in and near the root where it is growing. But the rest of the hair is dead. Making a

choice between dead or alive, it's mostly dead.

Hopscotch
6–12 years
596 words

From the Author

As the CEO for the Ontario Society for the Prevention of Cruelty to Animals (OSPCA), I find it hard to make time for my other passion: writing. (Although I must say that my job does require significant writing skills for the numerous publications produced by the Society.) Meanwhile, I spend my available time learning and gaining as much experience and skill as possible, with the intent of having a successful career in writing after retirement.

The idea for "Dead or Alive?" came when one of my sons asked this very question, and I was not able to answer it well! It seemed to me that there must be a fun way to give kids the answer. I researched several books I had on hand (my house is full of them!), and gave a great deal of thought to how the information could be presented in order to maintain the interest of a fairly young reader. (The topic, of course, does not lend itself to an age group beyond 13 years.)

I became wrapped up in the subject as I discovered the important and varied functions that hair had for animals—including humans. I then tested the article on my two sons, and it was well-received.

I was not daunted when my article was rejected by four magazines. As we are often told in this field: persevere! I felt confident that I had developed an interesting article—and sure enough, *Hopscotch* accepted it!

Bird Alarm

By Cynthia J. Breedlove

When the smoke alarm goes off for a practice test at home, you know it! The sound blares in your ear and makes you notice it. Did you know that birds have an alarm system, too? It does not tell them about fire, or of a car or building being broken into. The bird alarm warns about predators!

A predator is an enemy, a creature who would like to eat a bird, a nestling, or even eggs. In a bird alarm system, it just takes one bird to notice a predator. This bird will start the alarm by chipping in a loud, excited manner. Immediately, any bird in the area will join in, and soon a very loud and effective alarm system is doing its job.

Being still was one way to avoid being seen by an enemy.

One day I was taking a walk in our woods. I noticed the pleasant singing and chirping sounds I had been hearing had changed. The air was filled with excited, staccato chips of sound. I looked around and saw a group of birds gathered in one area, and all were giving their alarm calls. I walked toward them and saw something fly up to a hole in a tree and disappear inside. The birds followed, still calling the alarm. They fluttered around the tree with the hole for awhile, but soon all had left. I waited, watching the hole. I wanted to know what had alarmed the birds. When it was quiet, a screech owl looked out of the hole.

Another time on my walk, a robin started giving off an alarm. Other birds joined in. I looked around and spotted the neighbor's cat, slinking through the weeds.

Starlings are good alarm callers. Stepping out my back door once, I heard them start up the call. A downy woodpecker became perfectly still at the suet feeder. He heard the alarm. Being still was one way to avoid being seen by an enemy. A mourning dove came flying across the yard, trying to get to safety. A cooper's hawk came swooping down after it. They disappeared behind a tree, and then I saw a poof of feathers. What do you think happened?

One time I thought the birds were giving a false alarm. I found a group of them in a tree, all calling the alarm. I could see no danger. Then one bird fluttered above a limb. I used binoculars and looked at the limb. Stretched out on it was a snake.

Some birds do more than just call out the alarm. Crows love to find an owl in a tree. They will start up a loud alarm, and then take turns swooping down and diving at the owl. I have seen some owls just sit and take it. They ignore the crows and the crows finally leave. But some owls try to fly away from the crows. This makes the crows caw louder than ever and they chase the owl.

Since smaller birds can maneuver more quickly than larger birds, they are safe if they don't get careless.

The eastern kingbird and redwing blackbird are other birds that will give off an alarm call, and then do more about it. They will fly above a hawk who comes into their nesting area and dive bomb from above. Since smaller birds can maneuver more quickly than larger birds, they are safe if they don't get careless. Sometimes they even hit the hawk on its back. The hawk usually flies away as fast as it can.

During the nesting season, birds are very alert to danger. Even though we mean no harm, the birds still think of us as possible predators. That is why we should not go where we know a nest is. The time they spend sounding an alarm about us could be better spent finding food for their babies, and could even attract cats or other predators to the area.

The bird alarm system is a good way for the birds to stay safe. It is not a perfect way, or the predators would never get a meal! Usually it is sick or injured birds that get caught, birds who heard the alarm but could not get to safety quickly enough. Or it is a young bird, that cannot fly away, or has not learned enough yet to stay safe when it hears an alarm.

Next time you're outside, keep your ear alert to bird alarm signals. If you hear one, look around.

 See if you can see what the danger is. Is it a hawk, a snake, a cat? Or is it you?

Nature Friend Magazine
4–14 years
745 words

From the Author

I'm a birdwatcher. When I was young, my dad worked with banding birds. We would go along and help him. My love for birds lay dormant in me for quite some time, but around 15 years ago, I started watching birds again with my dad.

This was my third published nonfiction article on birds, reinforcing the saying "write what you know." Though I have many bird books for reference, "Bird Alarm" was based on personal experiences I had while on bird-watching walks. I picked out things I thought kids would notice, interesting things kids can relate to right away.

In my writing, I aim for the 10- to 11-year-old reader, because my son is that age. I try to avoid complicated words. I try to write stories and articles that will motivate children to go outside and experience nature instead of watching television and playing video games.

I am an Institute graduate who is still primarily involved in motherhood. I write as time permits, jotting down ideas to be worked on later. I write both fiction and nonfiction—I've had stories published in a Sunday school weekly paper, but I've had more success with nonfiction.

"Bird Alarm" was rejected by two other publications before it was accepted by *Nature Friend*. I revised it a bit after reading a few issues of *Nature Friend,* because the manuscript had a reference to a school alarm, and I knew many of their readers were home-schooled. So I revised accordingly. It was accepted as written.

The Black & Blue Ballet

By Amy Cooley

Turning Olive Leaves into Gold

The very first Olympic games were held in a city called Olympus in Greece over 700 years before Jesus was born. There was only one event—a running race. People from different towns in Greece came to try to win. The winner got a crown of olive leaves.

Over the years the Greeks added new events, like boxing, wrestling, chariot racing and throwing a discus. Even if the towns had been fighting each other, they would make peace for the time of the Olympics. All the people would come together to watch or compete.

The games went on for nearly a thousand years. Then after the Romans took over Greece, the emperor ordered that the games be stopped. There were no Olympics for the next 1,500 years!

Finally in 1896, the Olympics began again. They are now held every two years.

Today's Olympics are a little different from those held in ancient Greece. Now there are summer games and winter games. Some of the events in the Winter Olympics are skiing, ice skating, bobsledding, ice hockey and the luge (pronounced "loozh," this is like a small sled or toboggan). The winners of each competition now receive medals; gold for first place, silver for second and bronze for third.

In today's Olympics, people come from different countries all over the world. They come together peacefully even if their countries don't usually get along. Because the people compete without fighting, the games help all of us work toward world peace.

A few years ago Daniyel Cohen used to watch his older brother playing ice hockey. He played on the pond by their house in Massachusetts. "I remember when he would fall when I was little...I would watch him and I'd think, 'that could *kill*,'" says Dani.

Dani, who is now 9, got over being afraid of falling on the ice. Now he is training to be a figure skater. Someday he wants to skate in the Olympics!

Dani first tried skating when he was 7 years old. "At first I fell a lot," he says. His grandma took him that first time he went, and he had to wear his cousin's skates. The skates rubbed against his heel and hurt his feet.

Even though his feet hurt, Dani loved skating right away. "It was so much fun to slide across the ice," he said, "especially when I was wearing smooth pants. I would slide really far."

Last July Dani skated in a Pre-Juvenile competition at Lake Placid in New York. (Lake Placid has four huge arenas. The Olympic games have been held there two times.) Dani won a gold medal and a bronze medal in his competitions. Dani, who was in the third grade then, was able to beat boys who were 13 and 15 years old.

It took a lot of work for Dani to get so good in only two years. Today he practices for two and a half hours a day. For a while he would practice at six o'clock in the morning before school started. Now he mostly practices after school. He has a private coach, Thomas McGinnis, who is one of the best in the world.

The highest spin Dani has learned so far is the "death drop." To do it he jumps up and looks down while he is in the air. He lands on the foot opposite the one he jumped up on and goes into a sitting spin. At first spinning made him dizzy. "After you learn to do it right," he says, "it doesn't make you dizzy anymore."

When people are learning to do jumps and spins on ice skates, they fall down often. Dani points to a red mark on his knee. He says it is an ice burn. He also has bruises on his legs and a blister on the back of his foot. Dani says the ice is very hard when you fall, but that you get used to it after a while. "My coach calls it 'the black and blue ballet,'" Dani says, smiling.

Besides training on the ice, Dani also has *fun* skating. He belongs to the Skating Club of Boston. Every year about 75 of the skaters put on a show called *Ice Chips*. This year they did an ice circus. Dani was a clown. "We would do funny things. We would stick out our tongues and stuff, and then after that we would make funny faces and do all these funny things to each other and make each other fall down," Dani says. About 3,000 people came to watch the shows.

Sometimes when he skates in front of so many people, Dani gets a "tiny bit" nervous at first. When he is skating in a competition, however, he has to think about what he is doing, so he forgets about being nervous after a few moments.

Dani's best friend, Jimmy, has leukemia. Dani got a chance to do something special for his friend in a program called "Lace Up for Leukemia." If he raised the most money skating for leukemia, he would win two tickets to Disney World. Dani worked hard to raise $3,000. He won the competition and sent his friend on a wonderful vacation.

Besides skating, Dani also likes to play the piano. He takes dance lessons and learns tap and jazz and ballet. He also has his own fitness trainer he goes to three times a week. Last September Dani got his black belt in Tai Kwon Do, which is like Karate but without the weapons. These things also help him skate. In school his favorite subjects are music, gym, math and recess. "Oh, and I like science, too," he says. "I love dissecting things."

A person can't try out for the Olympics until they are 15 years old. If you want to be able to get into the Olympics, Dani says there is a lot you have to learn. One thing is that it is not always fun and that you can't always just play on the ice. It's a lot of work.

Before he started skating, Dani wanted to be an astronaut. Now he is not sure if he would have

time. He knows he will have to spend most of his time practicing on the ice. It takes a lot to become the best skater in the country, and maybe even the world, but that's what Dani wants to be!

Olympic Tidbits and Trivia

Did you know that when he was 12, Dick Button, the first American to win a gold medal in figure skating, was turned away by one coach who said he was too fat? He weighed 160 pounds. But by the time he was 16, he had won his first US title.

Q. What does the Olympic motto *Citius, Altius, Fortius* mean?
A. It is Latin for "Faster, Higher, Stronger," which is what each Olympic athlete tries to be.

My Friend
6–12 years
1,141 words

From the Author

I wrote "The Black & Blue Ballet" the summer before my senior year of college, while I was an intern at St. Paul Books & Media in Boston. One day, while I was working in the editorial department, Sr. Kathryn James, the editor of *My Friend*, asked me to interview a young ice skater. She was excited; I was a little scared. It was to be my first interview for a professional publication.

Sr. Kathryn had called the local skating rink to find a young skater to interview. She wanted someone training for an Olympic sport to teach readers about the upcoming winter Olympics.

The interview was great. Daniyel was bright and talkative. But he was still a kid. I knew it was time to wrap up when Daniyel started fidgeting and climbing on the back of his chair.

What helped me most during the actual writing was picturing my nine-year-old nephew. I pretended I was simply telling the story to him in a way he could understand.

Soap It Up!

By Amy O. Barish

You've just finished making a big stack of mud pies when you hear the call for dinner. You rush inside and quickly rinse your hands in the bathroom sink. As you slip into your chair at the table, your mom shakes her head. "Go wash your hands," she orders. "And try using soap this time!"

Queen Isabella of Spain bragged that she had only two baths in her life.

Your mother is right. Water alone won't clean the dirt off your hands. But add soap, and the dirt is washed away. Here's why.

Your skin is always making an oil called *sebum* (SEE-bum). Dirt gets stuck to this oil. Because oil and water do not mix, water by itself cannot wash away the oily dirt on your hands. The water rolls off your skin, leaving the oil and dirt behind.

But soap is a special substance. It has a water-loving side and an oil-loving side. The oil-loving side of the soap sticks to the oily dirt. The water-loving side mixes with the water. When you wash your hands with soap, the dirt and oil are lifted from the skin, and the water washes it all away.

Soap used to be made from two dirty materials—animal fat and wood ashes! Wood ashes contain lye. This strong chemical added a water-loving side to the oil in animal fat to produce soap.

You might wonder why people would think of mixing fat and ashes to make things clean. It may be that the first soap was discovered by accident. Legend has it that melted fat from animals sacrificed in fire mixed with ashes from the fire. Rain carried the mixture into a nearby river. Women who were washing clothes in the river saw that the ash mixture made the clothes come cleaner. Soap was discovered! This type of soap was used to wash clothes, but it was too harsh for the skin.

For many years in Europe, it was not the style for people to take baths. People thought water would make you sick. They didn't know that just the opposite is true. Queen Isabella of Spain bragged that she had only two baths in her life. Queen Elizabeth of England was a little better—she took a bath every three months. Later, people realized that dirt can carry diseases and that keeping clean is a good health habit.

It wasn't until around 1900 that soap could be bought in stores.

In colonial days people started taking more baths. But they couldn't buy soap. They had to make it themselves. Once a year the women would prepare lye from ashes they had saved. They would mix this with animal fat to make big batches of soap. Washing still involved carrying water from a well and heating it on the stove. Since cleaning was such a chore, people might only bathe and wash their clothes once a week.

It wasn't until around 1900 that soap could be bought in stores. Soon new cleaning agents called *detergents* (dih-TUR-jents) were invented. Detergents are made from man-made chemicals instead of animal fats and ashes.

In the past people used the same soap to wash their clothes, bodies, and hair. Today, there is a special soap for every need. There are detergents to wash dishes, wash clothes, and clean the carpet. Many soaps are just used on our bodies. Do you use a different soap to wash your hair, hands, and body? Do your parents use a different soap than you? How many different soaps and detergents can you find in your home? As you can see, it takes lots of soaps to keep our world clean!

Messy Mixture—A Dirty Experiment

1. Collect about ¼ cup of dirt outdoors and put it in a clear jar with a lid.
2. Add about 1 cup of water. Put the lid on the jar and shake it up.
3. Let the mixture settle for five to ten minutes. Is the dirt in the water? Where is most of the dirt?
4. Now add ½ cup of oil (vegetable oil will work) to the jar. Put on the lid and shake it up again.
5. After five to ten minutes look at the mixture. The oil layer will float on top of the water. Where is the dirt now? Is there more dirt in the oil or in the water?
6. Now add a big squirt of dishwashing detergent. Shake again.
7. Let the jar settle for five to ten minutes. Where is the dirt now? Does the oil layer look cleaner?

This experiment shows how dirt likes to stick to oil. Adding detergent should have cleaned most of the dirt from the oil layer, just like soap cleans the dirt from your oily hands.

*U*S* Kids*
5–10 years
592 words

From the Author

I am a mother earnestly writing while my children are at school. "Soap It Up!" is the only article I've sold so far; I have two other articles and a book making the rounds.

With a background in chemistry, I wanted to write science articles for young readers. Unfortunately, there aren't many children's science magazines that accept freelance work. The Children's Better Health Institute publishes about six magazines with some nonfiction articles; they especially like subjects related to health and hygiene. At first, I thought chemistry wouldn't fit, but then I remembered soap: it has a fascinating chemistry and is essential to hygiene.

I started my research in the children's section of the library, where I found books on the craft of soap making. With a few basic facts from an encyclopedia CD, my research was complete. (I have also used the Internet for research, but only for current-event topics.)

I included the most amusing or intriguing facts. Many involved the history of soap, which flowed through the article. I included only the simplest chemistry, but it is there. In order to catch the attention of the reader, I began with a common-day scenario using the second-person "you."

I didn't write for a specific age, but chose an age based on the final product. My seven-year-old test-read the article. I made about three revisions and the editor made his own.

In order to develop the activity, I tried to think of the most basic fact I was trying to teach: "dirty oil and water don't mix; soap allows them to mix." I used everyday materials to prove this point. I experimented in the kitchen to get the activity to work. What quantities of dirt and oil worked best? What type of soap worked best? It's essential to try out your experiment before you submit it.

I chose *U*S* Kids* based on age range. This is my only article that's been accepted the first place I sent it. I guess it was just a good fit.

Growing Up in Another Time, Another Place

By Peggy Wilgus Wymore

Read these clues. Can you guess what time and place this is?

- Families spend time together.
- Kids like acrobatics and music. They like playing with dolls and balls. They like racing and "playing war."
- Cats and dogs are favorite pets.

Sounds like today in America, doesn't it? But what about this:

- Some babies are given fried mice to chew while teething!
- Most children don't go to school!
- Children's heads are often shaved except for one lock of hair worn over the right ear!
- Kids don't worry about clothes because they don't wear any!

This doesn't sound like your life anymore, does it? Let's travel back about 4,500 years into the past. Go to the northeast corner of Africa along the Nile River. You are now in Egypt when the pyramids were built.

Suppose you are growing up in that time and place. What is your life like?

Your job may be to tie up the shafts of wheat and put them into bundles.

Whether you are rich or poor, your house is probably made of mud bricks and is one to three stories tall. Its size depends on your father's job. Is he the pharaoh (Egypt's ruler)? Then your mud brick home would be a palace with many rooms. Is he a nobleman or a scribe (one of the few people who could write)? If so, your house may have a private courtyard with flowers and a fish-pond.

Perhaps you live in one of the great cities, Memphis or Thebes. Your father or mother might be a weaver who makes cloth or might work in a bakery making bread. Then you live in a small house, close to others like yours, with doors opening to a dusty, narrow street.

Probably, though, your father is a farmer. If he is a rich farmer, you may live on a huge farm along the Nile. If he has a small farm, you may live in a tiny town near the fields.

All houses have flat roofs. Because of the hot weather, your family often goes to the roof in the evening to get cool. You might even sleep on the roof.

You probably believe in many gods and wear an amulet or figure of one of them on a necklace.

Wherever you live, it is on the sand. Except for a narrow strip of land along the Nile, every place is sand. The green land along the river is too precious to build houses on. This is the only place to grow all of the food for the country.

Because growing crops is so important, most families farm. At harvest time, everyone helps. Your job may be to tie up the shafts of wheat and put them into bundles.

If your father is a farmer, he does not work from June to September. The Nile floods its banks then, and all of the farmland is covered with water. At that time the pharaoh may order your father to work for him. If not, you have vacation time. Then you might take a boat trip down the Nile with your family. Or you might walk to the next village for a visit, with a donkey carrying your supplies.

Childhood is carefree and happy, but it is short.

Whatever the season, religion is an important part of your life. You probably believe in many gods and wear an amulet or figure of one of them on a necklace. Your parents say this protects you from evil and illness.

Childhood is carefree and happy, but it is short. By the time you are a young teenager, you'll be married. So you need training for life and work. You'll get much of this from your parents and some on-the-job training. Like most Egyptian children, you'll be expected to live your life just as your parents have lived theirs.

Right now, though, you're still growing up. You have time to play with your pet *miw* (pronounced me-you). Do you know what a *miw* is? It's a cat!

AppleSeeds
8–10 years
615 words

From the Author

I worked from an outline when I wrote this article. After gathering what seemed like hundreds of pages of notes, I went through and highlighted any fact that might be interesting to a child. Then I categorized the highlighted notes into topics such as houses, parents' occupations, climate, recreation, pets, religion, and schooling and put the topics into outline form. Next, I rearranged parts of the outline so each subject would move logically into the next. Then I wrote transition statements to connect the topics and paragraphs.

For my hook at the beginning, I tried to find some situations that today's children could find in common with those of ancient Egypt, and contrast them with "outrageous" practices that would make a child say "Wow!" The rest of the facts developed in the article continued in the vein of children in ancient Egypt being very different from today's children, thus (hopefully) keeping readers entertained.

I wrote in second person, asking readers to imagine themselves living in the time when the pyramids were being built. I used "you," "your," "your family," talking directly to readers as if they were actually growing up in ancient Egypt.

I wrote at least seven major drafts. The article started off at 1,000 words, and the one I actually submitted was down to 660 words. The final article, after editing, was 640 words long.

I read and reread *AppleSeeds'* guidelines and theme list to make sure I understood what they wanted. Then I followed all the advice about query letters in the front of the *Children's Magazine Market,* but used *AppleSeeds'* form.

Since I had never been published before, I remembered my Institute training and didn't mention it. Instead, I showed my knowledge of the subject by explaining that I had taught a sixth-grade section on ancient Egypt. From the *Children's Magazine Market,* I knew to word my query as a proposal for a "to be written" article (even though the article was already written).

This article was edited pretty heavily by *AppleSeeds*. The editor kept my tone exactly, with my ideas and facts, but some paragraphs and even sentences were rearranged, and some facts were edited out. When they sent the draft for my approval, I liked what they had done.

Watching a Beekeeper

By Joan Davis

I froze in place as a cloud of honeybees buzzed around my head and arms. My only hope was that the big fancy net I was wearing would keep the bees out. You see, my friend Frank is a beekeeper. He not only keeps bees but he loves them,

A few days later, the buzzing, vibrating boxes arrived at the post office. Each box was filled with more than ten thousand bees.

too. I joined him on this warm spring day to see how a beekeeper starts a new hive.

Frank needed some more hives, so he called a nearby bee ranch to order two boxes of bees. A few days later, the buzzing, vibrating boxes arrived at the post office. Each box was filled with more than ten thousand bees. A postal worker called Frank and asked him to please hurry and pick them up!

Honeybees had always seemed scary to me. But as I watched Frank work, I learned something. I learned that if you know how to handle bees the right way, beekeeping can be a great hobby.

We used string to tie our pants around our ankles to keep any lost honeybees from crawling up our legs.

Frank and I each wore a helmet and a net to protect us from bee stings. We used string to tie our pants around our ankles to keep any lost honeybees from crawling up our legs.

For hives, beekeepers use boxes with narrow wooden frames hanging inside. On each frame is a sheet of thin wax. The honeybees produce more wax from their bodies to make six-sided boxes, called cells, on these sheets. The queen bee lays eggs in some of the cells, and the bees store honey and pollen in others. Each cell is just big enough for a honeybee to squeeze inside.

Frank sprayed sugar water on the mass of bees in the center of the mailing box. For a few minutes, this makes their wings too sticky to fly. Then he reached in for the tiny box containing the queen bee. "Aha," whispered Frank, "and here she is." His voice was quiet but excited. He slipped the queen's box into his pocket to keep her safe. The queen is important to the hive, and the other honeybees will attack to protect her.

Then he smiled at me and said, "Not one sting. They must really like you!"

Moving quietly, he dumped the rest of the honeybees from the mailing box into the hive. After spraying the queen with sugar water, he took her out of the special box and placed her in her new home. He covered the top of the hive with a lid. Then he smiled at me and said, "Not one sting. They must really like you!"

Next, Frank opened a little door at the bottom of the hive. This would let the honeybees fly in and out to gather nectar and pollen for the hive. Honeybees use nectar to make honey. They use honey and pollen as food. Soon the queen would start laying eggs, and the hive would grow. Frank's work for the day was done.

Later in the summer, I saw Frank again. He proudly presented me with a big jar of sweet, tasty honey made by my friends the honeybees.

Highlights for Children
2–12 years
492 words

From the Author

When I wrote "Watching a Beekeeper," there was a great deal of media hype about Africanized honeybees and the danger they represented. My husband has been a beekeeper for several years, and people often expressed their fears about the bees to us. So I decided to write an article that would help present the other side of the story in a manner that would be appealing to young children.

I used my opening paragraph to capture their attention because most of us are afraid of bees, especially a whole swarm buzzing around us. From there I simply described the process of setting up the hive, adding a little information about bees as I went. First-person point of view worked well here because it kept the action happening like a story instead of sounding like a dry encyclopedia article.

My research was based on interviewing Frank, watching him work with his bees, and reading a couple of his professional beekeeping books. Obviously, there were a massive number of possible topics about beekeeping, but *Highlights for Children* seemed to like basic ideas with an interesting twist, so I decided to write about the idea of setting up a beehive.

Since the article was written with younger children in mind, I kept it short, simple, and to the point (not easy for someone as wordy as me, but my friend's advice was to keep it "lean, clean, and mean"). I was also careful to use active-voice verbs to make it more interesting. Children in this age group like stories and action. I have received several letters from children who enjoyed the article, which is quite gratifying.

I began seriously writing about six years ago after attending a local writers' conference, and with the encouragement of a good friend. I am currently pursuing my master's degree in history as a springboard to doing serious research and writing on ancient history.

Scary Science

By Barbara A. Tyler

Sometimes science can seem pretty spooky, but there's always a good reason for what happens—or seems to happen. See if you can figure out what makes this science experiment work.

The Ghost Coin

Can a coin disappear while you watch? Try this experiment and you won't believe your eyes!

You Will Need:

1 empty jar (32-ounce mayonnaise jar works well)
A coin
Cold water
A plain sheet of paper
Newspapers

Directions:

1. Cover your work area with newspapers and lay the plain piece of paper on top.
2. Place the coin on the paper and set the jar on top of the coin.
3. Look at the coin through the side of the jar.
4. Slowly fill the jar with water and watch what happens to the coin.

What Happened?

The coin disappeared because the jar of water forms a lens that refracts (bends) light.

You could see the coin when the jar was empty because light could travel from the surface of the coin straight to your eyes. As you added water, the light was bent away from your eyes, making the coin seem to vanish.

Jack And Jill
7–10 years
185 words

From the Author

I've been a full-time freelance writer for the past five years. During that time, I've published children's activities in *Jack And Jill, Guideposts for Kids,* and *American Girl.*

When I originally decided to write "Ghost Coin," I was researching optical illusions and science experiments to show my children. This one was such a big hit that I knew other kids would like it. I also knew from experience that *Jack And Jill* used science experiments, so I sent in a query. When the editor expressed interest, I did the experiment again, and started working on a rough draft.

I go through an activity step by step as I write a rough draft. That way, I know the steps are in order and I'm not leaving anything out. Then I go back later and tailor the piece to fit the market. With the exception of a title change, "Ghost Coin" ran exactly as I wrote it, and it was published with another experiment, "Eggs-tremely Eerie Eggs."

My advice to writers is trite, repetitive, and completely true: know your market! Anybody willing to do the work can make a piece fit a specific magazine. Start by *scrutinizing* your target magazine. In this case, I went to the library and read a year's worth of back issues, counted words, checked vocabulary, and studied how much depth was given to explanations. Then I wrote and rewrote my piece until it fit.

Knuckle Down That Taw!

By Beth Kennedy

Do you want to have fun? Find some *mibs*, grab a *taw*, and start shooting. These words may sound odd, but you probably know the game they're used in. It's been around for ages but is still enjoyed by people everywhere. What game is it? Why, marbles, of course!

The game of marbles dates back to ancient times. Historians think that children in Egypt, Rome, and North America may have played marbles thousands of years ago. In fact, signs of marble playing have been found in countries all over the world.

Abraham Lincoln is thought to have been an expert at a marble game called "old bowler."

Marbles from long ago were not like those of today. People used stones, clay balls, nuts, and fruit pits as the first marbles. Later, people made marbles from materials such as glass, china, and real chips of marble. This gave the game its present name.

Adults as well as children enjoy marbles. Some people say that Presidents George Washington and Thomas Jefferson liked to play. Abraham Lincoln is thought to have been an expert at a marble game called "old bowler."

How do you play marbles? Here are directions for "ringer," a game that is popular today.

Getting Ready

Find a large flat surface where it's safe to play. It can be outside or inside. Use chalk or string to make a circle that is ten feet from one side to the other. Inside the circle, place thirteen marbles in the shape of a cross. Each marble should be three inches from the next one. These target marbles are sometimes called *mibs*.

How to Shoot

Turn your hand so that at least one knuckle rests on the ground. This is called "knuckling down." Hold your shooting marble between your curled index and middle fingers. Aim, then flick the shooter with your thumb. Shooters are also called *taws*, and they may be larger than the target marbles.

Let's Play!

From outside the circle, shoot at the marbles in the cross shape. Try to knock them out of the circle without having your shooter roll out. Shoot again from the spot where your shooter stopped. Your turn ends when you fail to knock a marble out of the circle or when your shooter rolls out.

Has anyone ever asked you if you've "lost your marbles"?

Players take turns. The winner is the player who has knocked out the most marbles by the end of the game.

There are dozens of ways to play marbles. "Pot" games are played by aiming marbles at small holes, or "pots," in the ground. "Bombers" is played by dropping a marble to try to hit another marble.

This Game Has Endured the Test of Time

Sometimes people play marbles "for keeps." That's when the winner keeps the marbles that have been won—not just for the length of the game but for good. Since many players collect marbles as a hobby and don't want to lose them, most games are played just for fun.

Has anyone ever asked you if you've "lost your marbles"? This phrase means to lose your common sense or sanity, or to be foolish. Some people believe that this comes from a folktale in which a monkey steals a boy's marbles when the boy is not paying attention.

Whether or not any monkeys live near you, here's what to do if you're looking for fun. Polish up those *mibs* and *taws*, call your friends, and "knuckle down" to an exciting and historic game.

Highlights for Children
2–12 years
562 words

From the Author

This article resulted from an Institute course assignment. I wanted to write something unique for 6- to 10-year-old readers that would also be interesting to editors—not the "same old, same old," so to speak. I leafed through books until I came upon the game of marbles. My brother had played marbles for several years, and I remembered how the whole neighborhood of children participated in the games. As a teacher, I wanted to reintroduce the game during those indoor, in-clement-weather recesses we often have in Ohio.

In my research, I used an encyclopedia, a book about marbles, and a text on idioms and expressions of everyday language. That's where I got statements like "Have you lost your marbles?"

My instructor said my article was marketable, so I mustered up my courage and sent it to *Highlights, Cricket,* and *Jack And Jill. Highlights* accepted it first. They did quite a bit of editing, but it still sounded much like my original article. And my students have enjoyed playing marbles during snowy weather!

All in the Family

By Sandy J. Stiefer

OK, maybe you're thinking—what could a wolf pack and my family possibly have in common? Well, for one thing, wolf packs are made up of a father, a mother, pups of different ages, and maybe a grandparent. There may be newborn pups, one-year-olds, and two-year-olds. And that's the way it is for many human families around the world—with parents, toddlers, pre-teens, teenagers, and maybe other family members all living together.

Also, the wolves in a pack work together, play together, and depend on one another in many ways. They even care for and show affection for one another. Doesn't that sound a lot like a human family?

These are some of the most important ways wolf packs and human families are alike. But if you look closely, there are even more.

Mom and Dad—They're the Leaders

In most human families, Mom and Dad are the ones in charge. Same thing in a wolf pack. The mother and father are called the *alpha* wolves. Alphas are the leaders of the pack, and they control the rest of the wolves. When wolves mate, it's sometimes for life. If one dies, the other will often mate with a new partner. Usually, only the alpha pair mates and has pups.

Sometimes a pack has only one alpha. It may be male or female—just like in a home with a single human parent.

My Room—Keep Out!

You may have put such a sign on the door to your room. It's your territory, right?

A wolf pack also has a territory—a place it moves around in, hunting prey and raising pups. The pack tries to keep other wolves out of its territory by posting signs all around the edges. But wolves can't use words as you can. Instead, they raise a leg and sprinkle urine on tree trunks, rocks, and anything else that might be handy. The urine's scent is like a message.

Wolves from other packs then "read" those messages by smelling them. They know to stay out of that pack's territory. They may even pee on the same place, like leaving a note that says, "We were here too."

Baby on the Way

When a woman is expecting a baby, she may buy or make clothes and blankets. She also may fix up a room or other special place for the new baby.

A female wolf doesn't buy things, sew or knit, of course. But she does get ready for her babies. She digs a den in a hillside or at the base of a tree. Or she finds a cozy cave behind some boulders. Sometimes it's an old den. But she wants it to be "just right."

Your mom might say, "I don't like these green walls—let's paint the baby's room pink!" If a mother wolf decides a den won't be just right for her pups, she digs or finds another one.

It's a New Baby

When a human mom has a baby, she usually likes a little quiet time for a while so she can rest and get used to being a mother.

The mother wolf stays in the den with the pups for a few weeks after she gives birth. No one is allowed inside, not even the father wolf. If he comes to the entrance, she may bare her teeth and growl at him. She's very protective of her pups.

49

The father wolf brings food back from a hunt and leaves it at the den entrance for the mother wolf to eat. She will leave the den mainly for a quick drink of water and to go to the bathroom. And just as a woman changes a baby's diaper, the mother wolf also cleans her babies—she licks away her pups' wastes.

When five or six weeks old, the pups may explore outside the den for the first time. The father wolf and the others gather around with tails wagging. They lick the pups and make little noises.

That, too, is a lot like what usually happens in a human family. Grandma or Uncle Henry gush all over the new baby, kissing and cooing. New babies sure make a happy time for both human and wolf families.

What's for Dinner?

A human mom or dad brings food home for the family and then serves a warm meal. It's not a whole lot different with wolves.

After a hunt, Mother, Father, or one of the other adult pack members brings food home to the pups.

The pups gulp down their dinner faster than you and your friends can wipe out a pizza.

They don't bring it in a grocery bag, of course. Instead, they bring it in their mouths and drop it in front of the pups. Or they bring it in their stomachs. The pups poke the adult wolves in the mouth with their noses, and up comes a pile of warm and partly digested meat. The pups gulp down their dinner faster than you and your friends can wipe out a pizza.

Call the Baby-Sitter

Your parents probably left you with a baby-sitter when they went out for an evening. And that's the way it is with wolves.

Once the pups are big enough to be out of the den, the mother wolf goes out hunting with Dad again. One of the pack members stays behind to baby sit. Often it's an older brother or sister from last year's litter, or maybe a grandparent. Only difference is, a baby-sitting wolf doesn't get paid!

After the pups grow up, they leave to find mates and start families of their own. Some move nearby, while others may move hundreds of miles away.

So you see? Even though we're different in many ways, wolf and human families really do have a lot in common.

Ranger Rick
7–12 years
957 words

From the Author

The idea for "All in the Family" came from my six Siberian huskies. Their wolf-like behavior had triggered my interest, and for at least five years I studied wolves by reading everything I could find and watching documentaries. It occurred to me that wolf packs and human families have similarities, and the article was born. I wrote a couple of pages of a first draft and had my writing group critique it.

I'd always wanted to write for *Ranger Rick,* and their humorous animal profiles appealed to me. Their guidelines said they were open to comparisons of wild and domestic animals, but I thought comparing wolves to humans would be a unique twist. I also knew they required "expert" knowledge and I had no real experience with wolves. But I had joined Timber Wolf Alliance some time back and mentioned that in my query. The editor asked to see the article on speculation. I wrote at least 10 drafts before submitting it.

I'm an instructor for the Institute and a full-time freelance writer for adult and juvenile magazines and biographical reference books. I have two juvenile nonfiction books out. I've been a magazine editor, and I also teach writing classes.

I get ideas from my dogs, the world around me, and things I read. Articles suggest themselves to me as I do chores and hobbies, or see something when I'm out, or have a conversation with someone. I keep my eyes and ears and mind open.

The Mysterious Yawn

By Lee Ann Howlett

People do it. Most animals do it. Everybody does it. We all yawn, but nobody's really sure why we do it.

We begin to yawn about five minutes after we're born. We continue to yawn all of our lives. We do most of our yawning when we first wake up. We also yawn a lot just before going to sleep. You may think you yawn only when you're tired, but yawning actually helps to perk you up.

Did you know that birds, reptiles, and even fish yawn?

Some scientists think that yawning sends a fresh supply of oxygen-filled blood to a tired brain. Your heart beats faster, and your blood circulates more quickly when you yawn. Because of this, yawning helps to keep you alert. People usually stop yawning after they are in bed. This is because they have given themselves permission to fall asleep. They no longer need to yawn.

If you have a pet, you've probably noticed that dogs and cats yawn quite a bit. But, did you know that birds, reptiles, and even fish yawn?

In the animal kingdom, yawning can mean different things. For some animals, it's a way of showing who's in charge. Hippos and many apes yawn as a way of saying, "I'm the boss." Fish and lizards open their mouths in a wide yawn to scare off attackers. Chickens will stand on tiptoes and flap their wings while yawning.

Apes often live in groups in the wild. When the leader gets up in the morning, he yawns to get the other apes moving.

This is important to keep the group together and ready to travel.

Often, animals will yawn just before something important is about to happen. The yawn helps them feel more alert. Lions and other big cats will yawn just before getting up to search for food. Even lions in the zoo will yawn just before their feeding time.

Some scientists do not think that giraffes yawn. A student scientist watched giraffes in a zoo for over 35 hours. He never saw a yawn. This may have to do with the giraffe's long neck. Its head is pretty far from its heart. This may mean that a giraffe's breathing and circulatory systems are different from other animals.

Animals will often stretch when they yawn. People also do this. Scientists think that yawning and stretching are connected, but they are not sure how or why.

Hundreds of years ago, some people thought that yawning allowed evil spirits to enter the body.

There's an old saying, "Smile and the whole world smiles with you." Smiling is contagious, but not nearly as contagious as yawning. It's very hard to watch someone yawn without wanting to yawn yourself. You may have noticed this even when seeing someone yawn on TV. In fact, most of us can yawn just by thinking about it!

We've all been told that it's not polite to yawn in public. Hundreds of years ago, some people thought that yawning allowed evil spirits to enter the body. They began covering their mouths with their hands. Of course, we know that's a silly superstition. These days we cover our mouths during a yawn to be polite, or we try to stop a yawn by keeping our mouths closed. As you know, this is very hard to do!

The next time you start to yawn, remember that your body is just sending a message to your brain. Wake up!

Hopscotch
6–12 years
549 words

From the Author

The idea for this article came about from a newspaper article on the topic. Whenever I read or hear about something that interests me or arouses my curiosity, I immediately think in terms of explaining it to children in an entertaining fashion. I keep an enormous "idea" folder. I don't work from an outline, but I do take notes and highlight material from my research.

My writing for children has all been pretty much for the 8–12 age group. They're a tough audience, so I usually have several "hooks" or tidbits to draw them in, placed throughout the article. I also use humor whenever possible. The opening sentences for this article came naturally, since I've always wondered about this myself!

Keeping the article "understandable" for this age group went hand in hand with editing and revising. I read and reread the article and continuously "tightened it up." Instead of numerous details that could've been included on this topic, I backed up and took a broader view. This made the subject simpler to understand and kept the word count within limits.

I didn't sell this piece using a query. Once I have an idea, I prefer to flesh it out into an article. I had several magazines in mind for "The Mysterious Yawn," including *Hopscotch* (I had sold to them before).

I've been a librarian for over 20 years. I've published book reviews, poems, and juvenile nonfiction articles, and I produce a library newsletter.

Teddy's Bear

By Janeen R. Adil

Theodore "Teddy" Roosevelt, America's twenty-sixth president, was famous for accomplishing many important things while he was in office. Something he *didn't* do, however, made him just as famous. And because of it, one of the best-loved toys ever created was named after him.

In November 1902, President Roosevelt traveled south to settle a boundary dispute between Mississippi and Louisiana. While he was there, he took some time off to go bear hunting. Several reporters and a well-known newspaper artist named Clifford Berryman joined the president's hunting trip.

The hunters didn't have much luck. Finally, on the last day of the hunt, the president spotted a bear. As he carefully aimed his rifle, the animal turned around. It was only a cub! Teddy Roosevelt loved to hunt, but he refused to shoot this frightened little bear.

They sewed and stuffed the bear and added buttons for its eyes.

Clifford Berryman thought this was a wonderful opportunity for a drawing. He sketched a cartoon of President Roosevelt turning his back on the cub, unwilling to shoot the small creature. Soon Berryman's black-and-white drawing was appearing in newspapers all over the country. People everywhere liked the cartoon and thought it showed the president to be a kind-hearted man.

One of those who saw and enjoyed the drawing was Morris Michtom, a candy store owner in Brooklyn, New York. He and his wife, Rose, knew how to make stuffed toys, and the cartoon gave them an idea. The Michtoms found some brown plush fabric and cut out pieces for a bear with movable arms and legs. Then they sewed and stuffed the bear and added buttons for its eyes.

The Michtoms placed the new toy bear, a copy of Berryman's cartoon, and a sign that read "Teddy's Bear" in the front window of their store. The bear sold quickly, and so did the next few that the Michtoms made. When Morris saw how popular the bears were, he knew he would need the president's permission to continue using his name.

Teddy bears had become as important to children as blocks, dolls, and balls had already been for generations.

Morris wrote a letter to the White House and received a handwritten reply from Theodore Roosevelt himself. "I don't think my name is likely to be worth much in the bear business," the president wrote, "but you are welcome to use it." So the Michtoms went to work, making one teddy bear after another.

Since Rose and Morris made the bears themselves and still had a candy store to manage, they produced the bears slowly at first. Eventually they closed the candy store, and the Michtom family business became the Ideal Toy Company, one of America's biggest toymakers. Soon other companies in the United States and Europe were producing bears of all shapes, sizes, and prices. Some of the most beautiful stuffed bears were made in Germany by Margarete Steiff and her workers.

In just a few years, teddy bears had become extremely popular. Other items related to the stuffed bears were sold, too. Not only could one buy clothing for a teddy bear, but there were also bear puzzles, bear books, bear games, bear banks—all sorts of toys and amusements! Teddy bears had become as important to children as blocks, dolls, and balls had already been for generations.

Today teddy bears remain a favorite of boys and girls everywhere. Many adults love to collect and display them, too. Hundreds of millions of teddy bears have been produced since Teddy Roosevelt's hunting trip so many years ago. Who could have guessed that the story of an unlucky president and a frightened bear cub would have such a happy ending?

Spider
6–9 years
639 words

From the Author

"Teddy's Bear" began with a postcard. On a long-ago visit to the Smithsonian, I'd picked up a card showing the original teddy bear. I remembered hearing the story of Teddy Roosevelt and the stuffed bear's creation. It was easy to see that this article had "kid appeal" written all over it.

This piece was one of the first I wrote for children, and actually goes back a number of years. I researched it at a college library, using a few general books on the history of toys. I'm sure it took me quite a while. Today I complete my research much faster, thanks to a lot of practice—and to the Internet.

Once I choose a topic and do the background reading, I let everything "steep" for a while. I find that the article's opening always presents itself—probably through letting my subconscious have a turn with the material. Since kids need to be hooked from the outset, those initial sentences are crucial. Posing a question can work nicely, as can dropping an attention-getting name or a bit of intriguing information. (These same techniques, by the way, work with query letters and potential editors too!)

By the time I know what the opening will be, I also know how the article will fall into place. A piece like "Teddy's Bear" is easier because history has a sequence. I started at the beginning of the story, then told what happened next, and so on. To finish, I brought the subject back to the present—a child's frame of reference.

As one of my earlier pieces, this article did need some editing. Since then, I've learned more tricks of the trade. I try to use the active voice instead of the passive. I alternate short sentences with longer ones. And I favor non-idiomatic language, since it's better understood by younger readers.

As a former teacher, current mom, and avid reader, I believe quality writing for children is of great importance. To date, nearly a dozen magazines have accepted my fiction and nonfiction. I've also started working on longer book-length manuscripts. Writing for young people is my goal, my challenge, and my joy.

Danger on the Canal

By Carol Ottolenghi-Barga

C lang, clang!
Emily heard the familiar bell and raced down the path to the canal. Aunt Flo's and Uncle Fred's boat floated next to the lock that Emily's parents operated. Uncle Fred was unharnessing the mules that pulled the boat up the canal. Emily ran right into his arms.

"Do you know what today is?" she demanded.

Her uncle scratched his beard. "Saturday?" he guessed.

"I don't mean that!" Emily tugged his shirt sleeve. "Do you know what's special about today?"

"Well, it's June 6, 1848...don't think I know of anything special about today."

> *"Some folks think the railroads will put canal boats out of business. They might try to stop us from delivering this cargo."*

"Uncle Fred!"

He started to laugh. "Do you really think we would forget your tenth birthday?" he asked, ruffling Emily's brown hair.

Her parents hurried down the path from the house. "You're just in time for supper," Emily's mother called out. "Bring your things into the house, Florence. You and Fred will sleep in the front room tonight."

Emily frowned as her mother and aunt walked away. She wanted to ask Aunt Flo if she could ride up the canal with them, but now she'd have to wait.

"What's your cargo?" Emily's father asked Uncle Fred.

"Lumber and strap iron from Cincinnati, for the railroad they're building near Toledo," Uncle Fred answered. "Some folks think the railroads will put canal boats out of business. They might try to stop us from delivering this cargo."

Emily half listened as she balanced on a railroad tie like a tightrope walker.

"Careful, Emily!" her uncle hollered. "You'd better get off before you fall."

Emily sighed. Walking on the tie wasn't any harder than walking across the closed lock gates, which she did all the time.

"Do you want me to open the lock?" she asked.

"Good idea," her father said. "It can fill while we're eating."

Emily turned the big wheel that shut the gates behind the boat. Then she opened the gates in front of the boat. Water from the upper canal rushed into the lock.

As the lock filled with water, the boat rose. Emily knew it would take about half an hour for the water to be as high as the upper canal. She checked the gates, then ran into the house.

Supper was bean soup, corn bread, and her mother's secret-recipe birthday cake. Afterward Uncle Fred and the mules towed the boat out of the lock and onto the upper canal. Emily closed the gates behind the boat.

Back inside, her mother called, "Bedtime, young lady."

Emily groaned to herself. She still hadn't asked about the canal ride. Well, she thought, I'll pack a bag tonight, so I'll be ready to go if they say yes.

She finished packing and sat on her bed, too excited to sleep. She was listening to the water slap gently against the canal walls when she saw a lantern winking through the trees near the boat. Emily stood up.

"Uncle Fred must be checking the boat," she said to herself. "I'll ask him if I can go."

She ran barefoot down the path. But before she reached the canal, she heard the mules snorting nervously.

Emily froze. Uncle Fred wouldn't upset the mules. Someone else was on the boat!

Silently, Emily crawled across the lock gate, onto the boat, and near the mules' stalls. Two men stood there. One held a lantern; the other a torch.

"A little fire might convince other canal-boat captains not to help the railroads," said the man with the torch.

"Fire!" Emily screamed. "Some men set the boat on fire!"

As Emily watched, he touched the mules' hay with the burning torch. Yellow and orange flames leaped high, and the mules brayed with terror.

Emily thought desperately. She couldn't put out the fire alone. If she yelled for help, no one at the house would hear her—but the men would catch her, and the boat would burn.

The boat's bell! If she could sneak past the men, she could ring it loudly enough for everyone to hear.

Crouching low, Emily wiggled between the railroad ties until she touched the bell rope. Then she pulled it with all her might.

Clang! Clang! Clang!

The men yelled, and Emily dropped the rope. She ran to the back of the boat and climbed over, onto the lock gate.

Emily looked down at the black water. She had walked this gate many times, but night made the water seem deeper, the gate seem longer and skinnier than it looked in the daylight. She took a deep breath and scurried across.

When she reached the bank, Emily looked back. One of the men was climbing over the back of the boat onto the gate!

Emily darted to the lock's big wheel and turned it, opening the gate wide so he couldn't cross. Then she scrambled up the bank. Her family was rushing down the path toward her.

"Fire!" Emily screamed. "Some men set the boat on fire!"

Emily's family threw bucket after bucket of water on the flames. After the fire was extinguished, Uncle Fred put his big hand on Emily's shoulder. "Thank you, Emily. We could have lost the boat, our mules, everything."

"You were very brave," Emily's mother said. "What's more, you used your head. Ringing the bell was clever."

"Before all the excitement," her mother continued, "we thought you might like to take a birthday trip up the canal. The fire didn't do much damage, thanks to you. We can probably get the boat cleaned up in a couple of days. What do you think? Would you like to go?"

Emily grinned and said, "I'm already packed."

Spider
6–9 years
975 words

From the Author

I've been selling fiction and nonfiction for all ages since 1983. Often, my fiction arises from my nonfiction work. "Danger on the Canal" began with a series on the Ohio canals that I was writing for a business journal. Researching at the Ohio Historical Society, I thought, "This would be a cool thing to share with kids."

When I write for kids, I use as much dialogue as possible: it moves the story along faster, develops characters, and helps me see when I'm "preaching," which editors and readers hate.

By reading children's magazines and books, talking with librarians, and watching children react to stories, I learn who wants what and how they want it. To sell, I have to meet publishers' needs in terms of word length, language, style, topic. I stay current on potential topics and ways of handling them, new magazines and publishers, and age-related reading-competence levels.

I also spend a lot of time doing story research. As a writer, I have a responsibility to give kids as much truth as I can. That means knowing my facts—even when my stories are fiction. It's the truth in my stories—the real history, science, people, and emotions—that makes my fiction believable.

Cussing and Swearing

By Bob Hartman

Jamal jabbed the volume button two times, and then three. His little sister, Tamika, was screaming in the next room, and he couldn't hear the game on TV.

She was always throwing these tantrums. If she didn't get her way, or she didn't like what was for dinner, or she didn't want to go to bed, she'd hurl herself at the floor and just start screaming. What she said never made much sense, and anyway Jamal never hung around long enough to listen. He'd run to his room or down the street to the basketball court—anything to get away. But today he was trying to watch the game—the BIG game—and he wanted to do more than just watch the ball bounce up and down the court and drop into the basket. He wanted to HEAR!

So he jabbed the volume button two more times, and that finally brought his grandmother into the room.

"Jamal!" she shouted. "Turn that thing down!"

"And, Tamika!" she shouted even more loudly into the next room. "Stop your hollering and stop it right now!"

Tamika stopped—for a second or two, anyway—and then started right up again.

"Just wait till your mother gets home!" Grandma hollered back, as she marched through the doorway. But Tamika was running from room to room now, daring her grandmother to catch her.

Jamal sighed. He was never going to hear the game this way. So he punched on the "caption" button and just watched. A fight had broken out. Fists were flying and heads were butting while the ball lay alone in the middle of the court. Jamal couldn't hear what the players were shouting, and the "captions" dared not help, but he didn't have to be a lip reader to figure it out. He was just glad his mother wasn't there. She hated cussing and swearing of any kind, and always switched the TV off whenever she heard it.

Jamal was only nine. There was no way they would let him play.

The "refs" squeezed between the players, cheeks puffed out, whistles blowing, and soon each side returned, boasting and bragging and trash talking, back to their benches. And yes, there were a few more of those words, as well, framed in slow motion by the TV cameras.

Following a quick commercial break, the game started up again, and Jamal watched sadly as his team blew a ten-point lead and lost, at last, in overtime.

Jamal pulled on his shoes, picked up a basketball, and shoving the front door open with his shoulder, dribbled his way down the street to the local set of hoops. He was just going to shoot, in order to work out the frustration he felt at his team's loss. But the bigger guys were already there—high school kids with their shirts off and their backs gleaming.

Jamal was only nine. There was no way they would let him play. So, again, he sat and watched. And listened. And there were those words again, bouncing around between the pushing and the passing and the shoving. He went back home, finally, more frustrated than ever.

His mother was there to greet him when he arrived. But it wasn't much of a greeting.

"Jamal?" she asked. "Just where have you been? I

asked you to clean up your room while I was gone, and it doesn't even look like you've touched it! Your grandma tells me you've been sitting around on your backside all afternoon watching TV. And now, when we need you to set the table for supper, you're off somewhere playing. What do you have to say for yourself?"

As it happened, Jamal had a lot to say. He was frustrated and disappointed and angry. And all of that came out in his explanation—along with a few of those words he had heard on TV and down at the basketball court.

His mother's eyes opened wide. Her mouth turned down into an angry frown. If she'd been a cartoon character, steam would have shot out both her ears. But there was nothing funny about this situation. She grabbed Jamal by the collar and sat him down in the nearest chair.

"How many times have I told you, young man? That kind of language will not be tolerated under my roof! Your daddy's mouth was dirty with it, and I'll not have it coming from you, too. It shows no respect! No respect at all! Not for the people you're talking to, and not for the person who's doing the talking!"

"But the ball players do it!" Jamal argued.

"Those fellows down the street?" his mother snapped back. "They'll be down there twenty years from now, talking garbage and acting big and still going nowhere. You want to be like them?"

"But the ones on TV do it, too! I saw them. Today!"

"But if respect is what you want, then you need to talk with respect and say what you mean in respectful language."

Jamal's mother leaned back and crossed her arms and sighed. "And you think that makes it all right?" she asked.

Jamal shrugged. "Well, not all right. But…"

And that's when the screaming started again.

"Chicken?" Tamika shrieked from the kitchen. "We're having chicken again? I hate chicken!"

"That's enough, Tamika. Settle down, child." Jamal could hear his grandma calling. But it was no use. His sister exploded into another one of her tantrums, and he just shut his eyes and shook his head.

"Oh, you think that's bad, do you?" his mother asked. "I just hope you realize that's exactly how all those big basketball players sound when they're cussing and swearing! Throwing tantrums, that's all they're doing. Big men. Little girls. There's no difference. They sound just as foolish. And if that's how you want to sound, then you keep right on using that language. But if respect is what you want, then you need to talk with respect and say what you mean in respectful language."

Jamal's mother hurried into the kitchen to see to his sister, and Jamal just sat there for a while. He remembered the faces of the men on TV. He remembered the faces of the boys down the street. And then he thought about how his sister looked in the middle of her tantrums. How she looked right now.

His mom was right. He didn't want to look like that. Not ever. So he slipped off his coat, waited for the screaming to stop, and went into the kitchen to apologize.

My Friend
6–12 years
1,066 words

From the Author

I've been writing professionally for about 10 years and have had 20 books published since 1992. "Cussing and Swearing" was one of a series of monthly stories I wrote for *My Friend*.

When it comes to bad behavior, it's easy to tell children, "Don't do that!" It's harder to explain *why*. I wanted my main character to discover the "why" for himself in the hope that readers would make that discovery, too. That's why I started with the same excuses any child might make. "My friends do it. Bigger kids do it. Professional ball players do it. Everybody does it!" It was my way of saying, "I understand where you're coming from. I realize the pressures you face."

But I also wanted to show readers exactly how awful that behavior looks to others. Since nobody wants to look like their tantrum-throwing little sister, I thought that was an honest and convincing comparison. It helped enormously that, at the time I was writing the story, one of our local sports figures was being criticized in the media for exactly that kind of behavior!

The Flamelights of Oolumaree

By Bonnie Bisbee

Oora was green and scaly, and she had a long tail. But the United Planets Council put her in my class of humans at school. She learned our language, Earthish, pretty well. And she caught on to most of our lessons and games.

But many of the human kids thought that an *ammu* like her was strange. Some of them called Oora "Lizard Lips." And we were living on *her* world!

Ammus walked upright and developed a big brain.

I had come to this planet, *Oolumaree*, with my parents just a couple of months ago. They were part of a Universal Minerals scouting team. Huge dinosaurs used to live on Oolumaree millions of years ago, but they'd all died out. All except one type of small, gentle dinosaur—the ammu. Ammus walked upright and developed a big brain.

Like my friend Oora!

After school one day, Oora said, "I show you ammus' secret treasure?"

"Sure!" I replied.

I followed her through the forest, wondering what kind of treasure the ammus might have. The forest looked very different from forests on Earth. Some trees had pink leaves, like puffs of cotton candy. And the planet's twin suns gave everything two shadows.

Finally we came to a huge rock cliff with a misty waterfall cascading down it. Oora led me along a narrow passage behind the waterfall. Inside was a cave. It was lit up by hundreds of glowing stones! Each flashed a different color: ruby red, purple, aqua blue, or gold. "Lovely!" I whispered.

Oora's long tail twitched nervously. "*Maramoos—*flamelights," she said in a hushed, whispering voice.

Just then we heard voices. I figured that we weren't supposed to be in here. Sure enough, Oora pulled me back into the shadows. We crouched down behind a rock.

We peeked out quietly and saw a man and a woman coming toward us. Their uniforms showed that they were two Universal Minerals scouts. One of them whistled at the sight of the glowing stones. "This cave must have formed them somehow," he said.

"We could make a fortune selling these gems on other planets!" the woman said. Then she frowned. "But what will the ammus say if we take them?"

"Don't worry about them—the ammus will be declared Nonpersons at tomorrow's team meeting," the man said. "After all, they're not like us. They live in the forest like animals. They don't even use fire or build any shelters. So they shouldn't have rights like people. And they won't be allowed to own any mineral rights on Oolumaree."

"If humans take away flamelights, ammus will die!"

"Then Universal Minerals will claim the rights to all these sparklies," the woman said, smiling, "and we'll be rewarded for finding them!" She did a happy little dance.

Finally they left. Oora didn't talk as she walked me home. Her blue eyes looked worried. At my family's living unit, she said: "If humans take away flamelights, ammus will die!"

I gasped. What could this mean? I sure didn't want anyone to hurt Oora and other ammus. "Let's tell Jamar," I suggested. "She's the head of the United Planets Council here. If anyone can stop the Universal Minerals company, she could. I'll go with you tomorrow."

"Thanks, Yuki!" Oora's scaly lips looked like they were smiling. "See you tomorrow, then!" She disappeared into the forest.

Three months later Oora and I waited in the forest near the big rock cliff, along with other humans and ammus. It was dark. The waterfall tumbled softly.

We were waiting for a "surprise" the ammus said was coming. They said it would prove to us humans that the ammus needed the flamelights. "This had better be good," I whispered to Oora, "or the humans will start taking the flamelights. I don't think most people believe that you ammus depend on the glowing stones."

"Remember the hard lessons we learned back on Earth about upsetting the balance of life."

Oora stood stiffly beside me. "Surprise is good," she said.

Oolumaree's three moons came up, full and bright. The last moon's purple rays cast a magical light on the woodland scene. We were the first humans to see Oolumaree's Triple Fullmoon Night.

Suddenly something started moving. From behind the waterfall crawled thousands of flashing "stones." Spilling out into the forest, they looked like a sparkling river of fire. Then the "stones" sprouted wings and flew off among the trees!

"So the maramoos are really creatures!" Jamar said, smiling.

Spokesperson Rumanoo nodded. His big red crest made him look very important. "Soon we show you ammu city inside rock cliff," he said. "We ammus have carved many caves in the cliff for our homes and shops. But every year we leave them.

For a time we live simply in forest. Young maramoos crawl into our quiet, dark caves. They turn hard and still—like glowing stones.

"On Triple Fullmoon Night, maramoos awake as adults and they fly back to the forest. We ammus return to caves. Then maramoos make wonderful food in forest, sweet and thick."

"Like honey!" I said out loud. Jamar nodded at me and put her finger to her lips.

"You ammus should decide what is best for you and the flamelights; we humans should not interfere."

"Maramoos give us food. Is all we eat for many months. Maramoos help us; we help maramoos. For ages, it has been this way," he said.

For a while we watched the little living lights as they flitted through the woods all around us. Finally Jamar said, "I guess those glowing 'stones' would be hard to catch now!" Everyone laughed.

She went on: "This surprise should remind us to be careful before we take natural things from any world. Remember the hard lessons we learned back on Earth about upsetting the balance of life." She turned to Spokesperson Rumanoo. "You ammus should decide what is best for you and the flamelights; we humans should not interfere," she said firmly.

No one argued about her decision, though some scouts looked disappointed.

Then Rumanoo spoke up. "Oolumaree can spare some real glowing stones. We show you. We use them to light up our cave city. Have other useful minerals too. Here is deal—we give you some stones and minerals. You help us to reach stars. Is good deal?"

"Good!" said the team leader from Universal Minerals. Jamar nodded.

While the grownups went on talking, we kids— ammu and human—invented a fun new game called "Three Shadow Tag."

And nobody ever called Oora "Lizard Lips" again!

Ranger Rick
7–12 years
1,050 words

Champs

By James M. Janik

"Promise not to tell?"
I nodded.
"I cheat."
With those two words, everything changed. "You what?"

"I scuff the baseball."

"Why?"

"It makes it do crazy things. It flutters. It drops. I never really know what it's going to do." Jason grinned.

"No, I mean why cheat?"

"Why not? If we're in a tight spot...game on the line...needing a big strikeout, maybe."

"That's nuts, Jason. You're the best pitcher in the league. You don't need to cheat."

"Maybe not. But it never hurts to have a special trick up your sleeve."

I couldn't believe my ears. "How do you do it?" *Maybe it isn't really cheating*, I thought.

"I tape a piece of sandpaper in the palm of my glove. When I look to the catcher for the sign, I grind the ball into the sandpaper. It's easy."

"Sandpaper!" I screeched. "You can't do that! What if they check your glove?"

"Why should they? I'd only do it for the last out of a big game. Tomorrow being the championship and all...I might need an extra edge."

"But, with your fastball, you'd get them out anyway."

"Maybe, maybe not."

"What if they catch you?"

He stopped and glared at me.

"You're not going to tell, are you?"

"No, I won't tell."

Jason Bailey led the league in strikeouts every year. He led the league in wins, too. Why cheat?

"Look, man, don't go soft on me. Other guys do it."

"I don't know, Jason. You're not like the other guys. You're the best—without sandpaper."

"I plan to stay the best, too. I'll do whatever it takes to win tomorrow."

"Hey, look. I'm not asking for your permission. You asked me how I threw that pitch, I told you."

We walked home without another word. I'd grown up next door to Jason. We'd played ball on all the same teams. He'd always been the best pitcher. Always. I thought I knew him like my own brother.

At my front door, I asked, "When did you start?"

"Scuffing? I don't know. Month ago, maybe. I read about some pitching tricks in a magazine, so I gave them a try in practice. It took me a while to get the hang of scuffing."

"Have you ever done it in a game?"

"Nah, only in practice."

"Jason, don't do it. It's not right."

"Hey, look. I'm not asking for your permission. You asked me how I threw that pitch, I told you."

"Sandpapering the baseball is against the rules, Jason."

"Only if I get caught, Alex."

The clatter of silverware and the smell of hot meat loaf poured through the open kitchen window.

"Man, something smells good in there," Jason said, taking in a long breath.

"Yeah. Well, something really stinks out here."

"I shouldn't have told you."

"I wish you hadn't."

He stared at me, then whispered, "Maybe you're right, Alex. I'll think about it."

"Rest up! We'll need you fresh on the mound."

"Don't worry. Everything's under control."

Everything's under control, all right. Sandpaper!

I plopped a heap of mashed potatoes on my plate and smothered my meat loaf with ketchup.

"Did you get our income taxes finished?" Mom asked, passing a steaming bowl of green beans to Dad.

Jason stood on the mound, just one out away from winning the ball game.

I grabbed the bowl and spooned a pile onto my mashed potatoes.

"Finished it up just now," Dad answered. "What a relief! I'm afraid it's going to cost us, though."

"Oh? Sally, next door, says they're getting money back this year."

"Well, that's because Greg Bailey takes liberties with the tax laws."

"What does take liberties mean, Dad?" I asked.

"Jason's father takes deductions he's not really entitled to."

"Is that against the law?"

"Greg says it's his duty to take as much as he thinks he can get away with."

"But, is it against the law?"

"If they catch him, he'll have to pay a penalty."

"But, what if they don't catch him?"

Dad looked at me hard. "It's still wrong."

"Alex," Mom said. "Don't you think it would be difficult to sleep at night if you knew you'd been dishonest?"

"Yeah. I would think so."

Why didn't Jason?

The light breeze cooled my face at third base. I checked the sun. A high pop fly might be tough to see in the glare.

We were ahead by one run in the last inning of the championship game.

Jason stood on the mound, just one out away from winning the ball game.

Marty Edwards danced off second base after a

walk and a stolen base.

Curtis Corcoran dug his back foot deep into the batter's box. He whipped his bat around like a war club, smirking at Jason.

Jason got his sign and went into his windup. He kicked his leg and fired home.

"Stee-rike!"cried the umpire.

Jason still had good steam on his fastball, even after seven innings of pitching.

Curtis looked surprised by the high-octane heater.

"You can take him, Jason," Coach Dugan hollered from the bench. "We need a strikeout here."

Jason looked in for the sign again. He delivered. A slow-breaking ball, low and outside—right on the corner.

"Strike two!"

Great pitch! The hitter's set up for an inside fastball now.

"Let him have it," I hollered. "Bust him inside. End it right here."

Coach Dugan shouted, "Do whatever it takes to get this guy out, Jason!"

Whatever it takes? I remembered what Jason had said the day before.

Jason turned his back to home plate and fiddled with the ball inside his glove.

"Time out!" I shouted.

The umpires waved their hands above their heads.

"You're the best pitcher in the league," I whispered. "You always were. Even before sandpaper."

Jason glared at me, a look of disbelief on his face.

I pointed to the sun. "I need the glasses." I trotted into the dugout and grabbed a pair of flip-downs. Walking slowly across the infield, I pulled them over my hat. I stopped at the mound, pretending to have trouble adjusting the sunglasses.

Jason stood next to me.

Still fumbling with my glasses, I said, "Don't do it."

"What're you talking about?"

"Let me see the ball."

"No way. Not with one out to go."

"Have you been scuffing the whole game?"

"No." He glanced around.

"You've come this far without cheating, Jason. You can win it yourself from here."

"You don't understand..."

"No! You don't understand," I snapped. "It's dishonest. I don't want to win that way. Neither should you."

Coach Dugan climbed the steps of the dugout. The home plate umpire walked toward the mound.

"You're the best pitcher in the league," I whispered. "You always were. Even before sandpaper."

Jason frowned.

The umpire pushed between us. "We've got a game to play, boys."

I snatched the baseball away from Jason. The cowhide was clean. No scuffs. I flipped it back to him.

"Let's get this game going," the ump ordered and walked away.

I got right in Jason's face. "You—don't—need—the sandpaper." Our eyes locked for a moment. I wheeled and returned to my position.

Jason stared at me from the pitcher's mound. He slammed the ball into his glove and turned toward home.

I couldn't see his hands.

The umpire waved the hitter back into the batter's box.

Jason went into his windup. He checked the runner on second. He kicked high and hurled the baseball home.

Curtis unloaded everything he had at the speeding baseball. At the last moment, the ball dipped. Curtis fell to the ground from the force of his swing. He'd hit nothing but air.

"Strike three!"

The dugout emptied. Everyone cheered.

Jason tossed his glove high in the air. The guys lifted him onto their shoulders.

I stood at third base with my head down. I didn't feel much like celebrating. That last pitch had dipped way too fast. We'd won all right, but not without cheating.

Jason was on the ground, the whole team piled on top of him.

Just inside second base, I saw his baseball glove on the infield grass. I glanced at Jason, still buried in the pileup. I walked over and picked up the glove. It was there, all right. I touched my finger to the small scrap of sandpaper. It was coarse, like gravel.

"What're you looking at?" Jason asked, grinning broadly. His hat was gone, his hair all wild.

The guys still whooped it up behind him.

I searched his face. "How do you sleep at night, Jason?"

"Not so good last night. Even with all the tossing and turning, I still wasn't sure what I'd do."

"I saw it dip, man."

"Here, why don't you keep this?" He tossed the game ball against my chest.

I caught the baseball and looked it over. Clean and white—no scuffs?

"How'd you like that last sinker?" Jason said, grinning like a crocodile. "That's something else I've been working on. Forgot to tell you."

"Sinker?" I let out a whoop of my own and punched my fist in the air.

We were champs, fair and square.

Boys' Life
7–18 years
1,487 words

From the Author

The idea that cheating is acceptable if you don't get caught is common in our society, and kids absorb everything. I wrote "Champs" to address that issue. Winning by cheating is a shallow victory. Whether you're caught or not, you have to live with yourself.

Before "Champs," I had submitted other stories to *Boys' Life*. They were all rejected. I subscribed to *Boys' Life* and read each issue cover to cover for a year before offering "Champs." Now I do the same thing whenever I target a new market.

I chose Alex as my viewpoint character because I needed to keep Jason's secret sinker pitch a surprise, and because I wanted readers to discover the truth for themselves.

In my first draft, Jason had already perfected and used his scuffed pitch when the story began. The editors suggested I change the story to indicate that Jason had only been *thinking about* cheating at that point. That subtle change intensified the climax. Jason had to choose: cheat or compete? He learned Alex was right: the "edge" he needed was self-confidence, not dishonesty.

Intermediate Fiction

Treasure in the Trash

By Jeannie McGinnis

Zakaria watched from behind a mahogany tree as the American family drove away from the compound. He waited a few minutes, to make sure they were really gone, then ran to the fence and began to climb. The chain links didn't bother him. His feet were tough and calloused from nine years of going barefoot. His arms had plenty of wiry muscle from working on his family's farm, but no fat, and they lifted him easily over the fence. He tore his shorts a bit going over the top, but he didn't care. They had lots of other holes already. As long as he wasn't wearing his Sunday clothes, Mama didn't care, either.

The cans could be used for many things, but he hoped she would use them for cooking moi-moi.

Zakaria dropped lightly to the ground on the other side of the fence, and paused to wipe the sweat from his eyes. Then he headed for the treasure mine—the *Batures*' trash hole. *Batures*, whether they were American or any other kind of foreigner, threw away lots of useful kinds of stuff. Zakaria and the other kids in his northern Nigeria village looked through the trash hole when nobody was around. And today he had something special in mind.

Zakaria slid down the side of the four-foot-deep pit. He was careful to land on some scrap paper and avoid the pile of rotting mango peels and seeds. One of them was sprouting, and he carefully pulled it out and wrapped it in a wet peel to take home and plant.

The hole was full of tin cans and plastic bottles. He gathered them and threw them up into a pile. Mama would store oil, salt, and sugar in the bottles. The cans could be used for many things, but he

A broken flip-flop popped up from under a plastic bag, and he snagged it.

hoped she would use them for cooking *moi-moi*. He pictured her pouring the bean-cake batter into tins and setting them in boiling water to steam. His mouth watered as he rummaged around for more.

The biggest can he set aside for himself. That was the one thing he needed, but there was still something else to find. He took a stick and poked around in the trash.

A broken flip-flop popped up from under a plastic bag, and he snagged it. His older brother was learning how to make a popgun and needed a piece of rubber. He took the plastic bag too, so he'd have something to carry all his stuff in.

He had more than he could carry now, but he still hadn't found the one thing he needed most.

He kept a sharp lookout for the *Batures* and for the other kids in the village. If any of his friends came, he'd have to share his bounty.

Zakaria spied a sugar bag on the far side of the pit, and pulled it over toward him with his stick. He looked inside, just in case.

"*Kai.*" There was enough sugar left in the bag for tea for his whole family! All eight of them. He rolled the bag into a ball and pitched it up with the cans.

He had more than he could carry now, but he still hadn't found the one thing he needed most. He stirred the garbage with his stick, grimacing at the smell that came up. These people sure threw away a lot of food!

Finally Zakaria gave up and turned to go. He hooked his toe onto a ledge of dirt and began to climb out.

"Aah-hh," he gasped in disgust, as his foot slipped and he landed on his hands and knees in the rotten mangos. He scrabbled in the slimy mess, trying to get back on his feet. Something sharp stuck him in the hand and as he wiped the blood off on his shorts, he spotted a wire sticking out of the glop. That was it! That was what he was looking for! He tugged at it, but the wire wouldn't come loose.

He could hear a car coming in the distance. Desperately, he dug with his hands through the mango peels until he got a better hold on the wire.

Zakaria was already making plans for his next raid on the garbage pit.

This time he got it loose, and scrambled out of the pit. Stuffing his prizes into the plastic bag, he ran to the fence. He heaved his bundle up and over and climbed after it. The Americans' car pulled into the compound as he landed, but he didn't stop to look.

Zakaria grabbed his bag and headed for the river. He wasn't going home without washing first!

Later that afternoon, the air was filled with the hot, spicy smell of steaming moi-moi. Zakaria sat outside the hut, playing a small musical instrument and singing. His neighbors smiled and tapped their feet, and the little kids danced to the music. Mama was proud. Even though he was only eight, nobody in the village could play like Zakaria.

Zakaria was content. He'd found what he needed and his instrument was a good one. His brother was thrilled with the flip-flop, and promised to make Zakaria a popgun if he could just find a few more things. Zakaria was already making plans for his next raid on the garbage pit. He would wait a few days then go back. All he needed this time was an old ballpoint pen and a nail. That should be easy!

[Zakaria's instrument was a drum with an attached guitar-like wire for strumming. The story was accompanied by a sidebar showing readers how to make it.]

On the Line
9–14 years
873 words

From the Author

I am a United Methodist missionary currently living in San Jose, Costa Rica. However, I wrote "Treasure in the Trash" soon after returning to the United States after six years in Nigeria. Zakaria was a real little boy who was a friend of my daughter. I was constantly amazed at the creativity of African children and the wonderful toys they could make out of what we would consider trash.

After showing American children how to make this instrument at churches and schools, I decided to write this piece for Assignment 8 of the Institute's basic course. Zakaria was the obvious character for it.

After I wrote "Treasure in the Trash," I had to cut about 150 words before submitting it to *On the Line*. They published it without further revision.

I wrote this piece as an early writer and had not read sample copies of the magazine, but I always read sample issues before submitting now. At the time, since I had worked as a volunteer for the Mennonite Central Committee for several years in East Africa, I had a pretty good idea of what would appeal to the staff of a Mennonite magazine. "Treasure in the Trash" felt right to me. I was lucky, and very pleased, that they felt the same way.

I recently showed this piece to a colleague. Not only did she like it, but she subscribed to the magazine!

The Problem with Georgina

By Debbie Levy

"**S**how Georgina your room," Mom said. "Connie and I will have some tea." Connie is my mother's new friend. Georgina is her daughter.

"Let's play racetrack," I said to Georgina, pulling out my miniature cars.

Georgina shook her head. "I'd rather play cards," she said. "Old Maid is my favorite game."

Old Maid is the only card game I *don't* like. "We could draw," I suggested. "I have some brand new markers."

Georgina wrinkled her nose. "Markers are so childish. I always draw with charcoal. Don't you have anything to do that's fun?"

"No!" I said. She stuck out her tongue.

Next time, Mom and I went to Georgina's house. She took me to her room—or maybe I should say her stable.

There were toy horses everywhere in Georgina's bedroom. Little horses on a shelf. Big horses with manes and tails you could braid. Stuffed horses.

"Wow," I said. "I guess you like horses."

"I love horses," Georgina said. "I've been taking riding lessons for a year."

I knew what was coming next. "Do you ride?" Georgina asked.

I sat in a chair and practiced counting backward.

I think horses smell bad and their stables smell worse. But I just said, "Yeah, I ride—on a bicycle."

The next time we went to Georgina's, she had another friend over. "This is Samantha," said Georgina's mom. "I'm sure you three will have fun."

Samantha and Georgina set up a stable outside and brought out all of Georgina's horses. Then they skipped around yelling, "Neigh! Neigh!"

I sat in a chair and practiced counting backward.

"So how'd it work out, Nicki?" Mom asked as we drove home. When I didn't answer right away, she said, "Not great, I guess."

"Not even good," I answered, very quietly.

A few days later Mom told me that Connie would be visiting that afternoon. "But Georgina's going to her friend Samantha's house," Mom said.

"Thanks, Mom," I said.

The next time Mom visited Connie, I went to a friend's house. When Connie came over to see us, Georgina went to visit one of *her* friends. And on it went—for a while.

One day, many weeks later, Mom told me she had plans with Connie that afternoon. "Today," she added, "you, Georgina, Connie and I are all going to do something together."

I wasn't happy, but I didn't argue. Mom seemed tired, and I didn't want to make her feel worse.

After school that day, Mom and I met Georgina and Connie at the ice-cream parlor. "I would like a scoop of chocolate-chocolate chip, please," I told my mother.

Georgina made a face at my choice. "Rainbow sherbet, please," she said to her mother.

She doesn't even like real ice cream, I thought.

Georgina and I sat down at a table.

"So, uh—" I said.

"Well, um—" she said at the same time.

We both stopped. "Go ahead," Georgina said. "What were you going to say?"

Our moms were waiting for the ice cream. I looked closely at Georgina's mother. Her belly looked like my mother's belly: bigger than it used to.

"Is your mother going to have a baby?" I asked Georgina.

"Yes," she whispered. "Is yours?"

"Yes," I said. "Could you tell?"

"Sure," she said. "Are you excited about it?"

"Yes," I said, "and no."

"Actually, I'm a little scared," Georgina said.

"Some days I'm happy," I said, "and other days I want things to stay the way they are."

"What name do you want for your little brother?"

Our mothers came over with the ice cream.

"I don't like pieces of candy in ice cream, " Georgina said, looking at my cone.

"Good," I said as I bit into a chocolate chip. "Then you don't want any."

Georgina laughed and pushed her dish over to me. "Want to try my sherbet?"

I tasted it. Not too bad, for something not chocolate.

"What are you hoping for, Nicki, a brother or a sister?" Georgina's mother asked me.

"A brother," I said.

"How about you, Georgina?" my mother asked her.

"Oh, a sister," she said.

"Oh, of course," I thought. "The opposite of what I want." But when I looked at Georgina, we both laughed.

After finishing our ice cream, we took a walk. While our moms walked ahead, Georgina asked, "What name do you want for your little brother?"

"So far I think I like Daniel the best," I said.

She jumped. "My favorite for my baby sister is Daniella! Isn't that funny?"

"Sort of," I said.

We talked about how tired our mothers were lately, what we would do if the babies cried all the time, and what things of ours they would not be allowed to touch.

"Thanks for the taste of your sherbet," I said to Georgina when it was time to go.

"Next time," she said, "I'll try your chocolate-chocolate chip."

"Next time?" Mom said to me in the car. "You and Georgina found something to talk about?"

I nodded as Mom clicked her seat-belt buckle closed. "Yes," I said, thinking of the baby safely buckled up inside my mother. "We talked about Daniel and Daniella."

"Daniel and Daniella," Mom repeated. "Are they characters on a television show?"

"No!" I said, laughing. And I thought, "I can't wait to tell Georgina that one."

Highlights for Children
2–12 years
1,750 words

From the Author

The kernel of the idea for "The Problem with Georgina" came from my life and my children's lives. It's not an unusual issue: Mom has adult friends with whom she wants to spend time. Those friends have children, and the children can play together while the adults socialize. Great idea, right? But mothers might forget that their children have preferences of their own.

I chose the first person because I thought the protagonist's voice was important to making the story work and making it funny. I wanted the reader to hear the narrator's tomboyish, judgmental voice—not only in dialogue, but also in the narrative. I tried to keep my dialogue short, snappy, and colloquial without sinking into slang. (Slang is fine in the right context, but this wasn't it.)

When I wrote "The Problem with Georgina," I was in a workshop on writing for children. My classmates were underwhelmed; they were much more positive about other work I presented. But I did get some valuable feedback on dialogue from the instructor: keep tweaking until it's really concise, funny, and true to life.

My career as a writer is still very much a work in progress. It's easy to become discouraged, but if you're both honest and kind to yourself, you should make progress and develop your career.

Danger on the Red Planet

By Sigmund Brouwer

Journal Log—May 7, 2098: Tyce Sanders

Time is running out, and Mom wants me to write a report for a magazine on Earth. She thinks it will mean more to people coming from a guy my age than from any scientist. But I hardly know where to begin. I mean, everything is happening at once: my argument with Mom about religious stuff, how it seems my body is getting too weak to move my wheelchair and how Mom—a scientist herself—has just reported the oxygen level in the colony is dropping so fast that all of us barely have a month to live.

Let me say this first to anyone who might read this when we are gone. If you have legs that don't work, Mars is probably a better place to be than Earth. That's only a guess, of course, because I'm the only person in the history of mankind who has never breathed Earth's air or felt Earth's gravity.

You see, I'm the only person ever born on Mars. Everyone else came from Earth about six and a half years ago—12 Earth years to you—as part of an expedition to set up a colony. The trip took eight months, and my mother and father fell in love with each other during the voyage. Mom is a scientist.

Life could be worse, of course. On Earth, I'd weigh 90 pounds. Here, I'm only 34.

Dad is a space pilot. They were the first couple to be married on Mars. They exchanged their vows over radio-phone with a preacher on Earth. When I was born half a Mars year later, it made things so complicated on the colony that it was decided that no more marriages or babies would be allowed until the colony was better established.

Complicated?

Let me put it this way: Because of planetary orbits, spaceships can reach Mars only every three Earth years. (Only three ships have arrived since I was born.) And for what it costs to send a ship, cargo space is expensive—very, very expensive. Diapers, baby bottles and cribs are not exactly a high priority for interplanetary travel. I did without all that stuff, just like I did without a modern hospital when I was born. So when my legs came out funny, there was no one to fix them, which is why I'm in a wheelchair. Fortunately it was brought when I was 6.

Life could be worse, of course. On Earth, I'd weigh 90 pounds. Here, I'm only 34. That makes it easier to get around, at least when my body and arms aren't weak from lack of oxygen.

The other good thing is that I never have to travel far. Here, all 50 of us—mainly scientists and workers—live under a sealed dome that might cover four of Earth's football fields.

When I'm not being taught by my computer, I spend my time wheeling around the paths beneath the colony dome. I know every scientist and worker. I know every path past every mini-dome, the small, plastic huts where people live in privacy from the others. I've seen every color of Martian sky through the super-clear plastic of the main dome above us. I've spent hours listening to sandstorms. I've…

…I've got to go. Mom's calling me to join her for mealtime.

A Question of Faith

Our mini-dome, like everyone else's, has two office-bedrooms and a common living space, where Mom was waiting for me.

I strained to push the wheelchair. It was getting harder and harder to move. I worried that pretty soon I might not be able to move it at all.

I finally reached her. She handed me a plastic nutrient tube. Red.

Mom knew she could never force me to believe something if I didn't want to.

"Spaghetti and meatballs?" I asked.

She nodded. I've never tasted real spaghetti and meatballs, so I have to take Mom's word that the nute-tube stuff is not nearly as good as the real thing.

As usual, she prayed over it.

As usual, I didn't.

As usual, it made her sad.

"Our oxygen level is dropping faster and faster," she said. "I really want you to consider faith in God. If we have only one month left…"

"I believe only what I can see or measure," I said. In the colony, I was surrounded by scientists. All their experiments were on data that could be measured.

"But faith is the hope of things unseen," she said. "Otherwise it wouldn't be a matter of faith. We don't ever see your dad, but we know he loves us, no matter where his cargo ship is. Faith in God is like that."

"Mom?!" We had argued this many times.

Mom knew she could never force me to believe something if I didn't want to. No person can make another person believe.

I ripped off the top of my nute-tube and guzzled the red paste.

"I'm going," I said. Mom and I were good friends, but we were both grumpy from our disagreement and the oxygen problem. I needed time to myself.

Staring Into Space

By the time I wheeled to the center of the main dome 15 minutes later, I was sweating from the effort. Before it would have taken only a couple of minutes and hardly any muscle power. This oxygen thing was scary. But what could I do about it?

Around me, men and women scientists walked on the paths, going from mini-dome to mini-dome. They nodded or said hello as they passed.

I just stared at the purples and oranges of the clouds above the dome. One day other people on other expeditions might explore the huge volcanoes and vast canyons outside. Not us. We would be dead soon. Dad was piloting the next cargo ship, and it wouldn't arrive for two months—one month after the colony ran out of oxygen.

I kept staring up. My eyes drifted to the giant, dark solar panels that hung just below the clear roof. They turned the energy of sunlight into electricity. Part of this electricity powered our computers and other equipment. Most of the electricity, though, went as a current into the water in the oxygen tank. The electrical current broke the water (H_2O) into the gases of hydrogen and oxygen. The hydrogen was used as fuel for some of the generators. We breathed the oxygen.

"Either these carts are getting heavier," he said wiping his brow, "or there's even less oxygen in the dome than we figure."

But something was wrong with the panels. Nobody could figure it out. Taken down and tested, they worked perfectly. But back up on the roof, the panels were making less and less electricity each day. With less power, we had less oxygen, it was that simple.

As I gazed at the panels, thinking about the problem, I heard huffing and puffing. I turned to see bald-headed George, a computer technician, pushing a cart towards me.

He caught my glance. "Either these carts are getting heavier," he said wiping his brow, "or there's even less oxygen in the dome than we figure."

He pushed on.

Everybody is losing strength, I thought, *not just me.*

I felt my stomach rumble from the spaghetti and meatball paste.

Hang on, I thought as I remembered lunch. *If I'm getting weaker, how come I can rip open my nute-tube like always?*

I thought about it some more.

What if it's not me getting weaker, but my wheel-

chair slowly getting harder to push? And what if George's cart is becoming harder to move? I took a deep breath.

Weird, I told myself. *Why would things with wheels be getting harder to push?* I heard a squeak from high above. I looked up and heard another squeak. *From the solar panels?*

I glanced at my watch. Then I had a wild idea.

"Mom!" I shouted. "Mom!"

As fast as I could, I wheeled back to our mini-dome.

Finding Answers

Two hours later, Mom came back from her laboratory. I was sitting on my bed, because she had taken my wheelchair to the lab.

"Well?" I asked.

"Things unseen," she said smiling. "Microscopic particles of Martian sand that had gotten into the sealed dome over the years. We took apart your wheelchair axle and examined the grease that helps it turn. The sand has finally worn the axle down."

She high-fived me again, and I knew exactly what she meant.

"Wheelchair wheels," I said, "wheels on a cart and tiny wheels that let the solar panels follow the sun! The more sand, the harder it is for all the wheels to turn."

"Exactly," she said. "That was the squeak you heard. We were looking for the problem in the panels and all along it was the wheels. Technicians have already fixed the problem!"

She gave me a high-five.

"Things unseen," I said. "Things that are there but you don't know it until you know where to look." I grinned at her, finally understanding.

"Just like we don't know much about what's behind faith, but someday we'll find out?"

 She high-fived me again, and I knew exactly what she meant.

Family Clubhouse
9–14 years
1,479 words

Sapphire's Eyes

By E. M. Schumacher

"Nothing younger than 15," her parents had said. Both of them standing there side by side, their message was clear. *We're together on this one.*

Jessie frowned and wrinkled her nose in disgust. A dozen horses so far. Seven she tried out; three she wasn't even allowed to ride because they were too young, and two more her dad had said weren't worth a closer look.

Now they were on their way to the Farquharson's place to see a twenty-year-old Arabian mare. A horse that had been around and done it all, according to her dad. But one that really needed some attention now, according to her Mom.

Jessie didn't even feel like getting out of the car to look at it. *Some old half-dead bone bag, probably,* she thought, her mind still on the shimmering

---

Sapphire didn't look like much, and she was bony.

---

golden palomino her friend Kelsie had taken her to see. Now *that* was a real horse. The way it could run, slide to a stop and spin on the spot. So what if he was only three!?

But then when Mrs. Farquharson came over to the car and said, "I hope you brought your boots. We'll have to walk out to the pasture to get her," Jessie just couldn't say no.

Maybe it was because she knew Mrs. Farquharson from school, where she helped out in the office, and she didn't want to be rude. Or maybe it was curiosity—Jessie didn't know. She just followed her out to the pasture to get the flea-bitten grey.

Sapphire didn't look like much, and she *was* bony. Not too terribly thin, but out of condition, with a really big hay belly. She was covered in dust and mud. There were so many burrs in her long mane that Mrs. Farquharson said not to bother trying to pull them out now, because it would take all day.

The dust rose up in clouds and everyone was sneezing and spitting horse hair by the time they got the saddle on. Sapphire let them know she didn't care for any of it by dancing back and forth so much they could barely tighten the girth.

"When was the last time anyone rode her?" Jessie's dad asked.

Mrs. Farquharson said, "Let me think. Moira moved away about three years ago now. I rode her afterwards, but I have a bad back and I can't do much more than walk her." She stood there for a moment longer, then she smiled. "A year ago this spring," she said. "Yes. Just over a year ago."

Jessie's parents turned towards each other and frowned. Her mom said, "We'd really like to see someone ride the horse before we let Jessie try her. She's only taken lessons for about a year now."

"It's been nearly two years," Jessie interrupted. "And I'm a really good rider."

Mrs. Farquharson turned and smiled. "I'm sure you are. I tell you what, I'll ride her around once or twice at a walk just so your parents can see that she's safe. Then you can show us what you can do."

Jessie looked at her parents, who nodded. Then she took another look at Sapphire. *What a mess!* she thought. *All I want is that palomino.*

Mrs. Farquharson had to be at least ten years older than Jessie's mother. She had grey hair, wide hips and seemed about as stiff as anyone could be. Getting her up on the aged mare's back wasn't easy.

"Alice, are you sure you want to do this?" Jessie's dad must have asked about seventeen times as he pushed and pulled and strained to get her up there. Sapphire didn't help. She didn't want to stand still. At least not until Mrs. Farquharson dropped herself down into place in the saddle.

Then she acted like a lead line pony. She walked all over the paddock with her head nodding, acting like she was half asleep. Jessie just snorted when she heard her dad say, "Well, she's certainly quiet enough."

Like I need a horse that's half dead! Jessie thought as she buckled on her hard hat and climbed up into the saddle. *All I want is that palomino.* Then she gave Sapphire a neat little kick. "Give me something better than a walk," she said. Suddenly Jessie felt a surge from behind throw her forward. She slipped out of place and had to grab for the matted white mane just to keep herself on Sapphire's back.

"Jessie! You have to go easy with her," she heard Mrs. Farquharson call after her. "She'll go as fast as you ask her to."

Jessie could see the tears welling up in her eyes and she had to look away.

Sapphire was galloping straight for the paddock fence. "Turn her!" she heard her dad shout. Jessie didn't have the time to shorten the reins. Without thinking she leaned in the direction she wanted to go and Sapphire followed along. They took the corner so neatly that Jessie soon found herself centered and balanced again.

After that the mare slowed into the loveliest floating trot. Jessie tried one thing after another. Everything she'd learned was a challenge on the sensitive, well-schooled horse and she could tell that Sapphire knew a whole lot more. Things she still had to learn herself.

"Moira won too many high-point awards to count with that horse," Mrs. Farquharson said proudly as Jessie's mother handed her a cheque later that same day. Jessie could see the tears welling up in her eyes and she had to look away.

She couldn't remember when she had decided

that she didn't really want that palomino after all. Maybe while she was riding Sapphire. Or maybe just after she came off.

Jessie remembered jerking the reins, just a little, to ask the mare for one last stop. The sudden halt that followed had rolled her over Sapphire's withers and bumped her down, unceremoniously, on the ground.

Afterwards she had looked up, right into those soft brown eyes. She could tell that they were laughing. Old Sapphire, it seemed, still wanted to have fun.

Horsepower
8–16 years
1,008 words

From the Author

When I wrote "Sapphire's Eyes," I was working part-time as a freelance magazine writer. I wrote feature-length articles on local issues, articles and stories about horses, and whatever else I could sell or resell. I soon learned that reading sample issues is a must. It's like trying to sell fruit to a meat market if you don't.

It wasn't difficult to tailor this story to *Horsepower*'s length and readership requirements since I'd done lots of that in my nonfiction work. My goal has always been to write fiction, but it's much more difficult to get fiction published, so I decided to work on articles first.

For article research, I usually go directly to the source, either interviewing in person or over the phone. I also use the library, the Internet, and whatever other information I can get my hands on. Verifying information and making sure you have reliable sources is also very important.

After finishing a piece, it's good to put it down for a day (or longer if possible), then go back and do a final polish on it. I never stop editing.

Now I'm working on my first novel. I did much more work on outlining both the plot and characters. If you build them properly, characters have a way of coming alive, doing things, and taking you where you want to go. That, I think, is one of the biggest rewards in writing fiction.

A Place of My Own

By Judith Montgomery Inman

Naturally, I told my brother Charlie I would miss him when he left for college. Unless you're pretty hard-hearted, you can work up a little sadness when your big brother leaves home. But I had big plans for his room.

I was in the closet (I prefer to call it my art studio) of the room I share with my little brother, Daniel, when Mom broke the bad news.

"Aaron, we need to talk," she called through the closed door. The door stayed closed to discourage Daniel from wrecking my stuff. I didn't notice the serious tone of Mom's voice, because I was busy putting the finishing touches on a cartoon featuring my dog, Streak.

"Okay, Mom. But don't let Streak in." When I'm in my studio, Streak keeps watch outside with his paws and nose pressed to the crack under the door. He snuffles every so often to let me know he is still on the job and probably to make me feel guilty.

Mom's forehead creased like it does when she's worried or upset—not a good sign.

Mom squeezed through the door and stood behind my stool. I was just signing my name—Aaron Trainor—in the bottom right corner of my cartoon. I had drawn a pretty good likeness of myself throwing a stick for Streak to fetch.

"You and that dog." Mom laughed as she helped me find an empty spot on my bulletin board to pin my latest project. "Your drawings have really improved, Aaron. Your art teacher is going to be impressed next fall."

"Thanks, Mom. Just wait till you see the things I'll do once I move into Charlie's room." Charlie was studying to be an architect. He had shown me how to start working on the portfolio of drawings and paintings I would need to apply for art school.

Mom's forehead creased like it does when she's worried or upset—not a good sign. "That's what we

My heart sank. There went all my plans. I was still stuck with my little brother, Daniel the Pest.

need to talk about—Charlie's room." She ran her hands over the cabinets that held my art supplies. "Dad did a good job fixing up your studio, didn't he?" She smiled, but the crease stayed put.

By this time all my sensors were sounding a red alert. I put down my marker and stared at her.

She started again. "I'm worried about your grandfather." I could understand that. We had worried about Grandpa after Nana died two years ago. But he seemed more like himself when he came for Daniel's fifth birthday.

"Grandpa jokes like he used to," I said. "He said he has to be on his toes because now God and Nana are both watching him."

Mom smiled. "That's not what I mean." Then she explained how Grandpa had lost his drafting job because his company was using more computers and fewer people. Grandpa had drawn maps for a huge oil company ever since I could remember.

"Since he lost his job, Grandpa doesn't know how to keep busy. I'm afraid he's lonely, too. He agreed to stay with us this summer, and we need to put him in Charlie's room."

My heart sank. There went all my plans. I was still stuck with my little brother, Daniel the Pest.

"Aaron, what about it? I know you're tired of sharing a room with Daniel. Someday you boys will realize how much you love each other."

Have you ever noticed how most people who tell you to love your brother never had one, like my mom? Being an only child, she had never been humiliated the way I have been when my friends come for dinner and Daniel clowns around.

"But Daniel's so childish," I said.

"Well, he *is* a child. He's only five years old." She patted me on the shoulder. "Aaron, please make your grandpa feel at home. You two have always been pals."

As she left, I heard Streak give an extra-loud snuffle under the door. I decided to ignore my no-dog rule. I opened the door, and Streak padded in. He laid his head on my knee like he's done since he was a puppy.

"I'm sorry you lost your job, Grandpa."

I remembered the day Grandpa and I named him after Mom had banished him to the porch because he had chewed the sofa cushions.

"Yes sir, if dogs could blush, he would be red," Grandpa had said. "This is a very sensitive animal."

"Well, for sure Mom won't let him back inside after he tore a blue streak through the house."

"So that's his name!" Grandpa had scooped up the furry culprit. "Come on, Streak. I'll speak up for you."

In the kitchen, Grandpa and I had faced Mom's stern gaze. "Ellie, God watches over each sparrow that falls from its nest. This puppy seems a lot like those fallen sparrows to me."

Of course, puppies aren't one bit like sparrows. Just think of puppies plopping out of nests all over. But Grandpa is always saying things are like something else to make you think about them.

"All right, Dad. You win. He's got another chance." That night Streak slept under my bed, curled up in a slipper.

"Grandpa's here!" I heard Daniel shout. I went to meet him. I wanted to hug him like I always did. Instead I shoved my hands in my pockets and mumbled a hello. *I really want my own room,* I thought.

"I'm sorry you lost your job, Grandpa," Daniel said.

"Thank you, Daniel, but my job isn't lost. I know just where the job is. They just won't let me go to it anymore because I'm not a computer wizard." He set his bags down and rubbed his hands together. "But that's past. I've got big plans now."

"Is it another job, Grandpa?"

"No, Daniel. I'll be plenty busy helping you hunt for treasure and fishing with Aaron. And I know your mom has been itching to reorganize those kitchen cabinets of hers."

After dinner, I shut my studio door tight. I heard Grandpa putting his things away in Charlie's room. I tried to finish an ink drawing I had begun that morning, but the lines came out jagged and smeared. I wadded it up and tossed it into the trash.

During the next few weeks, I spent most of my time in my studio. Grandpa was up early every morning, helping Mom organize the kitchen. He got everything so tidy Mom was afraid he was going to label the milk carton. He asked me several times to go fishing with him. I was always busy, so he quit asking. He started clipping ads out of the Help Wanted section in the paper and making lots of telephone calls.

The first week in July, Grandpa announced that he had found a job. He dressed up every day and left early with his lunch in a brown bag. I thought I was glad, but by the second week I was starting to wish I had gone fishing with him. I remembered the fun we used to have.

One day I rode my bike out to the lake. I walked down toward the fishing pier and almost tripped over a fallen log in surprise. There was Grandpa, sit-

"It's just the place for you, Grandpa. Could I fish awhile with you this afternoon?"

ting on a bench by the pier. He had draped his suit jacket over the bench, and he was eating his lunch, looking out over the water.

I hid behind a tree so he wouldn't see me. He hadn't gotten a job! *Have I made him feel this unwanted?* I thought. I got a lump in my throat.

I pedaled home, ran to my studio, and bent over my drawing board. I drew a large square like a classified ad with careful block lettering at the top: FISHING PARTNER WANTED. EXPERIENCE WITH BOYS AND DOGS NEEDED. Then I drew Grandpa, Streak, and me fishing from the pier.

I grabbed my fishing gear and whistled for Streak. On the way back to the lake, I thought of Grandpa sitting on the bench all alone. I realized I hadn't heard him tell a joke in a long time. Having my own room didn't seem very important anymore.

At the lake, I fastened the drawing to Streak's collar and followed him as he ran and laid his shaggy head on Grandpa's knee. Grandpa took the classified ad from the dog's collar and looked at it a long time before he looked up at me.

"Yes sir, I knew this was a sensitive animal. He saw I needed a career change. What about you? Think I'll qualify?"

"It's just the place for you, Grandpa. Could I fish awhile with you this afternoon?"

Grandpa rolled up his sleeves and reached for a fishing pole. "Wouldn't start without you," he said. "And neither would the dog."

Pockets
6–12 years
1,455 words

From the Author

I wrote "A Place of My Own" for submission to *Pockets'* annual fiction contest. I sent for sample copies so I was familiar with the type of material *Pockets* uses.

Very few children live in ideal conditions. I decided my viewpoint character would be a middle child, under pressure from both younger and older brothers.

Every main character must want something so much that when he or she is thwarted, the story problem appears. If the character cares, the reader will care.

After establishing the viewpoint and story problem, I use both internal and spoken dialogue to reveal the character to the reader. Often we need to listen to what is *not* said. In the opening scene of this story, Aaron senses from his mother's body language that she has bad news.

Working from a brief outline, I wrote this story as a series of scenes. I knew the final scene first, and I worked toward that. When I revised, I cut out everything that digressed from my goal: a satisfying end for the reader.

A Peruvian Christmas

By Diana Conway

Emilio fingered the coins in his pocket as he wandered through the outdoor market of the Peruvian mountain village. What could he buy for *Abuelita* with 25 *intis*?

"Papayas!" the fruit woman called out. Emilio's mouth watered, but if he bought his grandmother a papaya for Christmas, she would insist he eat most of it. He wanted to get her a present she didn't have to share.

The perfume man's stall smelled like flowers on a church altar. Emilio couldn't imagine his grandmother smelling of anything but wood smoke, roasted corn, and bitter coffee. Soon he would meet her in the plaza, and they would go to Christmas Eve Mass. She didn't expect a present. He had secretly kept back a few coins from his job at the hardware store after school.

Beyond the perfume seller, a young man and his wife sold carved wooden llamas. The wife wore traditional Quechua Indian clothes. Under her many layers of colored wool skirts her belly was round as a papaya. Soon she would have a baby.

Emilio showed them his 25 intis. "Do you have anything for this price?" he asked. The carver shook his head.

Cathedral bells called the villagers to Mass, and Emilio still hadn't found a present. In the next stall, a woman sold weavings. *Sí!* He would buy Abuelita a new shawl to replace the faded black one she wore to church. He fingered a sky blue weaving, soft as a baby's skin.

"*¿Cuanto?*" he asked the vendor.

"Forty intis," she answered.

"Too much," he bargained.

"Thirty-five," she countered.

Emilio showed her his coins. "Truly, this is all I have."

"Is the shawl for your mother?" asked the vendor.

"For Abuelita," said Emilio. "She took me when my mother died."

The woman sucked in her cheeks. "*Pués,* because it's Christmas . . . ."

She wrapped the shawl with brown paper. Emilio's heart skipped as he placed the package in his school bag and hurried to meet his grandmother.

The stone church was dark as twilight inside and smelled of candle wax, incense, and damp wool clothes.

Abuelita was not in the plaza. Maybe she couldn't find a ride to town from their home five miles out in the *campo*. Or maybe she came earlier and was already at the cathedral. He went there to look.

The stone church was dark as twilight inside and smelled of candle wax, incense, and damp wool clothes. Townspeople wearing holiday suits sat on polished wooden benches. Country farmers and Indians stood in the back. Emilio didn't see Abuelita anywhere.

The priest read the ancient Christmas story. At the part about Mary and Joseph having to spend the night in a stable, someone pushed back through the crowd toward the door. Emilio recognized the young couple from the market.

"*Con permiso,* excuse me," whispered the carver

as he cleared a way for his wife. Emilio followed them out of the cathedral.

The carver spread his poncho on the ground next to the church wall and helped his wife lie down.

"Is she sick?" Emilio asked.

"The *wawa*," said the man in broken Spanish. "The baby comes early, I think." Deep lines etched his face like the knife marks on his wooden sculptures.

"She should go to the *clínica*," said Emilio, but the carver didn't seem to understand. "A doctor," explained Emilio.

The man shook his head. "Too much money."

Some women gathered around and took charge. They wore the same round felt hats as the carver's wife and spoke quiet words to her in Quechua. The carver and Emilio waited silently outside the circle of women.

Time passed without Emilio's noticing it. He forgot about Christmas Eve Mass. He forgot about Abuelita. Then two things happened at almost the same time. The brass bells rang from the cathedral tower, and the circle of women opened to take in the carver and Emilio.

A tiny baby squalled like a kitten in the cold night air. The women searched for a cloth to wrap her. Their woven wool carrying blankets were too rough for newborn skin. One woman started to rip her muddy cotton petticoat.

"*Espere!* Wait!" said Emilio.

People poured from the church, calling out Christmas Eve greetings. Emilio hoped someone would help, but they glanced at the Indians, then hurried the other way. He reached into his school bag, unwrapped the blue shawl, and held it out to the baby's father. For your daughter, *señor*."

"No," said the carver. "You tell market lady is for grandmother."

"I wish I had a present for you."

If Emilio could speak Quechua, he would have said that a Christmas baby must have a soft blanket. Instead, he just pushed the shawl into the carver's hands and ran away before he could change his mind.

He ran all the way to the plaza, gulping down the thin mountain air. Abuelita waited for him on a bench.

"I got here too late for Mass," she said, "but I know the Christmas story by heart."

Emilio sat down next to her. "*Feliz Navidad*, Abuelita. I wish I had a present for you."

She pulled him to her side and shared her faded black shawl.

"You are my present," she said.

Children's Writer
Writers for children
1,055 words

From the Author

Writers who live in Alaska, as I do, often get locked into regional themes. Recently an editor gently suggested that I draw on some other experiences in my life—for example, my time in Peru with the Peace Corps. The result was "A Peruvian Christmas," which almost sold to that editor. What can be more discouraging than a note that says, "This one was close. Please try us again"? Luckily, *Children's Writer* announced an inspirational fiction contest shortly after that rejection.

The subtext of my story was a parallel between the first Christmas (no room at the inn) and the social problems of contemporary Latin America. In rereading my manuscript, however, I found my message a little too obvious. There was a "bad" rich woman who insulted the Indian carver in the market. So I subsumed her into the indifferent crowd that "hurried the other way."

I retain many powerful memories from Andean Peru—the colorful markets, the handmade clothing, the painfully thin air, the gabble of Spanish and Quechua languages, and, above all, the social injustice. In the cathedral, middle-class people sat on benches while Indians stood in back. An Indian woman really did give birth on the street by my house in 1966. These separate memories, joined together and fictionalized as an event in a sensitive child's life, became my story.

It's important to belong to a support/critique group. Since I live in a "bush" community, I share my stories by mail with some faithful critics. One asked why I often write on "spiritual" matters although I'm not religious. I believe that people can make a difference in the world, and my strongest stories carry this message.

The Grass Is Too Tall

By Nancy Lammers

Jason dashed down the hall after the old German short-haired pointer.

"Dooley, want to go for a walk?"

"Oooo, Oooo, Oooo," Dooley moaned. His toenails clicked the floor and his liver-colored ears flapped like velvet mittens. Jason hurried home from school every day to walk the dog. Dooley was fifteen, but Jason tried not to think about him getting older and dying. The dog had been around since before Jason was born. And Jason had lived with Gramma all his life, since his parents died in a car wreck when he was a baby.

Jason passed the living room, and Gramma looked up from her computer. "While you're walking Dooley, why don't you take Gloria, too?" She picked the black toy poodle off the sofa.

They didn't need *another dog—especially a sissy toy poodle.*

"We've got two dogs now, you know."

Jason looked at Gloria, who was curly all over like a miniature lamb. *That was supposed to be a dog?* "I can't. We're going in the field. The grass is too tall for Gloria."

Gramma frowned. "All right. But she might surprise you."

Jason led Dooley outside. He wished Aunt Ruth hadn't given Gloria to them. Just because she had a traveling job. They didn't *need* another dog—especially a sissy toy poodle.

That afternoon Jason took Dooley on a longer walk than usual. When they got back he poured extra food pellets in his dish.

"Don't forget Gloria," Gramma said, handing Jason a small plastic dog dish.

Jason nodded and measured one cup of dog food. He wished he could forget Gloria. She was only two, which reminded him of how old Dooley was.

Dooley gulped food as if he were starved. His nose bumped the dish around the floor while he licked it. Gloria sniffed her food as if it might be poison. Finally she ate three mouthfuls and backed away. What a sissy, picky dog!

That night Gloria jumped on the end of Jason's bed and curled up against his feet. She made slurping sounds while she licked her paw.

Ever since she'd arrived, two days ago, she'd slept on a pillow in the kitchen. Jason waited for Gramma to walk in and tell Gloria to get down.

Instead, Gramma sat on the side of his bed and stroked Gloria's back. "You know, she's so little, I really don't mind if she sleeps with you."

Jason pushed up on his elbows. "But Dooley can't even sleep *by* my bed! You make him stay out in the den."

Gramma smoothed back Jason's hair. "Oh, Jason, I can tell how much you're hurting. I'll miss him too."

Tears stung Jason's eyes and he turned away. So what if Dooley had started having accidents? He was still the best dog in the whole world.

Gramma sat there a while longer, then she picked up Gloria and walked out of the room. "Goodnight, Jason," she said, and turned off the light.

Every day after school, Jason found Dooley and Gloria waiting inside the front door. He always pushed Gloria away. But, finally, one day she barked. She barked again. Louder.

"Jason?" Gramma called. "Take Gloria on a walk, too. She wants to go out, and I'm working on a poem."

"All right," Jason said, glaring at Gloria.

Outside, Jason headed across the field. Dooley ambled behind, but Gloria bounced over the tall grass like a fuzzy, black kangaroo. Jason watched as she chased a yellow butterfly. *And I thought she'd be too little for the tall grass*, he thought. *At first she hardly ate anything, but now she eats a lot. And today's the first time she ever barked. Gramma loves her—I guess that should be enough for me.*

On the way home, Dooley stumbled and fell, and his legs slipped when he tried to stand again.

Jason's eyes blurred with tears. "What's wrong, Dooley?" But he didn't have to ask. It seemed like ages since Dooley had raced squirrels and leaped over fences and jumped up in the back of Gramma's old pickup.

Jason slid his arm around Dooley's chest and heaved him up. Why couldn't Dooley swap places with Gloria and be the young one? It wasn't fair.

Back at home, Dooley slurped water from his bowl and flopped on the kitchen floor.

Gloria ran to Dooley and sniffed his face and ears. She wiggled between his front legs and rubbed her back against his neck.

Dooley poked his nose into her chest and licked her face. But then he yawned, stretched his legs out to one side, and closed his eyes.

Jason sat down beside the dogs. His chest muscles felt tight, and there was a lump in his throat. He swallowed, but the lump stayed.

He looked at Gloria. "You love him too, don't you?"

Gloria lifted her ears and turned her head sideways. She gazed at Jason, her whole body quivering. Bits of leaves and grass clung to her fur. Her eyes shone like wet, black marbles. She wanted something, and Jason knew exactly what it was. He'd pushed her away. He'd tried to ignore her. But in spite of that, here she was, acting as if she belonged to him. How many dogs were there that refused to give up?

He held out his arms. "Come here, you funny little dog."

Gloria bounded into his lap. Yipping, she plunked her front paws on his chest and licked his chin. Jason rubbed his cheek against her fuzzy side. Now it wouldn't seem right around here without her. But

when he looked over at Dooley, the lump in his throat grew.

Gramma walked into the kitchen. "How was your walk?" She patted Gloria's head, then knelt and stroked Dooley's side.

Gramma's sad, too, Jason thought. *Even though now she has Gloria, too.* He opened his eyes wide. *Gramma loves both dogs. Both dogs,* he realized suddenly. And he'd been thinking that if he really cared about Gloria, it'd mean she was taking Dooley's place. But that could never happen— Dooley was too special for that. Jason could have two dogs, couldn't he? Like Gramma. He sighed. At least for a while he could.

He patted Dooley's head. "The walk was great, Gramma," he said. Then he hugged Gloria. "And you're no sissy either. You're spunky."

On the Line
9–14 years
1,051 words

From the Author

I've been employed as a counselor with Big Brothers/Big Sisters, a temporary teacher, and a research assistant. The idea for "The Grass Is Too Tall" arose when our son gave his toy poodle to us. My husband, devoted to our aging German short-hair pointer, considered the poodle a sissy dog. When I recalled single-parent families I'd worked with, and how loyal the children were to the absent parent, Jason sprung into being.

Staying in Jason's head helped set the readers' age level. I focused on keeping the story short, but didn't consider actual length until the revision process. Then I summarized less-interesting parts and made scenes out of the more important material. The hardest part was writing an ending that was hopeful without being sentimental.

I sent the story out four times; it was rejected. I revised it again, and it won second prize in a local contest. I sent it out twice more with no luck. Two years later, after rewriting the ending, I sent it to six publications, and *On the Line* bought it. I attribute my success, mainly, to two creative writing courses, various workshops and conferences, and my weekly critique group.

Intermediate Fiction

San Luis Rey

By Annette C. Deamond

I never wanted to move to California. But my parents did. From the minute they mentioned it, they had that look. You know, the kind of look kids get when you tell them they're going to Disneyland. To Mom and Dad, California was one big Disneyland.

"Think of the new friends you'll make, Leah!" Dad said.

"I already have friends," I replied.

"You'll have adventures, then!" Mom said. She thinks a kid's life is like a story in a book, filled with magic and excitement.

"Our new house is earthquake-proof, hon."

The truth is, I had all the adventures I wanted back on the East Coast. I could go out with my friends and have fun, then come back home. Only now I had no home. Moving across the continent seemed more like a complication than an adventure. Nobody knew me in Southern California, where I'd just be another skinny blond kid on a bike. There were probably forty-five million skinny blond kids on bikes in Southern California.

In Southern California, all the neighborhoods are new. They look like models somebody just plunked down into the big dry hills. You walk down the street and *boom!* The neighborhood ends. Back home, the neighborhoods run together, all nice and cozy.

And let's not forget about California's earthquakes, for crying out loud.

"Our new house is earthquake-proof, hon," Dad said. Back on the East Coast, we had to have our basement waterproofed. Somehow it just wasn't the same.

So there we were, in all the confusion, men hauling our stuff from the moving van into that great, big box of a house. My mother wheeled out a bike with fat, muscular tires.

"Where's my ten-speed?" I howled.

"It's in the truck. This is a mountain bike," she said. "You can ride around in the hills. Explore!"

"But it's so big here!" I cried.

"Then don't go too far on your first day. Get to know your way around." She smiled. "I know this is hard for you, Leah."

"Thanks, Ma." I hugged her tightly, hoping that I'd find my way back. Sometimes my mother has a little too much confidence in me. She didn't know I'd left all my confidence back home.

I put on my Baltimore Orioles hat. How would I ever remember which house was mine? They all looked alike, big pink boxes. At least they had numbers on the houses, big yellow numbers, like in a cartoon.

"Hey! You must be the new kid!"

I pedaled to the edge of the neighborhood, two blocks away, where the houses just ended on top of one of those big dry hills. Across the road I saw this huge thing that looked like a church. But it wasn't like any church I had ever seen before. It stood stark white against a deep blue sky. Even the sky was different in Southen California, a weird, clean blue, not a cloud to be seen.

"Hey! You must be the new kid!" I almost

jumped out of my skin. I turned around. Was this supposed to be one of those new friends my parents told me about? It was too soon. I couldn't even tell if it was a boy or a girl. Black hair hung into black eyes on a wide, brown face.

"That's the old mission," the kid said. "San Luis Rey."

"Can we go there?" I asked.

"Come on!" The kid took off down the hill on a bike that looked as if it had been through one of those famous earthquakes.

"I'm from Baltimore," I said to nobody. The kid was far ahead.

The church loomed bright white into the big sky. It was funny to think that the Pacific Ocean was just a few blocks away. The air even smelled different here, not at all like the air at home.

"There used to be Indians at the mission," the kid said. "They had sheep and orange groves. They used to wash their clothes down there."

"Down there" was a dry hollow with bricks and cactus all around. What did they wash their clothes in, dirt?

"Some of the people around here snuck the stuff out of the church so it wouldn't get wrecked."

"There was water," the kid said, reading my mind.

We sat down by one of those empty brick pools. Big stone monster heads gaped at us. Somehow the heads seemed friendly, and a tiny lizard was even sunning itself in one of the mouths.

"They lived here until the soldiers came and chased everybody away, the Indians and the Spanish priests and everybody," the kid said. "Some of the people around here snuck the stuff out of the church so it wouldn't get wrecked. Statues, crosses, and holy things made of gold. After a while the old mission fell down."

"When was this?"

"Oh, a hundred and sixty years ago."

"What happened to the stuff?"

"The people got old and died. And their children kept it. But they knew it wasn't theirs. They just kept it for old San Luis Rey. Then," the kid leaned close with those big black eyes, "when the government returned the churches to the people, the old things started coming back. From all around, people brought back the old statues and the holy golden stuff."

"Cool," I said. "All of it?"

"Well, not all of it."

I dreamed that I was helping the friars hide statues under the piles of hay.

"Don't they know where everything went?"

"Nobody knows." The kid had a faraway kind of look. "We better go."

The kid jumped up on that ugly old bike. "My name is Pauli!"

Pauli was way ahead. The name told me nothing.

"I'm Leah!" I yelled and tried to keep up. It wasn't easy. Going up that bumpy brown hill took all my breath away.

That night I dreamed about friars in long brown robes with hoods and creaky wagons pulled by horses. I dreamed that I was helping the friars hide statues under the piles of hay. Beautiful wooden ladies, painted bright colors, were hidden under the hay, sneaking away under the stars.

When school started, Pauli was in my class. Pauli was a girl and even wore a dress one day. So Mom and Dad were right. I had found a friend. Pauli's parents were real nice. Her mother made tortillas from scratch and gave us gallons of lemonade. Her parents spoke Spanish, and I even learned a few words. Her father laughed and said that by the end of the year, they'd have me speaking Spanish fluently. They were like my parents, making promises as if they could see into the future.

All my knowledge of earthquakes had been built around TV disasters.

One night I woke to the sound of trains passing by our house. Only there were no tracks for trains to run on. There had been an earthquake, a minor one, a tremor.

"A WHAT!" I cried at the breakfast table. All my knowledge of earthquakes had been built around TV disasters. My parents explained that mild tremors are actually good. See, we're all riding on these giant plates. A hundred miles from our breakfast table, two of those plates meet. Only trouble is, each is moving in the opposite direction. If they bump along gently, we have a minor quake. The old Earth sort of gets some of that friction out of its system. When those plates stop gliding and start pushing and shoving, that's another story, one I hope to miss.

Pauli was excited that day. "Let's look around," she said.

"What for?"

"Sometimes things change after an earthquake." She leaned closer. "Where do you think those mountains came from?"

I followed her gaze east. The mountains were edged in silver light. There was nothing like that where I came from. Suddenly, I wanted always to see those mountains.

"You have to look real close," Pauli said.

We went down on foot into a dry wash. (If a storm comes up, you better get out of a dry wash real fast. The water comes down in buckets, rushing like crazy through the wash, moving stones and rocks and anything.)

"You get to know these places," Pauli said, "then after a quake, even a little one, you can see if anything is different. Look!"

Little hummingbirds darted all around us, feeding on tiny red flowers in the dry bushes.

A bit of earth had crumbled from a bluff. I never would have noticed it. I had to admit it was pretty neat, even if I really didn't know what was going on. Pauli was giving the little cliff the once-over.

"You think you'll find something really great, right?" I said. "Like dinosaur bones or something."

Pauli had a funny look in her eye. She glanced around. Of course, no one was there. The other kids were all inside playing video games or something. She leaned over and grabbed my arm.

"San Luis Rey," she said.

"Huh?"

"Just say it."

"O.K. San Luis Rey. San Luis Rey—Oh!" I knew then. Pauli expected one day to find a hunk fallen out of the cliff, and there in a little niche we'd see it. It would be old and dirty, but we'd know what it was right away. It might be tall, with golden leaves and angels. Or maybe it would be an old wooden statue, faded and patient, waiting to go home to San Luis Rey. I shivered in the sun. Little hummingbirds darted all around us, feeding on tiny red flowers in the dry bushes.

I shook myself. "What makes you think something could have been hidden around here?"

In 1769 Father Junípero Serra, a Spanish priest of the Franciscan order, began work on his vision of establishing a chain of missions that would stretch from San Diego north along the California coast. Each mission would be one day's walk from the next.

Father Serra and other Franciscan priests introduced Christianity and many aspects of the Spanish culture to the Native Americans. Music, agriculture, animal husbandry, arts and crafts all became part of mission life. In a sad twist of fate, the missionaries also brought diseases unknown to the Native Americans, whose numbers were greatly reduced by sickness and whose unique cultures were lost.

When Mexico gained its independence from Spain in 1821, California fell under Mexican rule. In 1834 a law of secularization put the missions into the hands of private citizens. Old Father Peyri, who had been in charge of San Luis Rey, had to retire. The Native Americans living at the mission followed him to his ship. As it sailed away, some waded out into the ocean and swam after it, so sad were they to see their beloved "Father" leave.

The missions' beautiful statues and works of religious art were stolen or carried away. Local families took some of them for safekeeping. Over time the beautiful buildings fell to ruins.

Eventually California became part of the United States, and in 1865 Abraham Lincoln returned the mission lands to the Franciscan order. Although some artworks were returned, even as recently as 1988, no one really knows the fate of most of the artifacts. San Luis Rey and the other missions were rebuilt and today stand bright white against the blue California sky, telling us of noble dreams and tragic outcomes.

Pauli shrugged. "People used to bury things for safekeeping. Gold and stuff. And now, when there's an earthquake, sometimes things get uncovered."

"What would you do if we found something?" I asked.

"What do you think we should do?"

"Well, we could wrap it up and sneak it back to San Luis Rey. Stick it in the garden. Nobody would know where it came from. We could leave a little note on it or something—"

"Like 'Surprise!'" Pauli laughed.

Not far away, the old white mission waited. It stood for something, long ago, on a big California hill. Earthquakes had not wrecked it; people had done that. Then, years later, other people had built it back up, shining white against that unbelievable sky. It seemed to say something to me, remind me of something.

I know, somehow, that Pauli is right. I will find something here, something wonderful. Maybe I already have.

Cricket
9–14 years
2,075 words

From the Author

"San Luis Rey" was my first story published in a national magazine. My work had appeared in small-circulation publications, but I had not written seriously for years, being busy with my children and part-time job. San Luis Rey itself led me back to serious writing.

While accompanying my husband on a business trip to Southern California, I visited San Luis Rey, drawn by some forgotten childhood memory, and decided to write a story about it. Having four children, I'd read a lot of children's literature, so I decided on that route.

So I had a setting and an anticipated audience. I knew from reading writers' guidelines that girls were "in." Since my story would be set on the other side of the continent, I decided to use a move as the conflict. The geology of Southern California is quite dramatic, so I used it to highlight Leah's situation and included a small earthquake. The history of the mission system also tied in with the general theme of upheaval.

I was thrilled by the story's acceptance and agreed to any changes the editors suggested. At first, Leah was rather sarcastic, her cockiness a defense against her fear of new surroundings. The editor at *Cricket* asked me to get rid of her flippant manner and make her more vulnerable. The editor questioned the earth tremor, so I researched seismic activity of the region. I had to fact-check several other issues at the library and make phone calls to San Luis Rey. After I revised the story and submitted research citing specific references, I was asked to write a sidebar.

For me, character and setting come first. I think of dialogue as the characters breaking free of the narrative. I hand-write a first draft until it's practically illegible, then rewrite it into my computer. The real beginning is the original inspiration. But it's the commitment that presents the opportunity to share that magic moment with others.

Intermediate Fiction

The Wreck of Monique's Antiques

By Sharelle Byars Moranville

"Mom, let's go!" Ignoring the rain, I hung out the van window. I pounded on Ellabelle's door, right over the spot that said MONIQUE'S ANTIQUES AND COLLECTIBLES.

Why did my mom have to name our van? Why did we have to schlep around in an uncool pink van, anyway, picking through people's trash in the middle of the night?

Mom said it was business; I said it was dumb.

With her slicker hood pulled up, Mom swept her flashlight along the bulging trash bags. Suddenly, she waved something over her head and ran toward the van.

What had she found this time?

A flowerpot. Mom had found a flowerpot.

Wow.

I sighed and leaned back against the seat. Why couldn't I have a normal mother?

Mom groped through the window with one arm, trying to hug me. "It's a really rare one, Tom! Worth a hundred dollars. At least!"

All I could think about was what if somebody I knew drove by and saw us?

"Mom," I said, as calmly as possible. "It's late. Can't we go home?"

"You used to love to go treasure hunting with me," she said.

"Come on, Mom. I've got homework."

The smile vanished from her face. "I'll sort through the rest of the stuff later." She opened her door and tossed a big, dripping trash bag onto the seat between us. "Maybe there's more."

I looked the other way and rolled my eyes.

With a gust, the rain began to pound down. By the time we got to the freeway entrance ramp, the wipers could hardly keep up.

Mom flipped off the radio and peered forward in concentration. Right before we got to the Brushy Creek overpass, a wall of wind and rain shoved Ellabelle into the next lane.

Suddenly, out of nowhere, a deer plunged into the beam of our headlights.

I hung in mid-air, suspended by my seat belt.

Mom braked and screamed as the van fishtailed crazily across the wet pavement. With a lurch that made my insides somersault, we bounced down an embankment. Ellabelle's windshield cracked and then shattered. The van balanced on two wheels before crashing on its side.

When the sound of crushing metal stopped, I heard the sound of gushing water.

I hung in mid-air, suspended by my seat belt.

I squirmed in panic, and the sudden movement made my head spin. The remains of Ellabelle's crumpled dashboard clamped my legs.

"Mom?" No answer. My voice came out in a whisper. "Mom?"

Then I saw her, slumped against the door. The van had landed on the driver's side.

"Mom!" I howled.

She mumbled something I couldn't hear. What I *could* hear was Brushy Creek rising. Fast.

Everybody knows Brushy Creek floods in a hard rain.

"Mom!" I reached down and tried to touch her.

In a flicker of lightning I saw the black water

pooling under her body.

"I'll get us out, Mom. I'll get you out." What I wanted to say was, *Don't die. Please don't die.*

It had been me and Mom for as long as I could remember. The two of us, taking care of each other. Best buds...until lately.

"Tom."

"I'm here, Mom. Don't worry."

Gripping the shoulder strap, I twisted and pulled, ignoring the pain in my right leg.

No use. The dashboard held my legs in iron jaws.

Now I wished with all my heart that somebody I knew *would* come by and see us. Even though we had been trashpicking in a pink van.

I reached for anything. My hand touched the trash bag Mom had tossed in the seat between us. Ellabelle's smashed front end crushed it too, but I worked my hand inside.

Lightning flashed.

A man's slipper.

I dipped my hand in again.

A paperback book.

I fumbled with the next thing my fingers touched.

Something on a cord. Its long, stringy length tangled with other stuff in the trash bag. I tugged.

Bulbs on a cord.

I coaxed the string of lights out of the sack.

"Christmas lights!"

And suddenly I had hope. Maybe there *was* a way out.

See, Uncle Ned and I had rigged up a thing called a "converter" to change the van's direct current to the alternating current that appliances use. Mom and I used it to test the old lamps and stuff before we drug them back to the antique shop.

"Hang on, Mom," I said. "Help's on the way. After all, if you drove by and saw Christmas lights at the bottom of a ravine on a stormy, summer night, wouldn't you stop?"

If I could just keep Mom talking to me, maybe she wouldn't die.

I think she said, "Sure."

But maybe not.

My hand shook as I reached for the converter outlet. *Who would throw out a string of Christmas lights that worked?*

I pushed in the plug.

The inside of the van exploded with light.

I yelped, and Mom twitched and mumbled something.

"See, Mom—"

Then the lights went out. But not before I saw Mom's fate.

How long would it take a person to drown? Would drowning hurt a lot?

Would she remember what a jerk I'd been lately? The lights blazed back on.

"They flash!" I screamed like an idiot. "They flash!"

I lifted myself up as best I could with my legs pinned and shoved the lights out the smashed window.

They lay on Ellabelle's side, pulsing like a bright heartbeat in the rain.

Almost at once, a car slowed down. Stopped. Backed up.

I screamed something majorly uncool like, "Help! Quick! My mama's gonna drown!"

Soon sirens wailed and lights flashed. The static of police radios drifted down to me.

Later, after we were inside the ambulance, the man who'd helped me onto the stretcher knelt between me and Mom. "Everybody's going to be all right, son."

I looked across at Mom.

Her eyelids drooped sleepily above the oxygen mask, but she managed to flash me a weak thumbs-up sign.

I reached for her hand. "Hey, Mom, I can't wait to get home and see what else is in that bag of junk!" What I really wanted to say was, *I love you. A lot.*

But her smile told me that she had heard. Really heard.

Guideposts
7–12 years
1,046 words

From the Author

The genesis of this story was a piece in our local paper about people who cruise posh neighborhoods the night before trash pickup looking for curbside "treasures." One of the "seekers" had fitted her van with an electrical outlet so she could test lamps.

I built this story around an action/rescue plot and a theme dear to every 12-year-old boy's heart: Why does my mom want to embarrass me to death? *Guideposts* helped me separate the gold from the dross and polish my final version.

Picture Your Pet

By Lynn Hartsell

David's new kitten is a ball of fast-moving, gray fluff. Rick's puppy has long, droopy ears. Jon's pony trots across the spring-green pasture. These images won't be forgotten because David, Rick, and Jon have taken pictures of their pets. You can do the same with your pet and your camera.

First, really know your camera. Read its book of instructions. How close can you get and still have a sharp picture? Is a flash attachment built in? Where is the shutter-release button? Practice until you know exactly how your camera works. Posing your pet will give you enough to think about!

Find someone to help with this project. Dogs and cats will be happier if a friend helps hold them in place until you are ready to "shoot." For a formal portrait, it's better to "stand-in" a toy animal while you are getting set up for the real thing. Toys don't wiggle!

Check the background. It should be as plain as possible to show off your pet. If you want to take a picture of your cat in her favorite chair, for example, and the upholstery is flowered, cover it with a plain blanket. Look for contrast in the background. A white, fluffy poodle looks sharp in front of a dark wood wall. A black cat is lovely with a white drape behind her.

Watch the animal's eyes before you press the shutter. The animal should look awake! Try making unusual noises to get that interested expression. Bits of cheese help keep dogs and cats from being bored while sitting for portraits.

Hold your camera steady while you press the shutter release. If you punch the button too hard, you will move the whole camera, and your picture will be blurred. Holding your breath when you "snap" the picture also helps keep the camera steady. Be sure your camera lens is clean. A dirty lens takes a blurred picture.

Ready for some action now? Try "panning" a picture of your horse or dog running. (Cats are usually too fast.) "Panning" simply means moving your camera in the same direction and at the same speed as the animal is moving. The picture will be sharp of the animal with a blurred background. A little blur might show up in a paw or hoof or floppy tail, but this just gives your picture a sense of how fast your pet moves.

You will enjoy showing your pictures to your friends, but they might be even more important sometime. If your animal ever is lost, it is very helpful to have a good picture to show what it looks like. You could even make picture posters to put up around the neighborhood.

Pick a time when your pet is feeling cooperative. All people have moods, so pick a time when you are feeling patient. Take lots of pictures, and one or maybe even two will catch that perfect picture of your perfect pet.

Boys' Quest
6–13 years
494 words

From the Author
   I write long and then cut until the desired length is reached. This results in a tighter, smoother piece than if I try to write "to length" from the start. I saw *Boys' Quest* as a natural outlet for an animal-hobby article. Luckily, the editor agreed.

Dirt Detectives

By Sally Eyre

You might call them detectives, or better, dirt detectives. They are digging for clues and seeking treasures. To the workers at the Fort Michilimackinac (mish-i-la-MACK-in-aw) archaeological dig, excitement comes in small sizes. It can be the discovery of a tiny glass bead or a piece of a fish bone.

"Most of the things we find have very little monetary value," says Lynn Evans, curator of archaeology for Michigan's Mackinac State Historic Park. "But they have tremendous value in terms of what they can tell us about the people who lived here."

"Remember, when you dig a site, you're basically destroying it."

Located at the northern tip of Michigan's Lower Peninsula, Fort Michilimackinac is the site of one of the longest ongoing digs in the United States. Some sort of excavation has occurred at the fort every summer since 1959. The work takes place in full view of tourists visiting the fort.

The fort at Michilimackinac today is actually an exact replica of the original. The first fort was deserted and burned down in 1781. The ground beneath the fort holds the treasure for which the crew is digging.

Careful scientific procedures are used in archaeological digs to make discoveries—literally handful by handful. "Remember, when you dig a site, you're basically destroying it," explains Evans. "Therefore, we need to know where everything we found came from."

In order to keep track of findings, the area being excavated is marked off in a grid. Every handful of dirt is run through a series of screens.

This way *artifacts*, no matter how tiny, can be found and recorded. At Fort Michilimackinac, history is preserved in layers of dirt. The top layer, representing the last one hundred years, is where a bobby pin belonging to a visitor from the 1950s might be found. The next layer of dirt might reveal chunks of plaster and nails from when the British destroyed the fort. The layer beneath this holds the most mystery for scientists. It represents the time when American Indians and French fur traders lived and worked here over two hundred years ago.

Archaeologists use other sources of information to help piece together the story behind a location. "We use maps, military correspondence, and supply lists, and we have access to fur-trade records," says Evans. "The idea is to take the archaeological discoveries, compare them [with] the documented record, and come up with one story." For example, the workers have discovered tools made out of bone that were used for food preparation by American Indian women. Other household items such as a birch-bark container used by Ojibwe

These treasures show archaeologists that the Ojibwe, Huron, and Ottawa nations all lived in the area.

women to store maple sugar also were found. These finds of domestic life seem to be supported by church records that show the marriages of Indian women to French fur traders.

Near Colonial Michilimackinac in the small town

Intermediate Nonfiction

of St. Ignace, another archaeological dig is in its seventh season at Marquette Mission Park. The park is the oldest known historical site in Michigan. This dig has revealed a wealth of information about the mission that the French Jesuit priest Father Marquette established there in 1671.

Charles Cleland, a professor of anthropology (the study of man) and curator of Great Lakes Archaeology at Michigan State University Museum, teaches a class in archaeology at this site. "We have found a huge variety of artifacts, such as bones, tools, sewing awls, spoons, and iron and brass arrowheads," says Cleland. These treasures show archaeologists that the Ojibwe, Huron, and Ottawa nations all lived in the area. The objects indicate that the Indians hunted (specifically for bear, deer, beaver, and moose), were impressive fishermen, and grew corn in abundance.

The discovery here of one of the earliest French coins minted in the 1500s reveals that American Indians were trading with the French for manufactured goods. The finding of an elaborately carved comb and a bangle for a necklace crafted with a beaver design illustrate the artistic nature of the Indian culture.

What does it take to be an archaeologist? "Patience," stresses Evans. "You have to be patient." "Archaeology is a science," reminds Professor Cleland. "To be an archaeologist, you have to be someone who can pay attention to detail, and you should have a good curiosity about the past."

Cobblestone
8–14 years
701 words

The Think Tank

By Patricia Daniels

Azy, a 21-year-old male orangutan, had been scoring 100 percent on the day's vocabulary test—until now. Now National Zoo biologist Rob Shumaker holds up some folded bags containing chopped fruit. "Okay, Azy—want to tell me what this is?" In front of the rusty-haired ape is a

Think Tank researchers are studying creatures as various as hermit crabs, leaf-cutter ants, and macaques.

computer screen showing some symbols. Each one stands for a word. Azy lifts his long, graceful hand and points to the symbol for cup. A buzzer sounds. The screen shows an hourglass symbol that means his answer is wrong.

For the first time this afternoon, Azy seems confused. Shumaker shows him the bags again, and again the orang points to "cup." On the fourth try, Azy figures it out. He points to the symbol for "bag," and Shumaker hands him the paper bags through an opening in the Plexiglas between them.

They hope to learn whether—and how— animals think.

Azy picks out the fruit and reluctantly hands back the bags when the biologist asks politely, "Azy, can I have those?"

For the last three years, Shumaker has been working with Azy and five other orangutans at the zoo's Think Tank building. In addition to these great apes, Think Tank researchers are studying creatures as various as hermit crabs, leaf-cutter ants, and macaques. They hope to learn whether—and how—animals think. Some of the scientists look at tool use. Others observe the animals' social life. Shumaker would like to know if orangutans can learn language.

Shumaker is delighted with Azy's mistake. "Azy's mistakes are more interesting than his right answers," he says. "When he saw the bags, he didn't pick a symbol that meant food, such as 'apple.' He

"Just like people, they have different personalities and learning styles."

didn't pick a verb, such as 'open.' He picked the one other symbol that meant an object, a container. I think his mistakes show that he's putting these words into categories in his mind. Maybe this can teach us a little bit about how he thinks."

Shumaker has known most of the zoo's orangs since they were born. "Orangs' mental abilities are the least understood of the great apes," notes the biologist. "We want to learn more about them, mentally. We also want to add to the quality of their lives by giving them some challenges, some mental enrichment. They all take part in the project voluntarily. None of them is ever forced or punished."

"The most important thing to know is that they are all individuals," he adds. "Just like people, they have different personalities and learning styles. When we started the project, I didn't think Azy would be the fastest learner. But I was wrong. For instance, though he doesn't use tools as much as

Intermediate Nonfiction

the other orangs, Azy turned out to be the best language student. He is very focused and hardworking. I can see him steadily building his knowledge, step by step, making connections."

What's the next step? "We're going to start putting words together into simple sentences," says Shumaker. "Then things will really get interesting."

Muse
8–14 years
493 words

From the Author

I came to writing from the other side of the desk: for 19 years I was an editor for several magazines and publishers, working on both adult and children's nonfiction. Most recently I was managing editor of Time-Life for Children, but in 1996 I decided to leave the corporate world and spend my time doing what I liked best. Since then, I've worked as a freelance editor and writer for Time-Life Books. I've also written two children's books for National Geographic: *The Earth* and *A Pocket Guide to the Weather*. Two more (*Oceans* and *Night Sky*) will come out within the next year. I also edited National Geographic's recent *World Atlas for Children*.

I have written three articles for *Muse,* and I've enjoyed doing all of them. The editors at *Muse* are friendly, professional, and have the highest standards for children's nonfiction. I first approached them with a list of five story ideas: they liked one on sleep research, and it ended up being a cover story. Another one I proposed later, on a historical incident at Niagara Falls, appeared in a subsequent issue.

For the "Think Tank" piece, the editors asked if I could write a short piece on the National Zoo's Think Tank to accompany a longer article on animal thinking. Working through the Smithsonian's Public Affairs office, I contacted Rob Shumaker, the scientist working with the Think Tank orangutans, and interviewed him.

In all my writing, but particularly in science writing, I like to tell a story. In the limited space (500 words) I had for this piece, I decided to focus on one key incident of the language session that said something about animal thinking in general. The other information about the Think Tank research was worked into a few sentences after the anecdotal lead. Once I had decided on the key incident, everything fell into place quickly.

Using the Old Bean

By Pat Perry

Crayons! By the time you turn ten, chances are you've worn down about 730 of them on paper, books, and (occasionally) on walls. Kids use so many crayons that over two billion crayons are made each year in the United States alone. That's a lot of crayons.

Did you ever wonder how crayons are made? Most crayons are created by adding color to a waxy substance called *paraffin*—an oil-industry waste product. The mixture is poured into molds with thousands of holes that produce the crayon's familiar shape.

Petroleum is a shrinking natural resource, so three environmentally minded Purdue University students decided to see if they could invent a crayon made from something other than paraffin. After many experiments, they invented an all-natural, nontoxic crayon, using a plentiful, renewable natural resource: soybeans!

Why soybeans? Soybeans produce an oil that can be used to replace paraffin in the making of crayons. The result is a brand-new, environmentally friendly product. A manufacturer liked the students' ideas and is now making the soybean crayons. The new crayons are called Prang Fun Pro Crayons.

How Do You Grow a Crayon?

Soybeans are one of America's most abundant and useful crops. They are planted in the spring, and the plants' seeds are harvested in the fall. The seeds are cleaned and later crushed into flakes, which are used to produce a crude oil. Some of the oil is refined and used in food products. And some of the soybean oil is shipped to a manufacturing plant for a much more colorful purpose.

At the manufacturing plant, the oil is heated in large tanks. The oil is then mixed with another all-natural product, called *fatty acids*, to create a strong crayon base—something you can hold onto.

Pigments—the reds, greens, blues—are added to the base to bring your favorite crayon colors to life. The colorful base is poured into a special mold, which is then surrounded by water to cool. Once cooled, the newly formed crayons are shot onto a conveyor belt, hand-placed into a dispenser, then wrapped and boxed.

What began as a bean is now a crayon, ready to be used in colorful and creative ways by kids across the country!

*U*S* Kids.*
5–10 years
376 words

From the Author

Let's face it: crayons are not the most interesting of subjects. But kids use them on a daily basis—on paper, walls, each other, and, on occasion, as food. Like many everyday items, we never stop to consider how they're made or where they come from. By focusing on the process in simple, easy-to-read language, kids can quickly gather relevant facts without feeling like they're in school.

My advice? Don't preach; kids get enough of that and they really don't respond to that approach. Keep it fun. Make history live. Condense your research into details young readers can visualize, focusing on the familiar and avoiding the technical. Above all, entertain and inform.

Spadefoot Toads: Desert Amphibians

By Esther Kiviat

What was that weird noise coming from behind my house? The concert of hoarse calls woke me about 3 a.m. one August night after two days of torrential rains.

Could it be the mysterious spadefoot toads I had read about? At the time, I was living by the desert grasslands near Santa Fe, New Mexico. I had hoped to see some spadefoots.

The desert spadefoot is a small olive-brown creature about two and a half inches long. It is an amphibian, related to other toads and frogs. Like its cousins, it eats insects. Most toads and frogs are found in wet or moist places, but spadefoots live in a desertlike environment. So they have to have special ways to survive in a dry world.

Secret Burrows

The spadefoot toad is named for the sharp, hard, black bump on the underside of each hind foot.

It uses this "spade" to bury itself by digging backward into the sandy soil. The toad can stay in its secret burrow for days, months, or even a year without eating, waiting for a heavy summer rain.

They looked like a bunch of kids blowing pink bubble gum.

The morning after the late night concert, I walked out to the big sandy ditch behind my house. Usually the ditch was dry, but it had a trickle of water in it this morning. Following the ditch, I soon came to a monster muddy rain pool.

Suddenly I saw five or six small brown toads swimming around in the puddle. They were floating on their bellies, legs stretched out behind them, their heads out of the water.

Every few seconds they called, inflating huge, balloonlike vocal sacs on their throats. They looked like a bunch of kids blowing pink bubble gum.

Calling for Mates

The hoarse calls were mating calls. As the males called, other toads, which were females, swam around them. Over and over the males tried to grasp the females. The females swam away, only to go back as the males called again.

This courtship game lasted several minutes. Finally, each male spadefoot succeeded in clasping a female from the back.

In the mud around the edges was a network of tiny toad tracks, the only trace of the adult spadefoots.

The clasping stimulates egg-laying. Then, when the female lays her eggs, the male is there to deposit his sperm on them.

Suddenly the pool was quiet. The calling males had all found mates.

That evening I caught one of the toads. At home, I put it into a fishbowl with about two inches of moist sand in the bottom. The toad quickly dug itself backward into the sand with its hind feet, making a wiggling, side-to-side motion.

After about sixty seconds, all I could see of it were its eyes. Then the toad closed them into little slits, and soon they, too, disappeared under the sand.

Young Toads

Wading into the rain pool the next morning, I found many small jellylike blobs attached to the grasses in the water. In the jelly were many clear eggs with dark spots inside.

On the next day I saw some newly hatched quarter-inch tadpoles clinging to the tattered remains of the jelly. The shallow pool was beginning to shrink in the hot sun. In the mud around the edges was a network of tiny toad tracks, the only trace of the adult spadefoots.

To survive, the tadpoles would have to change quickly into fully formed toadlets.

Each day the pool got smaller. By the end of the week, it had shrunk to a strip of water just a few inches wide, crowded with hundreds of fat-bellied, long-tailed tadpoles.

To survive, the tadpoles would have to change quickly into fully formed toadlets. They would have to be able to live on land before their watery birthplace dried up.

As the pool shrunk, many tadpoles' hind legs grew large enough to be seen easily. A few began to sprout front legs.

And then on the twelfth day, I found dozens of miniature spadefoot toads hopping around the edges of the puddle. Some still had long tails. Some had stubby tails. Others had none. All of them had four legs, little toady bumps on their skin, and two beady eyes on the tops of their heads.

Countless tadpoles had died. But some had won their race against the disappearing rain puddle.

I watched one dig itself into the sand nearby. There it would hide safely until heavy rains signaled it to meet other toads in a rain puddle. Then the life cycle would start over again.

Highlights for Children
2–12 years
728 words

From the Author

After graduating from the University of Missouri School of Journalism, my early career included public relations and newspaper reporting, photography, and radio script writing. Later, my husband and I owned and directed a children's nature camp in Dutchess County, New York, for 30 years. I earned a master's degree in early childhood education, taught children and teachers from nursery school through college, and worked as a school consultant in environmental education. I also wrote a children's book, *Paji,* about an Indian boy.

I love writing for children, and I've always been a writer. However, it was not until my husband and I retired and moved to Santa Fe that I was able to devote myself to writing and photography on a full-time basis. I wrote a nature column and feature stories for the daily newspaper and began to exhibit my photographs in galleries there.

We had spadefoot toads in our backyard in Santa Fe. The first time I heard the toads, I didn't know what the sound was. I went out at night to see if I could catch them. My interest grew from there. I sent an article proposal to *Highlights.* I rewrote the piece several times.

In 1985 I returned to New York's Hudson Valley, and I've been photographing its lush landscapes, wildlife, forests, and wetlands for many years. My book, *Changing Tides: Tivoli Bays, A Hudson River Wetland,* has just been published.

I have always been interested in the natural world. I feel it's something we're all part of and need to remain part of. I share and express what I find in nature through my writing and photography. I look for little details in nature, the things people don't ordinarily look at.

Contrary Mary

By Susan C. Hall

Mary Edwards Walker stood only five feet tall, her body resembling that of a young girl. But she had big ideas, contrary ideas. At least that was the way society in the mid-nineteenth century viewed them.

In 1852, at age 20, she announced her intention to become a doctor, her first contrary idea. Women physicians were practically unheard of in those days. Nevertheless, she enrolled in Syracuse Medical School the following year and received her degree in 1855.

She first opened an office in Cleveland where she met with resistance. Folks wouldn't go to a female doctor. So she moved her practice to Troy, New York, where she encountered a similar reception.

To the community, she appeared militant and offbeat.

It's possible she may have been better received had she been more conventional in the way she dressed. Mary hated women's fashions, calling them foolish, impractical, and even unhealthy because of the tight-fitting bodices and the brutally heavy, long skirts, which were usually worn over a bustle or a hoop. She favored a controversial style called a bloomer dress, which consisted of a jacket and knee-length skirt worn over full trousers, gathered at the bottom with elastic bands.

Few women accepted this fashion, but Mary appreciated the comfort and practicality of the outfit. Long after the fad had passed, she wore her bloomer dresses. To the community, she appeared militant and offbeat. Women doctors were rare enough. On top of that, this one dressed funny. Her medical practice floundered.

When the Civil War broke out in 1861, Mary heard tales of vast numbers of wounded Union soldiers being treated in under-staffed field hospitals. She thought this might be her chance to prove her capabilities and tried to join the Army.

They didn't accept her qualifications, and they wouldn't induct her into the service. Undaunted and determined to help, she worked as a civilian nurse for three years. Finally, in 1864 her efforts were rewarded. She became the first female assistant surgeon in the U.S. Army.

She frequently crossed enemy lines to care for the wounded Union soldiers. Members of the opposing Confederate Army didn't believe she was a doctor, thought instead she was a spy and arrested her. She was imprisoned for about four months, then released in a prisoner-exchange deal. She loved to boast that she was exchanged for a Southern officer with the rank of major who was six feet tall!

In 1865, President Andrew Johnson awarded her with what is believed to be the first Congressional Medal of Honor.

After the war, she set up a private practice in Washington, D.C. However, she spent most of her time promoting her contrary ideas.

The French and the English found her feisty, refreshing, and entertaining.

She wrote articles for fashion magazines pleading for dress reform. She pioneered women's rights, taking special interest in the suffragette movement. She hated liquor and tobacco, declaring them unhealthy, and even this idea was considered contrary. People in those days did not believe that smoking and drinking could affect the body adversely.

Mary wrote two books, brimming over with her opinions. She became well known as a colorful, spirited speaker, and she lectured tirelessly all across this country and in Europe. The French and the English found her feisty, refreshing, and entertaining, but Americans continued to view her with serious reservations.

"You can have it over my dead body."

As she grew older, she became more radical about dress reform and eventually began to overdo modification when it came to her own apparel. Photographs of her in later life show her in trousers, frock coat, bow tie, and top hat.

Gradually, even her friends and family began to view her as eccentric, and virtually no one had much regard for her ideas or her credentials as a physician.

In 1917, Federal authorities told her they were going to revoke her Medal of Honor because she had not fought on the battlefield and carried a gun.

"You can have it over my dead body," she thundered. She never relinquished the medal, though the honor was formally nullified by Congress.

She died in 1919, never getting a chance to vote nor see any real significant dress reform. She didn't live to see women become accepted in the medical profession nor alcohol and tobacco become recognized as threats to good health. However, her determination helped set the stage for many important reforms.

Note: In 1977, the revocation of Mary's Medal of Honor came up before Congress, and an Army review board recommended restoring it in memory of the determined little doctor with the contrary ideas.

Hopscotch
6–12 years
739 words

From the Author

After graduating from the University of Arizona, I spent several years writing commercials for television. I then married and raised a family (five children). As soon as they gave me some free time, I began to write and submit stories and articles to children's magazines.

I have an interest in medical history, and while researching other personalities in this field, I kept coming across references to a feisty little lady named Mary Walker. I finally decided that I could ignore her no longer.

I do my research at two different libraries. I guess I just read and read until I feel qualified to write about a subject. I don't work from an outline, but I use notecards, which I fill out as I read, then arrange in logical order.

My first drafts are always bad (and way too long), so I triple-space them and revise by scratching out whatever I possibly can and re-wording until I think it sounds right.

I did not query *Hopscotch*, but it was my first choice since I'd read samples of the magazine. I knew that *Hopscotch* liked articles about outstanding women and thought this article would work for them. So I submitted my article, tailoring it to the magazine's guidelines for length and age range. I felt that, should *Hopscotch* not want it, there would be other markets for it.

I've had more than 300 stories, articles, and activities published in a variety of magazines, including *Children's Digest, Jack And Jill, Turtle, Cat Magazine, Clubhouse, Clubhouse Jr., The Friend, Good Apple, Good Dog!, Guideposts for Kids, Highlights for Children, On the Line, Story Friend, Teen Power, Teens Today, Touch,* and *Venture.*

To Track a Thief

By Kathy Beveridge

Police identification ("ident") sections are part of the detective branch of a police department. Members of the ident section collect and record evidence at a crime scene (such as fingerprints, blood, hairs, fibres, and footprints).

Sometimes footprints left in snow or soft earth can be used to determine a culprit's size, weight, and movements. Distinctive nicks and patterns from the bottom of a shoe may later prove a suspect was at the scene of the crime. Use your new-found forensic knowledge to make and lift your own footprint.

Materials

- Several large pieces of poster board
- Several pieces of plain, white paper
- Can of PAM (kitchen cooking spray)
- Cocoa (e.g., Nestle Quik)
- Roll of clear, wide packing tape
- Scissors

Note: You may want to do this project outside—it can be messy!

Instructions

1. Put on your shoes or runners.
2. Put a piece of poster board on the ground—shiny side down.
3. Completely spray the bottom of one shoe with PAM.
4. Step directly down onto the poster board with the sprayed shoe. Hint: try not to wiggle or move as you do this.
5. Put all your weight on that foot for a few seconds (preferably without falling over).
6. Lift your foot directly up off the poster board (again, avoid wiggling).
7. Sprinkle cocoa generously over the footprint.
8. Move the paper around to coat the footprint evenly with cocoa.
9. Shake off the excess cocoa.
10. Cut a piece of tape that is a bit longer than your footprint.
11. Carefully place the tape over the footprint, pressing down gently and evenly. Hint: try not to "contaminate" the tape with your own fingerprints.
12. Lift the tape off the poster board. The cocoa should stick to the tape.
13. Put a piece of plain paper on the ground.
14. Carefully stick the tape onto the paper, pressing down firmly and evenly.

Voilà! You have successfully made, lifted, and preserved for posterity your own footprint!

A Step Further

Do you think salt or cornstarch would work well as dusting powders? What about flour or baby powder? Try them to find out.

Yes Magazine
9–14 years
328 words

From the Author

As a teacher, I've done many hands-on science and math projects in elementary schools. After seeing that *Yes Magazine* had an upcoming issue on forensics, I was very pleased to have my first-ever article accepted for publication.

Fish Talk!

By Shirley Zebrowski

Fish make sounds. Researchers have found that some fish grunt, click, or make other noises during courtship and defense displays. The reason behind the research is to pinpoint where and when fish are breeding so the region can be protected during this time. There has been much overfishing in all parts of the world and this study might be used to protect and increase the fish populations. Let's see what they found out!

We know that snapping shrimp snap and lobsters buzz. Groupers make a booming noise that can scare divers right out of the water! Because sound travels five times faster in water than in air, fish seeking mates must "talk" quietly. Otherwise, they would attract a predator instead of a mate.

Some sounds are made by *stridulating*, that is, the fish moves its spines and fins, to creek or make a rasping sound. The striped Parrotfish moves its fins rapidly to create sound. Most fish make drumming sounds by vibrating muscles against their swim bladders, which are air-filled sacs in their abdomens. These sounds can vary from the low growl of Cichlids to the chirp of the Damselfish.

Squirrelfish grunt when fighting. Seahorses snap when exploring new territory. The Gobies snort at intruders. The comely Shiner knocks to find a mate. African Jewelfish purrs to show aggression. The gray Angelfish moans when it recognizes a friendly fish. The Toadfish lets out a boat-whistle to get his mate's attention. The Bluestriped *Grunt* does just that by grinding his teeth—he grunts!

Researchers believe there may be as much, if not more, communication between fish than there is between birds. It's just because fish are underwater, where we are not usually present, that we think of them as silent.

Noise affects fish. Loud, low-frequency sounds are used to drive fish away from the pipes of hydro-electric plants. The fish in your aquarium may be suffering from the vibrations from the volume of your television and stereo. Maybe they are yelling "Turn it down" and you just can't hear them!

Skipping Stones
8–16 years
345 words

From the Author

I went fishing quite often with my father when I was a child. Of course, I made too much noise and Dad was always hushing me. It seemed appropriate that the fish were talking at the same time I was!

My choice of material is quite random. I love unusual facts about nature, and I try to see through young eyes. I have to be passionately interested in a subject to write a successful article or short story. I've accumulated an extensive library of nonfiction books, and if I live to be 100, I'll never write up all the ideas I have!

I guess I break the rules. I write slowly but only one draft, reworking as I go. If an editor asks for a different slant or an emphasis on a particular point, I do revise. Experience has helped me understand what juvenile magazines want.

In the early 1970s I was a student of the Institute of Children's Literature. Although at times I don't have a lot of time to write, I do write every day.

Get Squashed!

By Carrie Belknap

Looking for a fun sport to call your own? A game that every girl in the country isn't already playing? A sport in which it doesn't make any darn difference how strong or fast or tall you are?

If you answered yes to the above questions, then you should try squash. Don't turn your nose up. It has nothing to do with those odd-shaped gourds or zucchini your mom brings home from the produce stand. It's just a great one-on-one racquet sport.

Unlike tennis, squash is played in a smallish, confined space.

If you don't already know someone who plays squash, chances are that you've never even heard of the game. But if you're anything at all like the thousands of girls across the country who have taken it up, you might just get hooked the first time you swing your squash racquet and connect with that squooshy little black rubber ball.

Squash is definitely a game that requires some skill—it can take many years to become a really good player. But, even if you're not squashing your opponents, it's something that you can still enjoy from the minute you start whacking that ball. And that's why so many girls like it.

Unlike tennis, squash is played in a smallish, confined space. That means you won't spend your first few matches missing balls and chasing them all over the court. Even the first time you swing a racquet on the squash court, you should be able to play a fairly decent game without feeling totally frustrated.

Squash is an easy sport to pick up because the rules and strategies are relatively simple. Basically, you're just trying to hit the ball in such a way that the other player is unable to hit it back.

And there is a lot less worry about potential injury because squash is not a contact sport. The only danger looming is in the event that you or your opponent don't control your swing and someone gets hit with a racquet. But the sport's regulations are designed to avoid that kind of disaster.

So What Is So Special about Squash, and Why Would I Want to Play?

Well, first off, you might want to take up the sport because squash lets you take advantage of the strengths you already have without putting you at a disadvantage for the ones you lack (like being able to run at the speed of light for track). And you don't have to be any specific body type (as in needing to be tall for basketball or petite for gymnastics).

In squash, you improve on your existing skills. Do you have excellent hand/eye coordination? Or maybe you're quick to react. Perhaps you have two left feet and zero agility but a sharp mind that gives you the upper hand in determining strategy.

"You may not be overly quick, but if you can figure out where that ball is going, you don't need to be," says Frank Cushman, a squash pro who works with nearly 100 kids every season. "If you're willing to put something into it, you can be good." It's also great exercise—physically and mentally.

Where Did Squash Come From, and Who Thought It Up?

Squash was invented by a bunch of students, who were playing "rackets" at the Harrow School in England around 1830. In rackets, you hit a hard ball against a wall. The kids, playing with a punctured ball, found that the game was more fun because the ball "squashed" on impact and gave them a greater variety of shots. Before they knew it, their new game was a respected sport.

Squash came to the United States in 1882, when the headmaster of the St. Paul's School in Concord, N.H., decided it would be a perfect sport for his male students. Today, it is played around the world and is even more popular than tennis in England and Australia.

Because squash is an indoor sport, it first caught on in America in colder climates. It's very popular, for example, at colleges in the Northeast. But the United States Squash Racquets Association (the sport's governing body) has members in just about every state.

The standardized court size is 21 feet wide by 32 feet long with (here's the weird part) walls. That's right—walls. Unlike other racquet sports, in which opponents face each other and hit the ball over a net, you and your opponent stand side-by-side and hit the ball against a facing wall.

There's no net—just lines that define the zone in which you can hit the ball. In each play, the ball can slam against the walls many times, but it can only bounce on the floor once before you hit it. The game goes really quickly and is very physically demanding.

How Old Do I Have to Be to Play?

Well, if you're reading this, you're old enough to play. The only requirement is that you're strong enough to hold and swing a racquet.

Some kids start out as young as 6 or 7, learning at an early age the pattern that the ball usually takes. As they get older, they gain enough strength to really develop proper form. Ali Pearson, 13, took up squash when she was 7. Now, she competes in the under-19 category, and last year, she won the U.S. nationals. She had already won the Canadian nationals twice when she was 9 and 11.

Ali works hard at her game, hitting the courts at 6 A.M. for over an hour before heading off to school. She plays in matches several nights a week and in tournaments every other weekend.

Ali loves playing squash, she says, because, "I like working on one thing and then going to a match and knowing I've accomplished it." The appeal of the sport, she says, is easy to understand: "It's something you can do with your friends, and it's easy to pick up. It's just really fun to do."

What Kind of Equipment Do I Need, and Where Can I Go to Play?

A racquet, ball, protective eye goggles and a pair of sneakers are all the equipment you need to play squash. If your school doesn't have courts, start by checking the listings part of your phone book to find a place where you can get instruction and play matches.

You can also contact the United States Squash Racquets Association to find out the club that is closest to your home.

Cost varies depending upon location and frequency of play, but you can expect games to range from $15 to $50 a session. Want to lower the cost? Maybe you could trade some work at the club (cleaning up, helping out in the snack bar) for some time with a pro.

If you think squash would make a good team sport for your school, talk to the head of your athletics department. He or she may be able to find a coach and make group arrangements.

Ready? Go ahead—gear up, and get into the swing of things.

Girls' Life
7–14 years
1,165 words

From the Author

There are, of course, two great rules for journalists: Write about what you know . . . and don't be an expert—know just enough so that you can ask intelligent questions. These two tenets came together in an assignment to write about squash for the sports column of *Girls' Life*.

Squash was the sport played by my younger daughter, Rachel, who discovered it in her freshman year in high school, so I knew a little—but not too much. My main challenge as a writer who had never targeted a young audience was to get the right tone of voice. (I'm the editor of The Johns Hopkins University faculty/staff newspaper.) The information for readers ages 8–14 had to be comprehensive, appealing, accessible—and not off-putting.

Valuable research sources for the article were the United States Squash Racquets Association, Rachel's coach, and a number of sites on the World Wide Web.

Intermediate Nonfiction

What Being "Grounded" Really Means

By Marianne J. Dyson

Feeling negative? Tired of black clouds hanging over you? Build this device called an electroscope and find out how to be a more positive, well-grounded individual.

You Need:

1 tall clear glass jar
1 piece of Christmas tree tinsel
1 small paper clip
1 small piece of cardboard (a box lid)
1 helium-quality party balloon

Make an Electroscope:

Poke the paper clip through the cardboard so half of it is above the cardboard and half below. Loop the tinsel through the paper clip so both ends hang down equally. Place the cardboard across the top of the jar so the tinsel dangles into the jar. Trim the tinsel if necessary to keep it from hitting the bottom of the jar.

Ready, Set, Charge:

Inflate the balloon, tie it, and rub it quickly across your hair. Touch the balloon to the top of the paper clip. What happens to the tinsel?

Set the balloon aside. Squeeze the paper clip between your thumb and finger. What happens to the tinsel now?

So What Did You Learn?

Most things are electrically neutral—having about equal numbers of positive and negative electrical charges. But negatively-charged electrons are easily bumped out of place. For example, when you rub a balloon against your hair, the electrons are "stirred up." Their negative charges *repel* each other, mean-ing that the electrons spread out as far away from each other as possible.

They spread onto the balloon while it touches your hair. The electrons "ride" the balloon to the paper clip and then spread out through the paper clip and tinsel. The strands of tinsel (like strands of your hair) are charged negatively and repel each other. Glass and cardboard are insulators, so the paper clip and tinsel stay charged until you discharge them. Your touch provides a path so the negative charges spread out over a large area and balance the positives again. Providing this path is called *grounding the charge*. You don't want to provide that path for a lightning bolt!

Next time you're feeling dangerously negative, ground yourself before you zap someone!

Odyssey
10–15 years
346 words

From the Author

I left my job as a NASA flight controller to raise my children. The Institute's magazine writing course gave me the practice and confidence I needed to share my knowledge and experiences, and it led to my first published science article.

To expand my markets, I sought the advice of a fellow National Space Society member and contributor to *Odyssey*. My first sale was a direct result of that contact. More acceptances followed, and *Odyssey's* editor began to call me when she had "holes" to fill. I hope my electroscope will "spark" a few kids to get science degrees.

Assault on Fort Wagner

By George E. Hughes

The 54th Massachusetts Regiment had its baptism of fire on July 18, 1863. At twilight that day it led an assault on Fort Wagner, a Confederate stronghold on Morris Island in Charleston Harbor. The two forts located on the island—Battery Wagner and Fort Gregg, along with Fort Sumter, controlled the entrance to the harbor. If the Union forces could take Morris Island, the rest of the area would fall.

Who were these black men who would make such a sacrifice? They were educators, fishermen, businessmen, and farmers who had answered the call when the Emancipation Proclamation was issued in January 1863. Abraham Lincoln had given them the right to bear arms.

When they were within 200 yards of the fort, the Confederates opened fire with cannon and muskets.

The first stop of the 54th after leaving Massachusetts was Beaufort, South Carolina. For several months they spent most of their time drilling, digging ditches, building fortifications, and doing guard duty. Their time for "glorys," however, would come.

The bombardment of Fort Wagner started the morning of July 18, 1863. This continued until 7:45 P.M. when Colonel Robert Gould Shaw received the command to attack. As the regiment moved forward, the sea was to their right and the marsh to their left. Some of the troops had to march in waist-deep water just to maintain the formation. When they were within 200 yards of the fort, the Confederates opened fire with cannon and mus-

kets. Bloody gaps 20 feet wide were cut into the ranks of the 54th by these bursts of cannon balls and bullets. When they reached the fort, the 54th still had not fired a shot. Led by Colonel Shaw, they

History books can say that the men of the 54th did not die with their backs to the enemy.

fought their way to the top of the fortifications. As they did so, they heard Shaw cry out, "Onward 54th, onward!" Soon after, he was shot dead.

It had been reported that there were only 300 Confederates in the fort. Actually there were 3,000 troops. They had stayed in the shelters during the bombardment. Now the fighting was hand-to-hand. The flag bearer of the 54th was shot dead and Sergeant William Carney took the flag and, although wounded, carried it back to the safety of the Union lines without it ever touching the ground.

Of the 600 men the 54th sent into battle, 34 were killed, 93 captured, and 146 wounded or missing in action. Of the 3,000 Union troops that went into battle, approximately 1,500 were killed, wounded, or missing in action.

Although the Union lost this battle, the valiant efforts of the 54th proved that black men could and would fight. History books can say that the men of the 54th did not die with their backs to the enemy. After their courageous assault on Fort Wagner, it was said that when anyone asked "Will a slave fight?," the answer was, "Tell them, 'no.'" But, if anyone should ask, "Will a Negro fight?" Then the answer was: "Tell them, 'yes.'"

The following is an excerpt from a letter written by George E. Stephens, a black sergeant of the 54th, to Captain Luis F. Emilio, the officer in command of the shattered and torn regiment at the close of the battle:

Regarding the assault on Fort Wagner, I remember distinctly that when our column had charged the fort, passed the half-filled moat, and mounted to the parapet [wall of a fort], many of the men clambered over and some entered by the large embrasure in which one of the big guns was mounted, the firing substantially ceased there by the beach, and the rebel musketry fire steadily grew hotter on our left. An officer of our regiment called out, "Spike that gun." Whether this was done I do not know, for we fired our rifles and fought as hard as we could to return the fire on our right.

But the rebel fire grew hotter on our right, and a field-piece every few seconds seemed to sweep along our rapidly thinning ranks. Men all around me would fall and roll down the scarp [steep slope] into the ditch. Just at the very hottest moment of the struggle a battalion or regiment charged up to the moat, halted, and did not attempt to cross it and join us, but from their position commenced to fire upon us. I was one of the men who shouted from where I stood, "Don't fire on us! We are the Fifty-fourth!" I have heard it was a Maine regiment. This is God's living truth! Immediately after I heard an order, "Retreat!," some twelve or fifteen of us slid down from our position on the parapet of the fort.

The men-of-war seemed to have turned their guns on the fort, and the fire of the Confederates on the right seemed to increase in power. The line of retreat seemed lit with infernal fire; the hissing bullets and bursting shells seemed angry demons...

I care not who the man is who denies the fact, our regiment did charge the fort and drove the rebels from their guns. Many of our men will join me in saying that in the early stages of the fight we had possession of the sea end of Battery Wagner. Indeed, most of the colored prisoners taken there were captured inside the battery.

Footsteps
9–12 years
861 words

From the Author

I am a retired 25-year Air Force Sergeant. At present I am Quartermaster Sergeant for Company I, 54th Massachusetts Volunteer Infantry. After seeing the movie "Glory," I became excited about black history, and I contacted someone who was organizing a company. That was four years ago.

My company gives presentations to first- through fourth-grade schoolchildren. To keep younger students interested, I know I must be expressive in telling of the struggles these men had to endure. I show the weapons that they used, and wearing a uniform attracts a great deal of attention, too. I do not give these younger audiences a lot of dates.

The fifth- through twelfth-graders can remember names and dates. Fifteen minutes is about maximum if my presentation is to hold their attention. I usually allot another fifteen minutes for questions and answers.

I was contacted by *Footsteps* and asked to write an article. I did no major revisions, but let the editor have a free hand in making whatever changes were deemed necessary. This medium has given me the opportunity to impart previously unknown information about African Americans' participation in the Civil War.

During the last four years, I have tried to read everything I could about blacks in the Civil War. Re-enactments also provide much information, because I meet and talk with others who share my interests.

One reader encouraged me to keep doing what I do "because so much of black history has not been told." Hearing comments like that is very rewarding to me.

Microbes on Mars?

By Vicki Oransky Wittenstein

Have you ever wondered about life on other planets? Christopher McKay thinks about it a lot.

He started wondering about life on Mars and elsewhere in the universe when the Viking spacecraft landed on Mars in 1976.

"What I thought would be interesting to examine for several weeks turned into something I'm still studying twenty years later," he said.

Dr. McKay is a planetary scientist with the National Aeronautics and Space Administration (NASA) at the Ames Research Center in California. He is interested in exobiology, which is the study of whether life exists on other planets or moons, or elsewhere in outer space.

Dr. McKay studies life that survives in the harshest climates known on our planet. Then he determines where evidence of life might exist in hostile environments beyond Earth, particularly on Mars. NASA uses this information to decide where to search for evidence of life on Mars and elsewhere.

Dr. McKay has scuba dived under the ice cover of Lake Hoare in Antarctica, observing tiny life forms

---

Although most of the continent is ice-covered, these freezing-cold valleys are not.

---

called algae that live on the bottom of the lake. In Siberia, he has drilled deep into the permanently frozen soil, which is called permafrost, to study frozen organisms that have survived there for millions of years.

He and his team often travel a week before arriving at remote locations, such as the Gobi Desert in Mongolia. They camp and explore for a month before helicopters come to take them home.

Antarctica

Dr. McKay's first exobiology mission was to the dry valleys of Antarctica. He wanted to see which forms of life could live in that harsh part of the world. If Mars ever had life, its last survivors might have been similar to the tiny life forms in these valleys of Earth.

Dr. McKay believes that Mars once had the water and sunlight needed to support life.

Although most of the continent is ice-covered, these freezing-cold valleys are not. They are Mars-like in appearance and climate, with dry soil and no plant life. The valleys have ice-covered lakes, like those that might have been on Mars long ago.

From some of NASA's pictures of Mars, scientists think the planet's surface must have been shaped by flowing water. To have had flowing water, the planet must have been warmer than it is today—maybe warm enough to support life. But now the planet, like these Antarctic valleys, is cold and dry.

To study some of Antarctica's toughest survivors, Dr. McKay built instruments to measure the growth of tiny life forms that live inside rocks. They are called *cryptoendolithic* organisms.

"*Crypto* means hidden, *endo* means in, and *lithic* means rock—organisms hidden in the rock," he said. "If you look at the rock's surface, you can't see them because they are living beneath the surface."

Intermediate Nonfiction

Using the findings from his instruments, Dr. McKay then determined how well these Antarctic organisms might grow in even colder temperatures, like those on Mars. Since these organisms live in very dry climates, he has placed similar instruments in deserts around the world.

Where to Search?

Dr. McKay believes that Mars once had the water and sunlight needed to support life. But where do we search for evidence that life existed? Dr. McKay thinks the best places are the bottoms of dried Martian lakes.

"The main thing we learned in Antarctica was that life survives under the ice covers of lakes in the dry valleys," he said. "A similar situation could have existed on Mars. That's probably the kind of place

---

Would we find the same life forms that exist here on Earth?

---

where life survived long after the surface of the planet died. Even if the surface never had life, there could have been life underneath ice covers like these."

NASA is planning a mission to Mars to collect rock samples and bring them back to Earth. Dr. McKay hopes the samples will come from a site that once was a Martian lake.

What will Dr. McKay look for in those first samples from Mars? He hopes to find fossils—the imprints of life. But what excites him even more is the idea that dead remains of tiny life forms might be frozen in Mars's permafrost.

On Earth, Dr. McKay has studied frozen organisms by drilling more than seventy-five feet into the Siberian permafrost. These organisms are about 3.5 million years old.

In the same way, the extreme cold at Mars's south pole might have preserved similar tiny life forms. "They may be frozen, they may be corpses, but their actual remains could still be there," Dr. McKay said.

What would these remains reveal? Would we find the same life forms that exist here on Earth? Or would we find something totally different?

"Imagine finding another life form that's built out of different building blocks than life on Earth,

something we can't fathom," Dr. McKay said. "That could really be revolutionary!"

Highlights for Children
2–12 years
791 words

From the Author

I am not a scientist—I wasn't even a science major in college. I practiced law for several years before beginning to write both fiction and nonfiction for children. Which all goes to show that if you like research and are interested in a topic, you can write about anything. In fact, even subjects I think I will never want to learn about become interesting once I read more about them.

The idea for this article came while I was researching another article about NASA's Sojourner mission to Mars and came across Dr. McKay's name. I was so fascinated by his research that I decided to write an article about searching for life on Mars. I telephoned NASA to ask who they suggested I interview, and they recommended Dr. McKay. I knew then that I was on the right track.

With Dr. McKay's permission, I taped the interview over the telephone and later transcribed the tape. The transcript was invaluable—I would never have remembered important concepts by just taking notes, and it was critical for quotes. I also read numerous articles and books.

Having written other science articles for *Highlights,* I felt my audience was its older readers. I telephoned the science editor and e-mailed him my ideas.

I didn't outline first, but I knew the most important areas I wanted to cover. I combed through the transcript and other sources, and developed the main points.

The hardest part about the writing was finding age-appropriate language to describe difficult concepts in only 800 words. I edited, then re-edited, and then edited again! I often cut phrases I liked so I could squeeze under the word count. Dr. McKay reviewed the piece for factual content.

The reward was receiving a fan letter from a boy who was very interested in life on other planets, and wanted me to wish Dr. McKay good luck!

What a Hoot!

By Diana Loiewski Weir

It was dusk, and I was in my front yard on the way to the mailbox when I looked up and saw the wing span of an unusually large bird in flight. It swooped down gracefully and landed on a branch high up in an old oak tree. Its eyes were not on the sides of its head like a typical bird. Instead they faced forward and were circled by white feathers. I recognized it instantly.

Quickly, I ran into the house and yelled, "Hey kids, an owl!" They grabbed their coats, and we ran back out together. "Look," I said, pointing up into a tree, "That's a barred owl. We're lucky to see one. They don't usually come out during the day."

"It doesn't have a neck!" Catherine, my six-year-old, exclaimed.

The owl can swivel its head 180 degrees towards its back in either direction.

"Yes, it does. You just can't see it because it is covered by feathers," I told her. The owl sat perched moving its head and listening.

"Mom, it looks like it can turn its head all the way around," Catherine said.

"You're right. It can't move its eyes up and down or side to side, but the owl can swivel its head 180 degrees towards its back in either direction. And its beak faces downward so that it doesn't get in the way of its vision."

Owls are a part of a group of birds that hunt animals to eat their flesh. Included in this group are eagles, hawks, and vultures. Many species of owls adapted to hunting at night because there is less competition for the same food. Owls are particu-larly successful night hunters because they have more rods in their eyes than humans, which improves night vision.

I looked up at the beautiful barred owl in our oak tree and wondered where it lived.

Owls have acute hearing, yet their ears are not symmetrical. One ear is lower than the other, so the owl adjusts its head until it hears the sound equally in both ears. This also lets it line up the prey's position. Then it swoops in with its talons (sharp hooks) at the ends of each of its toes that are designed for piercing flesh, grabbing, and grasping.

The owl has very fine down on the tips of its feathers that absorbs flight sounds. This stealth advantage helps the owl track a mouse, squirrel, snake, or other animal as it moves noisily over leaves and other ground debris in the night.

Even though owls are silent in flight, their reputation is anything but quiet. They are famously known for their hooting sounds and feared for their blood-curdling screams. The barred owl, which lives chiefly in the woodlands in the eastern half of North America from Canada to Mexico, can be identified at night by its loud "whoo-whoo."

I looked up at the beautiful barred owl in our oak tree and wondered where it lived. Catherine wanted to know why it didn't fly south with the other birds. Owls don't need to migrate because they are great hunters. And their downy feathers are sufficient to keep in body heat.

"How can we find where it lives?" Catherine asked.

Intermediate Nonfiction

Owls eat their prey whole, I explained, and after digestion they bring back up any fur, feathers, or bones that are not digestible in the form of a pellet. So we began looking for pellets under large oak trees or beneath trees that appeared to have large, leafy nests and discovered an owl's roost!

*Connecticut's County Kids
Parents
564 words*

From the Author

I'm fascinated with the world around me, and my natural curiosity drives my writing. As a child I played with worms and frogs, and I even collected insects. Three years ago, after I'd been writing on nature topics for 10 years, *County Kids* offered me a chance to write a nature column.

My column covers common wonders that people rarely consider, and I typically look no further than my very own backyard for ideas. "What a Hoot!" was based on an experience that inspired me to reflect on different adaptations of owls.

When researching a topic, I use many resources: the Internet, other naturalists, even encyclopedias. However, with this topic, I began at the library, reading bird books. I then drafted my idea and let it sit for a day. Usually I have two or three drafts before I begin to revise. I love revision, because I enjoy playing with my leads, endings, and even the content. Next, I find someone who is willing to read my piece and comment honestly. Then I make any changes and send it off to the editor of *County Kids*.

My column has won two first prizes from the Medill School of Journalism. I have three nonfiction books out now, and have even appeared on Fox's *Pet News* with my own amphibian zoo!

Stephen Bishop's Road to Freedom

By Michael Maschinot

Stephen Bishop dropped a pebble into the pit. The stone clattered against the sides for what seemed like an eternity before its echo died, but there was no sound of its hitting bottom. He raised his lantern and peered into the darkness. On the other side of the pit, a passage curved down into the depths of the cave. Who knew where it led? Who would ever know? The bottomless pit blocked the way, and there was no getting around it.

Stephen trudged back up to the mouth of the cave, fearing that if he stayed below too long, the boss would miss him. Every day from dawn to dusk, he worked in the cave with the other slaves, digging saltpeter for the army to turn into gunpowder. It had been a long time since he'd seen the sun.

That night, while the others sat around the fire swapping stories, jokes, and insults, Stephen lay on his straw pallet on the cabin's dirt floor, thinking about the bottomless pit and what might be beyond it. The more he thought, the more certain he was: his freedom lay on the other side of that pit.

He heard the rich voice of Old Samuel, who could barely walk but could still swing a sledgehammer. "River Jordan's deep and wide," sang the old man. "Milk and honey on the other side. All my trials, Lord, soon be over."

Stephen crept out of the cabin and went to the boss's toolshed. There he found an ax and an adz, and under the light of the full moon, he hiked deep into the woods, so far that no one would hear him. His bones ached from the day's work, and he longed for sleep, but the excitement of his plan made his heart beat furiously.

Like the other slaves of Mammoth Cave, Stephen had lived his entire life without trying to escape, though he wasn't closely watched. Compared to others he'd heard about, his life was bearable. He had corn pone and beans twice a day and a ham bone once a week, and he was seldom beaten. Most important, he was near his wife and child. Charlotte worked above ground on the boss's plantation. Stephen knew many men who were separated from their families, and if he was caught trying to escape he'd be sold down South and would never see Charlotte and Thomas again. That would be the worst cruelty of all.

At the halfway point, Stephen realized there was no turning back.

In the woods, Stephen found a tall, straight birch tree and, with a few strokes, brought it crashing down. He cut off all the branches, then split the trunk down the middle. He chopped notches at two-foot intervals along the two halves. He then cut the branches into equal sizes and carefully wedged them into the notches, pounding them with an ax head so the branches wouldn't fall out. When he looked over his handiwork, he knew the makeshift ladder was more than long enough to reach across the bottomless pit.

Stephen carried the birch ladder all the way back to the cave and followed the rocky passage to the pit. Laid from one lip to the other, the ladder made a perfect fit.

Now came the hard part. Tying his lantern to his belt, Stephen sat on the ladder's edge and let his legs swing out. Don't look down, he told himself, and he thought about Old Samuel's hymn. "Milk and honey on the other side," he tried to sing, but he couldn't catch his breath.

At the halfway point, Stephen realized there was no turning back. The ladder sagged in the middle, but he told himself not to hurry. One more shinny, and another, and another, and then his legs kicked out against the far side of the pit. No one has ever been here before! he thought as he groped to the edge and pulled himself up.

What lay in the darkness at the bottom of Mammoth Cave? The sloping path wasn't an escape passage—if Stephen had only wanted to run away, he'd have tried to long ago. But that road to freedom was dangerous, and with a wife and child, he wouldn't risk it. Instead, Stephen would use his discovery to buy his freedom. Once news got out that someone had crossed the pit, people would flock to the cave to explore the new passages. And Stephen would be their guide, the only person who could navigate the winding hallways and mind-boggling mazes. Above ground, Stephen was a slave, but in the cave, he was king.

Soon he found sights more magnificent than he'd dreamed possible. He came upon passages so tight he could barely squeeze through and domes so huge that his lantern light didn't reach the ceiling. He found stalactites and stalagmites that looked like sculptures and, in one room, a formation that looked like a frozen, crystal waterfall. Later he found an underground river full of white fish with no eyes. As he crossed it, he imagined it was the Jordan of Old Samuel's song.

While exploring Mammoth Dome, the largest room in the cave, Stephen came across the shattered remains of a lantern. He was heartbroken to think that someone else had been there before he had. But it turned out that a miner, working in a room above, years before, had dropped the lamp four hundred feet to the floor of Mammoth Dome. Although some parts of the cave had been explored by Native Americans thousands of years earlier—in fact, two perfectly preserved, mummified bodies, whose age could only be guessed, were found within its depths—Stephen Bishop was probably the first person to set foot in many of its rooms.

Stephen made his discoveries known, and soon the great cave became a popular attraction. Since only Stephen knew its secrets, many visitors insisted that he be their guide through the hidden fairyland. He would lead them across the bottom-

less pit (the birch ladder having been replaced by a permanent bridge) and tell stories of how he'd found the different parts of the cave, using light tricks to enhance the show. He saved every penny he made, and in a few years, he'd collected hundreds of dollars.

Stephen's dream was to take his family to Africa, and though he never moved there, he did save enough to buy their freedom. He even bought a piece of land near the cave, where they spent the rest of their lives.

A century and a half later, people still come to see Mammoth Cave, which became a national park in 1941. Guides still lead tourists to the bottomless pit, the crystal waterfall, and the other wonders,

and they still tell the story of Stephen Bishop, whose lantern first lit the way.

Cricket
9–14 years
1,131 words

From the Author

I got the idea for this article on a visit to Mammoth Cave. I immediately knew that the combination of Stephen's courage and the exotic setting would make an exciting yarn for older children. In addition, he is an African-American role model who is unfamiliar to most readers. I had long admired *Cricket*'s articles and knew it would be the right market for this article.

One of my challenges in writing the article was how to portray the slave's lifestyle. In many ways, the slaves of Mammoth Cave were treated more humanely than their counterparts in the deep South. But I had to take care not to imply that Stephen and his workmates had it easy, or that even a benevolent slaveowner was morally justified. All slaves faced the risk of separation from their families at any time, and I chose this as the impetus behind Stephen's pursuit of freedom.

I was asked to revise the article twice. The editor wanted me to expand on the descriptions of the wonders of the cave. There was also some concern about the abrupt change in point of view at the end, but we ultimately decided that it was a necessary part of the story.

Bonsai

By Veda Boyd Jones

Imagine a miniature tree, no bigger than a computer screen, that your great-great-grandfather had planted. Did he find a sprout, its growth stunted in the shadow of a large tree? Knowing it would never get large, did he rescue it, take it home, and plant it in a little pot?

Miniature trees are called bonsai (bon sigh). The first bonsai were grown in China hundreds of years ago. Then the hobby of raising tiny trees became popular in Japan.

Traditionally, the oldest boy in a Japanese family cared for the bonsai. He watered it; then he clipped and shaped it to resemble an old tree. It lived outside except for celebrations like birthdays when it was brought into the house and set in a special place for all to see and enjoy. Many bonsai are family treasures and are passed down from grandfather to father to son.

Japanese custom was to dig up a naturally dwarfed tree from the wild. Extreme cold on mountains stunted a tree's growth, and sprouts that grew in the shade of bigger trees were naturally dwarfed. These were dug and transplanted to pots. Although some bonsai are still dug, horticulturist David Massey of the Ozark Bonsai Nursery says, "Nowadays many are started from a seed or a clipping from a big tree."

Bonsai means "tree on a tray" in Japanese. Pots for bonsai are really shallow trays with feet that keep the pot off the ground. This allows air to get to the roots and water to get out. Only a small amount of soil is used in the tray.

American soldiers in Japan after World War II saw the beauty in bonsai and brought miniature trees back to the United States. The popularity of these living sculptures has increased since then.

Today bonsai clubs have sprung up.

David says the miniature trees come in three sizes. "You can carry the smallest ones in one hand. The next size can be carried with two hands. It takes two men to carry the largest bonsai."

David uses special tools for clipping and shaping his bonsai. "You want the bonsai tree to look just like an old tree in the forest, except it is tiny and looks like a fairyland tree. It should have a big trunk and well-shaped limbs."

By shaping the bonsai, the owner creates a living art work. Why not try your hand at this living sculpture? You can purchase a bonsai at many nurseries and florist shops.

When you move from one house to another, you could never pack up a big tree that your father had planted in the backyard. But you could transport a bonsai to your new home. Just think, you could give it to your grandchild someday.

Boys' Quest
6–13 years
461 words

From the Author

I saw bonsai trees at the home of a friend whose son owns a bonsai nursery. I scheduled an interview and read several books on the history of bonsai and how to care for them. I took pictures, asked tons of questions, and wrote the article, choosing only the quotes I thought would interest a young reader. I chose *Boys' Quest* because I knew they were looking for short nature articles.

Animal ER

By Geoff Williams

T he boxer was a bloody mess. But this fight didn't take place in a ring, and this boxer wasn't wearing gloves. This boxer was a dog.

Dr. Andy Sokol had seen boxers in the emergency room before, as well as collies, cocker spaniels, German shepherds and beagles, not to mention cats, gerbils, guinea pigs, iguanas, hamsters and hedgehogs.

"We call her the miracle dog."

The veterinarian had treated many injured animals, but nothing quite like this. A neighbor had shot the boxer through the nose.

All other patients were now put on stand-by in the waiting room while Dr. Sokol and his two assistants huddled over the examination table, operating on the wounded boxer.

They saved the animal—named Angel.

"We call her the miracle dog," says Dr. Sokol, who patched the wound and gave medicine to stop the infection that had started to spread.

The bullet, Dr. Sokol says, "missed the brain and the vital tissues of the ear. It just landed in the right spot."

That bullet is still in the dog's skull. But Angel is alive and happy and wagging her tail, as if nothing had ever happened.

Welcome to Grady Veterinary Hospital in Cincinnati, Ohio, one of a handful of animal clinics with its own 24-hour emergency room.

Emerging from the Shadows

One minute Dr. Sokol may put an iguana's eye back in its socket; the next, he might see an obese ferret or a cat with leukemia.

Most vets work regular hours, say 9 A.M. to 5 P.M. Not Dr. Sokol.

"You get the most interesting cases at night," says Dr. Sokol, who works from 7 P.M. to 7 A.M. Most people are either at work or school during the day. After sundown, owners and their animals emerge from the shadows.

It's Never Dull

Snow, a Siberian husky, has eaten some Flex All, a muscle relaxer for humans, but a potential poison for dogs.

"Let's give him apomorphine, some activated charcoal and an IV catheter," Dr. Sokol says to his veterinarian technician, who serves as a nurse.

Five minutes and eight stitches later, Magnum's paw will be fine.

Apomorphine is a medicine that will make Snow vomit the poison. Activated charcoal will keep Snow's stomach from absorbing too much Flex All. And the IV (short for "intravenous") catheter tube inserted in a vein will quickly carry medicine into the dog's system, allowing him to head home soon to a proper diet.

An hour after Snow's visit, with the emergency room quiet as a library, Dr. Sokol stitches up a police dog's paw. Magnum is a Malinois, a type of German shepherd, and the dog is in a deep slumber. Five minutes and eight stitches later, Magnum's paw will be fine.

Next, a worried man hauls in Mickey, a black Labrador retriever. Blood covers both the dog and owner. When Mickey shakes his head, blood flies everywhere.

"It's a puzzle," Dr. Sokol says of his job. Pets can't explain what ails them, so the vet must fit the pieces together.

In Mickey's case it wasn't difficult—it's soon determined that he has only a cut on his left ear—but other patients require X-rays. Sometimes X-rays display the strangest things, especially in dogs' stomachs.

Some animals die because their owners aren't able to pay for treatment and don't bring them in.

Dogs are like vacuum cleaners; they'll slurp up anything. Dr. Sokol has taken care of canines that have swallowed bones, balls, blankets, birdseed and entire loaves of bread; they've gobbled up string, Christmas tinsel, screwdrivers and drill bits, socks and underwear. The bigger the object, the more likely it is to be life-threatening.

Fortunately, most owners bring in their pets before it's too late.

In the Beginning

When Dr. Sokol was 3 and living in Birmingham, Ala., his dad bought him a dog named Snuff that was part beagle and part German shepherd. His father noticed how much the boy and puppy bonded, and said, "Oh, you want to be a dog doctor."

"O.K.," Andy said, and somehow the conversation stayed with him through elementary and high school, four years at Auburn University in Alabama, then four years studying veterinary medicine.

Living and Dying

It happens almost every night, and tonight it's a chow-shepherd puppy.

A woman brings in the black dog, explaining she found it on the road. It's laid on the table, and an ominous silence falls over the room—you almost hear your own heartbeat. Blood drips from the animal's nose and mouth.

Dr. Sokol says in a sad, cracking voice, "Dead on arrival."

Some animals die because their owners aren't able to pay for treatment and don't bring them in. While not all critters can get free help—though clearly vets would give it if they could—some end up getting just that. Angel's owner never paid for her care, for example.

Happily, there are owners willing to help their pets no matter what. (It's people such as this who ultimately pay for the nonpayers through higher costs.)

Dr. Sokol tells about a family and their hamster that had a tumor on its belly: "For the last six months they've been coming in, getting treated. We didn't think he was strong enough to stand the surgery, so we've been doing injections, and they've had to have spent $300 on this hamster.

"But they're taking care of him, and that's great."

Road to Recovery

Nobody meant to back the car over Cozy the cat. When he was brought in, his eyes seemed ready to fall out, his head was swollen, and his jaw, knocked loose, was hanging open.

"Have a pet," Dr. Andy Sokol says. It doesn't matter whether it's a dog, cat or goldfish.

But when the doctor picked up the cat, Cozy purred and purred. A little work and the animal was on the road to recovery.

"That's one thing about animals. They don't care that they look deformed," Dr. Sokol says quietly. "The cat felt good, so he purred and played. And that's what's great about animals. They just want love and affection and attention."

If you're interested in becoming a veterinarian, you can start learning right now.

"Have a pet," Dr. Andy Sokol says. It doesn't matter whether it's a dog, cat or goldfish. The important thing is to "pay attention to the pet, read about the pet, watch it, take care of it. Don't make Mom and Dad take care of it—you take care of it."

When you're 16, get a part-time job at a veterinarian's office, Dr. Sokol says. (He did.) The work might not always be glamorous—unless you enjoy cleaning out dog and cat cages—but you'll quickly be able to decide if this is the career for you.

JOB FACTS: VETERINARIAN

EDUCATION: Math and science courses in high school; two to four years in college meeting pre-veterinary requirements, typically chemistry, zoology, animal science courses; four years in veterinary school; and four more years if you specialize.

OTHER REQUIREMENTS: You have to like animals, but you ought to like humans too—you're going to see plenty. Must be able to remain calm when nobody else is. Must be able to stand the sight of blood and deal with animals' deaths on a daily basis.

DUTIES: Performing general check-ups and examinations; administering medicines; operating on animals.

SALARY: $30,000 to $35,000 for starters. Rates for specialists like veterinary dentists, surgeons, or dermatologists (skin doctors) can climb higher than a cat stuck in a tree.

JOB OUTLOOK: Wonderful. People will always have pets, so there will always be a need for vets. Also, zoos are always looking for quality doctors.

FOR INFORMATION: Contact the American Veterinary Medical Association, 1931 North Meacham Road, Suite 100, Schaumburg, IL 60173.

Your school or local library should have lots of books on veterinary medicine. Try The Best of James Herriot, a collection of work by a famous veterinarian and author. (His best-known work is All Creatures Great and Small.)

Check out the "Veterinary Medicine" merit badge pamphlet (BSA Supply No. 35004).

Boys' Life
7–18 years
1,294 words

From the Author

I've wanted to write for about as long as I can remember, and I'd say I started writing seriously when I was 10 years old. My 154-page book was never published, nor was the one after that, nor the several movie screenplays I tackled in high school. But the practice paid off, I guess: today, I'm a features reporter at a newspaper and a free-lance writer for a variety of magazines, including *Entrepreneur* (a business magazine), *Life,* and *Boys' Life* (the Boy Scouts magazine).

The idea for "Animal ER" came from the phone book. It sounds funny, but the Yellow Pages have a ton of story ideas. Sometimes I'll just thumb through the phone book looking for ideas. That's how I came across the Grady Veterinary Hospital, which advertised a 24-hour emergency room.

I spent an evening at the hospital, from 6 P.M. until midnight. Whenever I could, I'd ask the doctor and his assistants questions, letting my tape recorder take my notes. But mostly I tried to stay out of the way and watch the action—and, of course, write down everything I saw!

I thought the anecdote about Angel would be the most fun to write, so I began with that. The anecdote about Cozy had a warm, fuzzy feeling to it, so it made a nice ending. In the middle, I tried to tell something of a story about how Dr. Sokol's shift in the emergency room goes.

If you spend too much time writing a detailed outline, you can take the fun out of writing. And writing is fun. So is rewriting, if you like words and enjoy shaping and reshaping sentences, telling a story in the best possible way it can be told.

I wrote one draft of the article, then started rewriting (and rewriting and rewriting) until I felt I was finished. I write pretty much the same way for adults and for kids, but when I write for kids I instinctively keep out adult words that younger readers won't understand.

When I was a boy, trying to write novels, I made up places and people and wrote about them. And I had a great time. Now I go to real places and meet real people and write about them. I'm still having a great time.

Navigating by the Stars
Make a Cross-Staff and Find Your Latitude

By Mary Morton Cowan

O f all the stars we see from the northern hemisphere, the North Star is unique. Long ago people named it Polaris, for it always stays close to the North Pole. In the 1400s, sailors used Polaris to help locate their position on the high seas. A simple instrument that was already available for this purpose in 1494 was a cross-staff, that is, a board marked with angle readings and a crosspiece for sighting. With it, sailors and navigators anywhere north of the equator could determine the angle between the horizon and Polaris. The larger the angle, the farther north they were. They were actually measuring their degree of latitude.

Try your hand now at making a cross-staff and measuring the approximate latitude where you live.

You Need:

- a 54-inch-long board (about 2 inches wide and 1/2 inch thick)
- thin cardboard (from the back of a pad of paper)
- nails (long enough to nail 3 boards together)
- saw, hammer, and clamps
- scissors, string, protractor, thumbtack, and pencil

To Make Your Cross-Staff:

1. Saw your board into 5 pieces: one 26" shaft, one 18" crossbar, one 6" bar, and two 2" spacers. Cut 2 cardboard filler pieces, each the size of the 2" spacers.

2. Assemble the crosspiece. Place the 18" crossbar on your work surface. Lay the shaft across the center of it, forming a cross. Put the 2 small spacers on the 18" board, next to the shaft. Add the cardboard filler pieces. Place the 6" bar on top. Be sure to keep the crosspiece at right angles to the long board. Clamp it in place while you nail it together (2 nails on each side). Do NOT allow nails to touch the long board. That board should slide freely through the opening.

3. Mark your scale of degrees. Poke a thumbtack into one end of the board and knot a string around it. Push the centerpiece close to the other end. Stretch a string over the top of the crosspiece and hold it firmly. Center your protractor at the corner of the long board, with the angle line on zero, and read the angle. Mark a pencil line on the board where the crosspiece intersects it, and write the number of degrees next to the line.

4. Move the crosspiece closer to the protractor and mark every five angle degrees (25°, 30°, 35°, 40°, etc.), keeping the string tight as you work. The closer you get to the protractor, the larger the angle will be. When finished, remove the string.

Locate Polaris. Wherever you are in the Northern Hemisphere, Polaris is the only star that is in the same place in the sky every night (and all day, too, but you can't see it then!).

In the northern United States, you can see circumpolar constellations all year long. Circumpolar means that they circle Polaris, sort of like a compass that draws circles around a point. Two important circumpolar constellations to know are the Big

Dipper and Cassiopeia. The easiest one to spot is the Big Dipper. The two stars on the outside edge of its bowl (farthest from the handle) point directly to Polaris. (Polaris itself is part of a dimmer constellation—the Little Dipper.) Across from the Big Dipper's handle, past Polaris, is another bright constellation, called Cassiopeia. It is shaped like an "M" or a "W." In the far southern United States, the Big Dipper is below the horizon in the fall so that you cannot see the pointer stars. In that case, look for Cassiopeia. Polaris will be below it.

Once you have found Polaris, take your reading. Standing still, hold your cross-staff up to your eye. BE CAREFUL not to poke your eye or glasses. Keeping the board horizontal, move the centerpiece back and forth until its tip meets Polaris. The angle reading should be close to your degrees north latitude.

You may want to check an atlas to see how close your reading came to your actual latitude. If you travel far from home, take your cross-staff with you and check the latitude where you're visiting!

Calliope
8–14 years
665 words

From the Author

Since completing my first Institute course, I have had 40 articles and stories published, plus one historical novel.

I write frequently for the *Cobblestone* group. I review their theme lists and choose topics that interest me. Specific themes trigger ideas, and query deadlines force me to work efficiently. Sometimes, now that the editors are familiar with my work, they request a piece. Such was the case with this article.

Calliope's editor suggested an activity about celestial navigation. She assigned a page limit and a deadline. Within that framework, I was free to explore. That issue's theme was the 1494 Treaty of Tordesillas. Research showed that 15th-century navigators used cross-staffs to locate their latitude. Why not show middle-grade students (*Calliope*'s target audience) how to make one?

Before I wrote my article, I made a cross-staff. I would never describe how to make something I had not actually put together and tested.

Most of any how-to article is taken up in step-by-step instructions. You may think research time is wasted for a few opening sentences, but it's a *must* for gathering ideas and knowing your topic—and it's fun!

My first drafts tend to be about twice the maximum length. This article took five or six revisions, but the result was worth it. The editor made very few changes. To help an artist illustrate it, I submitted detailed sketches and diagrams. They appeared almost exactly as I had drawn them. My bibliography listed five primary and supplementary sources.

Because *Calliope*'s readership is nationwide, describing how to locate Polaris was a challenge. Circumpolar constellations aren't always visible everywhere in the U.S. Also, I had to make sure my cross-staff was long enough to cover the southern latitudes. My biggest challenge was testing the cross-staff—the week before my article was due, the weather was atrocious! Not a single star could be seen for five consecutive nights!

The final version of "Navigating by the Stars" excluded a lot of interesting details, because a short article can include only the most pertinent facts. But I saved my research folder. There are other ideas in there!

White Knuckles Over Niagara

By K. C. Tessendorf

Funambulist! Oh, how Harry Colcord rued the day he'd met one.

Eager to horn into the wages of fame, Colcord now feared he had sold his young life to Monsieur Blondin, famous funambulist—high-wire acrobat. Chicagoan Henry (Harry) M. Colcord was no daredevil or athlete, but a slightly built, white-

---

Trembling and pale, he subdued a clamoring impulse to run away as fast as he could.

---

collar clerk and agent who slid along on a smile, a handshake, and a shoeshine, selling his product, "The Great Blondin!"

But on this day, August 17, 1859, Harry stood unwillingly as point man in a crowd crowning the cliffs on the Canadian side of the Niagara gorge below the falls. Trembling and pale, he subdued a clamoring impulse to run away as fast as he could.

Harry's frightened eyes were presently engaged with Blondin's friendly encouraging eyes as the slim, muscular aerialist, carrying a long balancing pole, strolled up the final length of the rope pathway stretched 1,100 feet across the wild torrent of the Niagara River 190 feet below. Blondin's saunter from the United States side had been accented with a few circus-type stunts from his repertoire.

The three-inch braided rope swayed in the wind currents of the gorge behind the nonchalant daredevil. Harry felt sick, for it had been advertised that in half an hour he would ride on Blondin's back across the fearsome chasm.

"Blondin" was an appropriate stage name for Frenchman Jean-Francois Gravelet. He was fair, blue-eyed, and light-haired. Blondin was thirty-five and had been in the United States four years with a troupe of acrobats employed by master showman P. T. Barnum. In 1858, Blondin visited Niagara Falls as a tourist. It was there that he conceived a funambulist's dream of slinging a rope pathway between the two countries over the Niagara gorge.

In the spring of 1859 Blondin left Barnum, and with Colcord came to Niagara Falls determined to create a personal aerialist theater.

Getting tying rights on both shores was difficult and required the hefty sharing of profits. However, a public-spirited merchant agreed to provide the thick, expensive rope for free. He even winked kindly when he said that if Blondin changed his mind and never used the rope, he'd understand.

Installed and anchored at either end by wide-spaced guys (ropes), the heavy strand sagged about 20 feet in the middle of the span. Since the gorge is normally windy, the rope moved sluggishly sideways and up and down.

A huge crowd with mixed emotions of hope and fear was present on June 30, 1859, to witness Blondin's historic walk. Stepping out at 5 P.M. clothed in silk tights, Blondin revealed early on that he was a showman, not just a hiker.

The daredevil reeled the rope back, sat down, and took a drink.

A quarter of the way out, Blondin stopped, yawned, and stretched before lying down on the rope and placing the 38-foot balancing pole across

Intermediate Nonfiction

his chest. He even appeared to snooze for a few minutes. Neatly arising, not using his hands, Blondin casually ambled out to midpoint, pausing on the swaying strand to unroll a coil of thin lead-tipped rope.

He patiently dangled the rope 180 feet down to a waiting boat, where a small bottle was attached. The daredevil reeled the rope back, sat down, and took a drink. Resuming his journey toward Canada, Blondin abruptly performed a backflip somersault, raising the tempos of many hearts throughout the crowd. Then he ran lightly up the mooring as the applause from both banks momentarily suppressed the roar of Niagara Falls.

"The Great Blondin" announced that he'd walk back, too. Carrying a camera, he went out and tied his pole to the rope. Freestanding in perfect rhythm with the rocking footing, he took pictures like an airborne tourist. He then briskly walked to the American side.

The business of daredeviltry requires the addition of new thrills, mostly because the crowds demand it.

Blondin soon reappeared with a chair that he balanced on the rope and stood on. After that he called it a day!

Blondin went on to cross the falls weekly, adding new stunts. All of his crossings were heavily publicized by Colcord. On July 4, Blondin crossed in a heavy sack of blankets, blindly feeling his way. On his return he walked backward. He bicycled. Once he came out pushing a wheelbarrow bearing a small stove. In midair, Blondin fired the stove and prepared, cooked, and ate an omelet. At least once, he stood on his head on the rope.

The great funambulist crossed at night with Roman candles spouting from his pole tips to mark his progress. A locomotive headlight shining on the rope went dark as Blondin was en route. But it is likely that this had been arranged by the canny daredevil, who emerged unfazed.

The business of daredeviltry requires the addition of new thrills, mostly because the crowds demand it. In early August, Blondin told Colcord, "Harry, here's a stunt that will complete our fortunes! I'll find a man and carry him over." Harry also thought

it was a great idea, and advertised a princely sum for the person who completed the trip on Blondin's back. There were several suitable applicants, but after looking at the swirling depths of the gorge, each one quietly walked away.

Then Blondin proposed, "Harry, you're a small man like myself. I can carry you. Be a good fellow and come along."

Harry blushed and stammered—he couldn't say yes or no. But at a meeting of the star and his agent with the press, Blondin cheerfully announced that he would carry his friend Harry Colcord on his return from Canada on August 17.

The news caused a sensation. It was apparent that a big crowd would come. Harry was hooked—wiggle as he might!

On August 17, after landing on the Canadian side, Blondin realized that Colcord was in a state of terror, hardly responding to him, staring into the gorge where the roiling water sped by at 42 miles per hour. So Blondin firmly took hold and led his companion out to the brink beside the rope as about 100,000 people called encouragement.

In a daze, Harry M. Colcord, apprentice daredevil, mounted Blondin's back, wrapped his arms around Blondin's neck, and placed his feet into harnessed stirrups. It was a load! Colcord weighed a little less than Blondin—136 pounds. The balancing pole added about 40 more pounds. As Blondin walked out, Colcord tightened his embrace. As Blondin barely grunted to release his grip, Harry, by supreme will, obeyed. Harry remembered the moment:

"Out over that horrible gulf I heard the roar of the water below and the hum which ran through the crowd. As we cleared the brink the hum ceased—the strain had spread to them.

"Do not attempt to do any balancing yourself. If you do we shall both go down to our death."

"Blondin walked on steadily, pausing for one brief moment at each point where the guy ropes joined the main cable. The line was a trifle steadier at these points....Blondin halted at the last resting point before the middle span and yelled above the roar of water and wind, 'Harry, you are no longer

Colcord; you are Blondin. Until I clear this place be a part of me—mind, body, and soul. If I sway, sway with me. Do not attempt to do any balancing yourself. If you do we shall both go down to our death.'"

As the rope *really* moved, onlookers saw that the pole tips, which usually moved slowly, were now whipping up and down "like the wings of a bird in rapid flight." And Harry thought they swayed sideways with the river flow!

"Blondin was now running just as a boy runs in order the better to keep his balance when walking on a railroad track. We were nearing the point where the joining place of the first guy-line from the opposite shore offered us a breathing space. Finally Blondin's foot was planted on the knot that joined the lines. I was sucking in some air when suddenly the rope was jerked from beneath Blondin's feet."

The pair, near the end, managed to maintain their balance. Blondin was wringing wet with sweat, almost done in. Ashore, hundreds reached out their hands. The bandsmen were too emotionally overcome to hold a tune as the dogged pair rushed the crowd on American soil.

During the wild celebrations that followed, the president of the New York Central Railroad hailed the heroes. He gave Colcord a $1,000 check. Then the president offered the finest gesture a railroad baron could make. With a twinkle in his eyes he presented a second $1,000 check if Harry would promise not to do it again. Harry eagerly accepted.

What a happy ending!

Highlights for Children
2–12 years
1,404 words

From the Author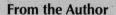

Though I was superficially aware of M. Blondin's high-wire showmanship at Niagara Falls, it was after I read in depth about his daredevil activities that I became enthused about Blondin and followed the urge to write about him—striking while the iron was hot.

I was certain much had been published about the high-wire artist, and a special approach would be needed. I have access to the Library of Congress and other federal libraries, which inspires me to be painstakingly accurate. I've read letters from young readers that began: "I love history..." but that is far from the norm. Many disdainfully consider it "that stuff."

I try to select historical situations where, without slipping into historical fiction, I can present a young, or young-seeming, protagonist. For "White Knuckles," I selected Harry Colcord, not a youth but green and innocent for the task his Hercules assigned him. I introduced him in the first paragraph and outlined his crisis. Then, trusting I'd set the hook for the reader, I was free to roam in narrative, being sure at some points to include strong "I was there" accounts. I ended on a pleasant note: Harry gets $2,000 and doesn't have to face the crossing ordeal again.

I sent my article to *Highlights for Children* when I (coincidentally) learned that an editor I respected had been hired as senior history editor.

As a writer, I'm a storyteller. For a long time I wrote history pieces for adults. Then Atheneum allowed me to write seven books of popular history for older young people. When I leaf through those books reminiscently, I find they are an organized string of stories. Not a bad approach!

Trouble in Thailand

By Elaine Masters

N a-shay, 10, squats on the kitchen floor beside the fire, watching her mom fix school lunches. Her mother stuffs cooked rice into two small plastic bags and whirls them tightly shut with rubber bands. Then Na-shay and her cousin, Palasak, 12, slip the bags of rice into their shoulder bags and start down the road to the school, about an hour away.

Why are simple mountain villagers raising a crop that could destroy a family in the United States?

Are drugs a problem in a remote mountain village like hers?

Absolutely. Na-shay and Palasak are members of the Lahu tribe in northern Thailand. They live in an area called the Golden Triangle where Laos, Myanmar (Burma), and Thailand meet. This is the area where most of the heroin sold in America is grown. And more and more, it's also where some of the heroin ends up.

Why Grow Drugs?

Why are simple mountain villagers raising a crop that could destroy a family in the United States? Or a family in Thailand, for that matter?

Part of the reason is money.

When Na-shay's mother was a little girl, opium poppies grew around the village. Na-shay's mother and the other children in the village worked in the poppy fields with their parents. When the plants bloomed, the farmers slashed the green seed pods with sharp razors. A milky sap oozed out. The farm-

ers collected the sap and swirled the milky juice onto sticks. Then they held the gummy balls over fires to harden in the smoke. This sap is what heroin comes from.

They did this because there was no way for farmers to get other, heavier crops—such as rice or beans—to market. There were no roads out of these mountain villages then, but traders came to the village to buy the sap. Although they paid the villagers very little, it was better than nothing. Na-shay's grandparents were able to buy things they wanted and needed, like sugar and t-shirts and knives.

Whose Problem Is It?

This was 20 years ago. At that time, the drug problem in America was getting worse: 24 million Americans used an illegal drug each month. Fortunately, the problem seems to be getting better. Now, 12 million Americans use drugs, half as many as 20 years ago. That's the good news.

But there is bad news, too. Drug use among kids is actually increasing. In fact, one out of every ten junior high students uses drugs at least once a month—the highest rate in five years.

Today many young people are becoming addicted.

At first the government of Thailand said drug use was America's problem. But then traders built factories along the border so they could turn the opium into heroin. Now the villagers had a fast—and available—way to shoot up. Before that, only a few old men had smoked the opium to ease their aches and pains. But today many young people are becoming addicted. And crime is increasing, too.

"It's gotten really bad in our village," Palasak says. "When I was little, we didn't lock our doors. We didn't even have locks. Now we padlock everything."

"The heroin makes them crazy," says Na-Shay. "They have to have it every day. So they steal everything they can. Then they sell what they steal to get money for heroin."

The drugs have had an effect on Palasak's family, too. A few years ago, his father was sent to prison for drug trafficking.

What's the Answer?

While he was in prison, Palasak's dad became a Christian. When he was released, he was made headman (mayor) of his village and has helped the villagers make different, better choices.

The American government has also helped, building roads into the mountains. Now the villagers can grow and sell coffee, tea, marigold seeds, peanuts, ginger, dried mushrooms, and bamboo shoots. They don't need to grow and sell heroin anymore.

Other countries are helping, too. Germans helped string wires for electricity and drill wells for safe water. Zimbabwe sent teachers to show farmers how to grow new cash crops.

But the supply of heroin has only been reduced, not eliminated.

Today most of the opium is grown across the border, in Myanmar. The government there neither wants nor accepts help from other countries. But for the poor mountain farmers who live there, growing and selling opium is still the only way to make a living.

Most of the heroin produced in Myanmar travels to America on new routes through China, instead of Thailand. But some of it does come to Thailand, and that's why Na-Shay and Palasak still have locks on their doors. And teens in Thailand struggle with drugs much like teens in the U.S.

What Can You Do?

Drugs are a big problem. But you *can* fight back. Here's how:

1. **Don't cave in.** If your friends are pressuring you to try drugs, get new friends. You can live a while without friends, but you can't live very long with drugs.

2. **Don't experiment with things that hurt your body.** Heroin can kill you. So can sniffing glue or nail polish remover. If a substance changes your heart rate or breathing, or if it makes you feel dizzy, it's not good for you. God says your body is the temple of the Holy Spirit (I Corinthians 6:19). Respect it!

3. **Don't keep secrets.** It never feels good to snitch on your friends, but you might save a life if you do. If you're sure a friend is using drugs, or if you know where drugs are being sold, tell your parents or your teacher.

Horrors of Heroin

Charlie, a young man in a Virginia drug treatment center, knows first-hand the damage drugs can do, especially heroin.

"My big brother was doing drugs," he says. "I always thought he was way cool. Then he got me to try marijuana. I think I was about 8 years old. One day, he laced it with heroin. Man, I felt no pain. From then on, I just kept wanting more."

"Feeling no pain" describes it well. Opium is made into morphine, a controlled drug (regulated by the government) used in hospitals after major surgery and at other times when pain is extreme. The street version is heroin.

It's Charlie's "wanting more" that causes the problem. Opium products are addictive. The user continues to need more and more to satisfy his craving. Charlie's brother couldn't stop and eventually died.

"After a few years of taking heroin, he couldn't think about anything but getting high. His brain didn't work right. He dropped out of school. He wouldn't eat. When he died, he was just skin and bones.

Three thousand kids start smoking cigarettes every day.

"That's when I decided to get treatment," Charlie says.

Bad News

Why do kids do drugs?

Sometimes they think it's cool. Sometimes they're curious.

"When my dad caught me smoking weed, he

was really mad," says Benny, 12. "He asked me where he had gone wrong. It didn't have anything to do with him. I smoked because I wanted to see what it was like."

But, unfortunately, research shows the younger someone starts using drugs, the harder it is to kick the habit. And that isn't all . . .

Marijuana is the most commonly abused drug by kids ages 10 to 17.

Three thousand kids start smoking cigarettes every day. These kids are 65 times more likely to try an illegal drug—like marijuana—than kids who never smoke.

Marijuana is the most commonly abused drug by kids ages 10 to 17. In fact, one in four high school students has tried it.

The number of eighth-graders who have used heroin is small, less than two out of a hundred. But that's still twice as many as five years ago.

Drug-related illness, death, and crime cost the U.S. $67 billion a year, almost $1,000 for every man, woman, and child.

Guideposts for Kids
7–12 years
1,304 words

From the Author

I've been writing since I was in the third grade. I've published adult Christian books, middle-grade fiction and historical fiction books, picture books, and board books.

I've been visiting the Thai tribal areas for 20 years, teaching the people that God loves them and giving helpful hints about hygiene and child care. Opium and heroin are major factors in village life.

My team of evangelists stayed at the house where Na-shay and Palasak lived. Na-shay was shy and would not talk to me until I bribed her with candy and strawberries, telling her I would use the information for an article for American children. (On my last trip to the village, I took Na-shay a copy of the magazine in which this article appeared, and she was enchanted to see her picture in its pages!)

I used present tense in the opening paragraph to give a feeling of immediacy and a sense of a continuing situation. I chose *Guideposts for Kids* after meeting the editor at an SCBWI national conference, subscribing to the magazine for a year, and submitting many fiction pieces (which were, alas, all rejected). I queried them with this article idea before I left on one trip, and they were interested.

Guideposts for Kids asked for three or four rewrites before the article was accepted. After publication, I was pleased to receive a letter from a girl who said, "I don't know why anyone would take drugs after reading your article."

An Honest Mistake?

By Mark Galli

I really, *really* wanted to see a Bulls game. It was Michael Jordan's last season, probably, and I really, really, really wanted to see him play in person.

One of my friends had a couple of tickets to a Bulls game, but something came up and he couldn't go. He said he'd sell me a ticket for 20 big ones. OK, it's not that much. But after helping pay for my car insurance, and going on the youth group ski trip, well, I was broke . . .

Twenty bucks is nothing when I'm caddying. In the summer. This was February.

I could have baby-sat.

Nah.

I could have waited until my allowance rolled around. My dad pays me 50 bucks every three months, but the next installment wasn't until April 1.

Too long.

So I decided to beg.

"Dad, you gotta take me to see Jordan! Greatest player of all time. It's his last season. Come on. It could be a bonding experience for us."

"Sorry, Josh. Our last 'bonding experience' cost me 35 bucks a ticket, 'cause you 'really, really' wanted to see a hockey game. You slouched through the whole game and afterward said it was just 'OK.'"

"I'll take you to the game, but you have to pay for your own ticket."

"Come on, Dad, I really, really want to see the Bulls."

My dad's eyebrows bent—not a good sign. "And last year, you really, really wanted a set of weights, which is now collecting dust in the garage. And before that, you really, really wanted go fishing with me, but you couldn't even find your pole the last time I invited you to go."

"Dad, this is different. Honest." I'd run out of arguments, so I just gave him my most sincere stare.

He stared back and then smiled and shook his head. "OK, I'll make you a deal. I'll take you to the game, but you pay for your own ticket."

Three *twenties? Where did that extra one come from?*

Well, that was half a miracle—to get my dad to take me to a basketball game, not exactly a sport he loves. But I still didn't have the cash.

I was getting desperate now, so I prayed.

"OK, God, I know this is kind of selfish, but I gotta be honest. I really want to see the Bulls this year. Just once. Any way you can make that happen? Amen."

Two days later, the full miracle occurred. I had driven over to 7-Eleven to pick up some milk and spaghetti sauce for my mom. The bill came to $5.32. So I gave the clerk a 50-dollar bill (it was all my mom had), and the guy gave me my change: "Sixty-eight cents makes six dollars, seven, eight, nine, ten, and two twenties makes fifty. Thanks."

I pulled into the driveway before I remembered to count the change—something my mom always tells me to do at the store, but a lot of times I forget. I knew she'd ask as soon as I got inside, so I pulled out the change. I counted the coins, the four one-dollar bills, and the three twenties.

Three twenties? Where did that extra one come from? My heart thumped. My mind whirled. An answer to prayer? Well, if it was, I decided it would be me and the Lord's little secret. So I didn't tell anyone—at first, anyway.

At the Bulls game, my dad shouted above the crowd, asking me where I got the money for the ticket.

I mumbled through a mouth full of popcorn, "I just found $20 I didn't know I had."

"I don't think God is a cosmic Robin Hood, stealing from the rich to give to the poor."

They were nosebleed seats; you needed a telescope to see the players. But we did walk down to courtside for warm-ups. Jordan was the man, all right. Thirty-two points that night against the Hornets. When my dad sprung for a slice of pizza in the fourth quarter, I thought *he* was the man.

About a week later, I was bragging to Jeremy about seeing the Bulls, and he asked where I got the money, 'cause he knew I was broke (because I had asked him to lend me the $20 in the first place), and so I told him.

"Uh, hello? Josh? You OK upstairs?" It seemed like his freckles were twitching. I hate it when that happens, 'cause it means he's irritated.

"What are you talking about?" I tried to act innocent.

"That's called stealing."

"I didn't take it. The clerk just gave it to me. It was an honest mistake."

"It was an honest mistake on his part. It was stealing on your part."

"Give me a break. 7-Eleven's not going to miss a stinkin' twenty. That franchise pulls in millions and millions a year."

"That's not the point."

"But it's obvious God answered my prayer." I was desperate.

"I don't think God is a cosmic Robin Hood, stealing from the rich to give to the poor."

"Yeah, but, you don't underst . . . "

"The facts are simple, Josh: You kept something that didn't belong to you. Period. End of Ethics 101." There went those freckles again.

I'm not as stupid as I look. Everything Jeremy said I'd already thought about, but not too much. I mean, would you? But now I had to think about it. I didn't sleep too well that night, and, I'll be honest, I was even too scared to pray about it.

I decided to get a second opinion. My girlfriend, Rebecca, wasn't exactly understanding: "You give that $20 back or I'm not speaking to you again! I'm not going with a thief." I could've sworn her blue eyes turned red.

OK, maybe I am as stupid as I look. But I thought there must be somebody who would understand. So I decided to get a third opinion. I asked my dad—without letting him know what was really going on, of course.

I told him we were talking about ethics in youth group, and we talked about a man who really wanted to watch Tiger Woods at the Western Open (my dad really, really loves golf), but he didn't have enough money to buy a pass, but he discovered on his VISA bill that the computer store had accidentally given him an extra $50 credit, so he was debating whether to tell the store what had happened, or use the extra to go to the tournament.

My dad leaned back in his chair and stared at me for about a minute and then said in a calm tone, "This guy who really loves Tiger Jordan should probably give the $20 back to whomever he got it from."

I just stared at my feet. "Yes, sir."

Now that I look back, I can't believe I wasn't

"Sorry, it'll mess up the count for the day."

---

more honest with myself. I knew it was wrong all along, but somehow I'd convinced myself it wasn't wrong.

Anyway, I felt pretty stupid about it, told God I was really, really sorry, which I was, and told him I'd do anything I could to make it up.

That's when the idea of babysitting popped into my brain. I tried to shove it out, but it just came back in again and again, so I told my mom to tell her friends I was available for the next couple of weeks.

So I sat for a few kids, made 25 bucks, went down to 7-Eleven, talked to the manager, told him my story, and handed him a twenty-dollar bill. I felt like an idiot and I felt kind of good at the same time.

But he refused to take the twenty. "Sorry, it'll mess up the count for the day."

"What?"

"I believe you, and I'm glad you told me, but we clear our books every two weeks, and that $20 is ancient history now. It would be more trouble than it's worth to enter it into our books."

On the way home, I felt excited. I thought maybe this was God's way of rewarding me for being honest, and that he wanted me to use the twenty to get this new baseball cap, which I really needed.

And then I thought, *Nah*. The next Sunday, I dropped the twenty in the church offering plate,

and went home and watched the Bulls on TV from the best seats in the house.

Campus Life
13–19 years
1,358 words

From the Author

The theme for "An Honest Mistake" began in someone else's head. The editor of *Campus Life,* a magazine for older Christian teens, was desperate for a fiction piece on honesty. I'd written a couple of stories for the magazine, and he wondered if I could create a 1,200-word story—in two weeks.

Since I'd only been writing fiction for a year or so, I was a little intimidated, but with a total of 15 years of writing experience, I thought I'd at least give it a try. The other challenge was this: I had to teach a lesson—that honesty is the best policy. To start with a moral is often a formula for fiction disaster. I also recognized that all good fiction is moral, but makes a point subtly and with nuance.

I began by pondering where honesty had been at issue in my life as a teenager (the memory of receiving too much change came back quickly) and what type of things happen when one is honest (thus the twist ending). Then I simply had to set up a situation in which the main character was sorely tempted to keep the money.

I chose first-person viewpoint because it allowed me to create an engaging character and to avoid preaching—the character had to come to his own conclusions about honesty. And I knew the story would have to be funny or at least light. A serious story about honesty would drift easily into cheap moralism.

What surprised me was how fast the story came to me, especially since honesty is not a theme that naturally would have occurred to me. This experience showed me that, as a writer, I have more ideas and themes in me than I imagined.

The Horse of Her Dreams

By Cynthia M. Schuckenbrock

Susan nervously circled her pony. Unfortunately, one circle brought her too close to Janet.

"What are you doing here?" Janet demanded. "You're not jumping that decrepit old beast are you?"

"Cut it out," Susan said, her cheeks burning. "Dash started from nothing. He's . . ."

"You and that pony are nothing," Janet interrupted as she wheeled her pony away.

"Susan?" A familiar voice interrupted her seething thoughts.

"Dad? Oh no . . . What are you doing here?" Susan asked.

How could she hope to compete against them on a borrowed pony?

Her dad looked down and skittered farther from the droppings by his feet. "I told my boss you were jumping today and she insisted we come. I guess she's a what-you-call, 'equestrian.' Look good for me, O.K.?" He turned back to the stands. "Oh," he called over his shoulder, "good luck, tally ho, or whatever they say."

Susan cringed as peals of laughter rang behind her. It just figured that Janet would have heard.

"I've got to get away from here," Susan muttered, reining her pony away from the arena and toward the practice field. Susan watched horses and riders sailing over practice jumps. How could she hope to compete against them on a borrowed pony? And why did her dad have to choose today to finally come and watch her ride? Before, he'd always been too busy.

Susan felt a nudge at her stirrup. She bent down and stroked the graying muzzle of the little red pony. "Dash," she said, stroking his neck, "I think you're marvelous. I'm just so nervous."

A small chestnut pony with a coat like a worn out rug glared back at her.

She and Dash had come a long way.

Three months earlier her instructor had called her aside after a lesson.

"Susan," she said, "a friend of mine, Linda Patterson, bought back her old pony, Dash, for her son. Dash was badly mistreated. He needs a lot of hard work. She'll provide all of the feed and board and pay a stipend besides. Would you be interested?"

Susan couldn't wait. She imagined herself on a gray mare that would sail her over jumps and into glory.

Her instructor led her down to the two end stalls. Out of one door looked the horse of her dreams.

"Is that Dash?" Susan asked, hoping beyond hope.

"No," her instructor said, "that's Dancer. This is Dash."

Susan peered over the stall gate, then jumped back as hooves landed heavy thuds against the stall wall beside her.

A small chestnut pony with a coat like a worn out rug glared back at her. An hour later she was still trying to get close enough to snap on a lead.

Finally she gave up. "Tonight," she told the pony, "I'll just feed you. At least then you'll have to show me your head and not your hooves."

Susan dumped feed into the trough, as the pony glared at her. Very slowly, Dash began to edge closer. Susan stayed still. At last, Dash began to eat, never taking his eyes off of Susan. She reached a tentative hand to stroke his nose. He bared yellow teeth. Susan jerked back her hand, but held her ground. The pony began to eat again, and once more Susan put out her hand. The pony glared, but this time, he didn't bite.

By the time Dash had finished eating, Susan was gently scratching behind his ears.

By the end of the first week, Dash stopped trying to kick and bite.

By the end of the first month, Dash whinnied when he saw Susan.

Susan had been surprised and delighted at the changes good care brought. Dash's red coat took on highlights of gold. He was a marvelous little jumper. Only his gray muzzle hinted that he was over twenty years old.

Only one jump left and suddenly her mind was blank.

The feeling that her stomach was trying to tie itself in yet another knot brought Susan back to the present. Finally, her number was called.

As Susan entered the jumping arena, Janet rode up. "Good luck!" she called. "A clean round and you win the event." Then Janet laughed as if she'd made the funniest joke in the world.

Susan ignored the insult as she and Dash trotted into the arena, their heads held high.

Susan turned toward the first jump. She felt as if she were in a dream. Over the first fence clean. The second, the third . . .

Susan felt herself becoming part of the rhythm of jumping. The fourth, the fifth . . . they were still clean. They sailed over the sixth and the seventh jumps. Then Susan froze. Only one jump left and suddenly her mind was blank. She couldn't remember which way she was supposed to go over the jump. Frantically, she made a decision and sailed over the last jump, clean.

The crowd was silent. Susan knew she had chosen wrong. Stunned and humiliated, she rode out, the sound of Janet's laughter ringing in her ears,

while the announcer intoned, "Number fifteen, DISQUALIFIED."

Once alone in Dash's stall she threw her arms around his neck and began to sob. "Dash," she whispered, "I'm so sorry. I'm so sorry I let you down."

Dash lowered his neck and gently butted her chest as if he understood.

"Hi, honey!"

Susan could tell by her dad's face, he didn't even understand what had happened. It made her feel like crying all over again.

Beside him stood a lady Susan didn't know—his boss. The boss said, "How about getting sodas? When I'm showing, I forget I'm thirsty until someone hands me a cool drink."

"Sure," said Susan's dad. "Be right back."

"I know it's a tough time for you right now," the woman said gently, "but I had to finally meet you. I'm Linda Patterson. Your instructor has given me glowing reports of Dash's progress. You've done a great job."

Susan hesitated as she sorted through what the woman had just said. "You're Dash's owner? And you're my Dad's boss?" Then Susan's head dropped. "I'm so sorry. I messed up. The last jump . . ."

"You messed up a jump," Mrs. Patterson said, "but you've completely turned around Dash. I can't thank you enough for the wonderful job you've done. My son wants to start riding him next week."

Susan felt crushed. She had lost a blue ribbon and Dash in one day.

"I'd like to propose a toast: To my new rider!"

Mrs. Patterson continued, "You know how busy we've been at work? I don't have time for my own horse right now. You may have seen her. She's in the stall next to Dash. Her name is Dancer. If you'd be interested in riding and showing her, I'll provide new tack and a new habit before next month's show. Would you be able to ride her?"

Just then, Susan's dad arrived with the sodas. Mrs. Patterson turned to him and said, "Before we go back to work, I'd like to propose a toast: To my new rider!"

"I'm so proud of you, Susan," he said, grinning at

her while they drank.

After they left, Susan walked to Dancer, as if to tell her the great news. Immediately, Janet appeared in front of Dancer's stall.

"Here," she said, tossing a copy of the course toward Susan. "Thought you'd like a reminder of your ride."

"No need, Janet," Susan said. "Mrs. Patterson said that after today I won't be riding Dash anymore."

Janet gloated. "Boy, she must have been furious!"

"Well, not exactly," Susan said. "Mrs. Patterson is really proud of me. Now I'm going to be riding Dancer in the horse classes."

The look on Janet's face was almost better than winning the blue!

Stable Kids
6–14 years
1,243 words

From the Author

I developed "The Horse of Her Dreams" while taking an Institute course. To establish the habit of writing each day, and to reinforce what I'd learned, I wrote a second story paralleling each assignment. This was one of those "practice" stories.

The story was based on a real incident: a girl jumping a jump backwards. Horrible for her, to be sure, but more of an incident than a story. I asked myself, "*What if* her father came to see her?" and "*What if* his boss was there?" and so on, to create a story from the incident.

I researched markets in the *Children's Magazine Market* and chose my readership age based on the markets available for horse stories. Essential to meeting the word limit was deciding what the real story was: rehabilitating an old pony, or Susan's story? Once I chose Susan, I made the word limit. I chose third-person viewpoint to explore interaction between the characters.

This was my first published piece. The greatest thrill was when the editor told me that she'd received many fan letters about it!

A rejection slip (I have a *huge* stack!) just means a piece wasn't right for a certain editor at a certain time. Write to the best of your capabilities, practice your craft, and find the right editor!

The Funeral

By Toni L. Herzog

I'm lying on my bed counting the ceiling tiles in my room. I'm pretty sure that there are 110, but I keep on counting them anyway. Because I'm not really thinking about the ceiling tiles. I'm thinking about Mrs. West. I wonder where she is. Well, I know where she is. She's dead. She is in the ground by now. I suppose. But I wonder where she really is. If she's looking down on me. And I wonder what she thinks of me now.

I went to her funeral today. And I cried, probably harder than I should have. Because I was crying for more than just her death. I was crying for the way I behaved toward the end of her life.

I used to sit in her office during my study hall. She would try to grade papers, but we'd start talking and she'd end up telling me some fun story about when she was in college or how she met her husband. It seemed amazing to me to think of her being that young and carefree. You don't think of teachers like that. But when she'd talk about those days her eyes would light up and I'd see a bit of romance in them. And I suppose I also thought I saw a bit of myself in them. A bit of what I wanted to be.

She was only thirty-five when she discovered she had a tumor in her brain.

She knew me pretty well. She said she had been like me once, even though it was hard to imagine a mature, self-assured woman like her ever being as shy and backwards as I am. She encouraged me to speak up in class when I knew the answer, not to be afraid. And she even talked me into joining the staff of the school newspaper, she said I had a tal-

ent for that sort of thing. And above all else, she assured me that no matter how strange and awkward I felt now, I would turn out fine. I would grow up and be a real person just like her. And she made me believe it.

She was only thirty-five when she discovered she had a tumor in her brain. It was large, too large to do anything about. She found out about it in the summer, and she didn't come back to school that fall.

My friends, Robin and Melissa, went to see her. She was bedridden by then and they cleaned her house. Her hair was falling out, they told me. And she had gained weight and didn't look like herself. It

The bravest thing I did, even though it wasn't very brave at all, was send her a letter.

was hard to imagine, hard to believe. This was the sort of thing you read about or see in a tear-jerker movie. But I'd never actually known anyone with a brain tumor before. And it petrified me. She had a husband and a son. And she was only thirty-five.

Robin and Melissa made more than one trip to see her. They took it upon themselves to clean the house on several occasions. Her husband, Bill, was very appreciative, as he had much more on his mind than keeping up with the housework. Robin told me that Mrs. West had been asking about me and that I should go with them, at least once. And I knew she was right.

But I was scared. Scared to see her like that—my teacher, my friend. She had always seemed so "in control," always had all the answers to my questions. And I didn't know what I could possibly say to her now. I also feared what expression might shape my face upon first seeing her. I didn't want to hurt her like that. And I also, however selfishly, didn't want to face what was happening to her.

The bravest thing I did, even though it wasn't very brave at all, was send her a letter. I told her how great the school newspaper was going, and that I was appointed to be the editor next year. I said how well I was doing in all of my classes. I said things that I thought would make her proud. And I said I was sorry I hadn't come to see her yet, and that I hoped she was feeling better. Of course, I knew she wasn't. But I didn't know how to address the issue. I guess I still don't.

She wrote back to me in a jagged handwriting I barely recognized. She was glad things were going well for me. And she wrote, "Please come to see me soon." Those words haunt me now.

I wrestled with a terrifying guilt.

I wanted to go see her. I truly did. I wanted her to know I cared for her. But no matter how I pleaded with myself, I couldn't do it. I was just so horribly scared. And the more months that passed, the more frightened I became, and the more resolved I became not to go. And I never did.

I waited in a line with hundreds of other people, students and adults alike, to pass by her body at the funeral today. And I wrestled with a terrifying guilt. Because I'd known all along that I would go to the funeral. And I guess knowing that was my way of making it seem all right, my way of justifying the fact that I never went to see her. It was as if I had thought she'd be there waiting to talk to me or something. But standing there in line, I realized that none of that was true. It wasn't all right. She wasn't there anymore. And it was too late to ever do anything about it.

I didn't look at her long. I glanced past her puffed-up, misshapen face rather quickly, because she didn't look at all like the woman I knew, and I had to struggle to remind myself that it was really her.

Her son, who was not much older than me, waited to greet people at the end of the casket. I was crying when I reached him, and I felt dumb. And completely weakened. Because he wasn't crying. Her own son wasn't shedding a tear. He was strong and incredibly well-composed for a boy his age at such a tragic time.

"Thanks for coming," he said, looking me warmly in the eye.

There were a million things I wanted to say to him. I wanted to tell him about every time she'd ever made me laugh, or smile, and every word of confidence she'd ever handed my way. And I also wanted to tell him how horrible I'd been, how I'd not gone to see her even after she asked me to, as if thinking that somehow he could grant some forgiveness on her behalf.

But words were hard to come by. And most of them seemed rather meaningless to me in that strange, empty moment during which I felt so lonely, holding nothing inside me but a useless sense of remorse.

"She meant a lot to me," I uttered softly.

"What's your name?" he asked

"Amy Brewer," I told him.

He looked upward for a moment, trying to think back. "You were one of her students," he said. "I know I've heard her talk about you."

I only nodded. I still wanted to tell him everything, how very sorry I was for his loss, and what a wonderful person she was. But I think he already knew all that. And a nod was about all I could muster through my tears.

"She's in a better place now," he said to comfort me. And how odd I felt, knowing that I was the one who should be comforting him, and yet it was happening the other way around. He amazed me, the son she'd raised. And I thought how very proud she would be for the strength he was able to show. It made me admire him.

I hope that she's watching me, and that she's understanding my pain.

And so I count my ceiling tiles again, wondering if perhaps there aren't 112 now. My eyes are tired, and losing interest in the ceiling. I let them close.

I can only hope that she understood my absence. But on the other hand, how could she? And how could I not have gone to her? Tears come to me again there in the lonely confines of my room, the coming dusk beginning to throw a dull shadow over my bed. And I can't get the tears to go away. Because now that she's gone I recognize the full scope of my mistake. I am full of painful regret. And it is something that cannot be undone.

Death is permanent, and love is useless unless it is shared.

The only comfort I can take is that she is with God now. She was very sure about that, I am told, and rested comfortably with the idea that God was taking her for some particular reason that we just couldn't know right now. I hope that she's watching me, and that she's understanding my pain. If anyone could, it would be her. And if she is watching me, she knows full well what I have learned today—that death is permanent, and love is useless unless it is shared.

With
15–18 years
1,518 words

From the Author

I've always wanted to be a writer, but I didn't seriously pursue the dream until I was 28. Now, five years later, I have had more than 35 short stories and articles published, and I have sold three romance novels, all published under the pseudonym Toni Blair.

"The Funeral" is a special story to me because it draws on my own life. I was very close to a teacher who died, and I was too afraid of her death to be there for her in the end. So writing this story was a therapeutic exercise, as well as an artistic one.

I chose to make the protagonist younger than I was when this actually happened. I'd been selling short stories to magazines for adolescents/young teens, and I wanted the story to fit the market. I've found that "fitting the market" is one of the most important tasks for writers of any genre.

I selected *With* as a market for this story because they had bought reprint rights from me for another story of a similar length and style, with a similar type of lesson.

I chose first-person viewpoint because it reads powerfully. The reader *becomes* the character, and this is effective in reaching younger readers. I decided to fill the story with internal monologue because the girl's thoughts and feelings are mostly what the story is about. After all, it's much more about what she *didn't* do than what she *did* do.

Although I didn't revise "The Funeral" for content after I wrote the first draft, I went through it countless times, polishing. I can't say I ever feel that a piece of work is definitely "finished," because I am always improving as a writer and can always go back and make improvements.

The Love Song

By Melanie Marks

"So, Robin, do you know what I mean?" Ryan asks. He puts down his guitar and turns to me.

"Sure," I say as I reposition my fingers on the frets. "It's like me and Scott."

"What's like you and Scott?" he asks with a puzzled look on his face.

"Well, what you were saying," I tell him, feeling my face start to flush. It's possible I've missed the gist of his ramblings. I was messing with my guitar and only half-listening.

Normally, I tune into every word Ryan utters. But tonight I've been pretty intent on getting down this song I'm working on. Also, it's around 2 A.M., and Ryan has a way of getting philosophical in the wee hours.

I thought I was following the conversation—obviously I wasn't. He'd been talking about how people can like each other one way and not in another, then suddenly change their minds and like them the other way as well—but how eventually it might end up ruining the great thing they had in the first place.

I got the impression he was talking about him and Kelly Baker. He'd had this on-again, off-again relationship with Kelly, and now it looked like she wanted it on again.

Ryan's such a "guy." He'll never just come out and say exactly what he means. But then again, I tend to do the same. Maybe that's why we're such good friends.

Ryan stares at me intently, waiting for my response. Furrowing my brow, I take a half-hearted stab. "It's just that relationships change," I tell him. "Like how Scott and I used to be . . . dating or whatever, and then for a while we hated each other, but now we are friends . . . sort of."

Ryan gives me a sympathetic smile. "You still like him."

"No. I don't. Not like I used to."

"Yeah you do. You were on the verge of tears when he came with Tammy to the concert tonight."

"I was not," I deny emphatically. But to be honest, it makes my blood chill thinking of Scott and Tammy together.

"Well, you looked really hurt," he says and pauses. "Robin, the guy's a jerk—get over him."

I knew Scott had been seeing other girls and lying to me about it.

"He was really nice to me later, though. Maybe you were in the mosh pit, but we talked for a long time. It was nice."

"No, I was there. I saw." Ryan stares at me a moment, then shakes his head. "You're like an abused puppy or something. You let him kick you around and just keep going back for more."

I know what he's saying is true. Whenever Scott is even remotely nice to me I start wagging my tail, happily gobbling up any attention he throws my way. I don't know why I'm like that with him. I think it has a lot to do with Scott being my first boyfriend. I'm not sure if I miss him or just miss having a boyfriend.

"Well, I broke up with him. That's not letting him kick me around."

Maybe that's not a big deal to Ryan—but it is to me. It was hard to do. I knew Scott had been seeing other girls and lying to me about it. But it's one thing to know you need to break up with someone. It's another to actually do it.

"It's late," I tell Ryan. "I should go."

When I get to my house, I flop into bed still wearing my clothes. Life is totally cruel. When I was with Scott I was miserable. Now that I'm without Scott I'm still miserable—and I'm lonely as well.

Tonight he told me the only reason he was with Tammy was to make me jealous—and then he mentioned he'd asked her to next weekend's school dance. He said he misses me—that he realizes he should have treated me better. He seemed sincere, but it's no secret that he can be a good liar. Ryan's probably right: I should just get over him.

A few nights later I'm over at Ryan's again. We're down in his basement, working on a new song. That's how we got to be friends. We discovered that we're both into playing the guitar.

"Look, Robin, you don't need Scott. I'll take you to the dance."

"I don't feel like writing a love song," he says.

"I know what you mean."

It's around 11. Ryan and I have been at this for hours. I should finish some homework but I don't want to go. It's fun hanging with Ryan even if we don't get anything done. Sometimes I wish we weren't such good friends. Maybe he'd look at me as more than a bud.

"Maybe we should write a song called 'Love Sucks,'" he suggests.

"Yeah. Or maybe 'Scott Sucks'—that sounds good."

"Are you upset he asked Tammy to the dance? Trust me, you're better off without him."

He always says this, but he doesn't understand. Ryan has Kelly and many other girls beating down his door for a chance to be his girlfriend. What if Scott's the only guy who'll ever be interested in dating me?

We go upstairs to raid the fridge.

"Scott hates school dances," I say and make a huge mess opening a bag of chips. "I'm sure he only asked Tammy because he knew I wanted to go."

"You want to go?" Ryan makes it sound like the thought's inconceivable, but then he turns reflec-

tive. "Look, Robin, you don't need Scott. I'll take you to the dance."

I raise my eyebrows. "You would?"

"If you really want to . . . do you really want to go?"

"Yeah. But you hate dances."

Ever since I've known Ryan he's avoided school dances like the plague.

He shrugs. "I guess that says something about our friendship."

Tingles run through my body. "Yeah . . . I guess."

I remember that earlier today I'd overheard Kelly saying she was going to make Ryan take her to the dance.

"I heard Kelly say she wanted you to take her," I tell him.

"Yeah, no kidding." Ryan sighs. "Look, do you want me to take you or not?"

"Of course I do."

"OK, then," he says. "Shut up about Scott and help me find something edible."

On the night of the dance, I'm nervous. It takes me over an hour to get ready. I still can't believe it: Mr. Ryan I-don't-go-to-school-dances is taking me to the dance. I mean, maybe that's not a big deal. Friends do things for friends. But a school dance—that's something he's never done for anyone else. It makes me feel special.

When he shows up at my door, he's wearing a suit—and looking great.

"You look pretty," he tells me. And the way he stares makes me believe him.

I hadn't realized he was thinking of this as a date.

Ryan takes me out to dinner first—and not to the pancake house. (That's where we usually eat—Ryan loves crêpes.) Instead he takes me to a romantic little Italian bistro. When it's time to pay, I try to put in my share, but he won't let me.

"It's a date, Robin."

I quickly put my money away. Until this moment I hadn't realized he was thinking of this as a date. I just assumed he was taking me to the dance as a favor.

The dance is fun. We goof around, talk to friends, and I would be having a great time, except I keep seeing Scott and Tammy all over the place. Only

131

three days ago, he begged me to forgive him, to give him another chance. He said he was miserable without me. Watching him slowdance with Tammy, I feel sort of sick. He sure doesn't look miserable.

With a sympathetic grin, Ryan touches my arm. He caught me. I had a wistful look on my face while watching Scott.

"Dump the jerk for good."

"You want to dance?" he asks.

Ryan takes me in his arms and we dance. Out of the corner of my eye, I see Scott watching. He's looking hurt. For a moment I feel bad—like it's wrong for me to be having a good time without him. But I close my eyes and try to forget about Scott. Instead I think about Ryan—about being in his arms, about what a good friend he is.

When the dance is over and it's time to leave, I look up at Ryan. "I wish this wasn't over so soon. I had a good time."

Ryan stares at me. "Yeah, me too."

When we get to my house, Scott's car is parked in the driveway. He gets out as soon as we pull up.

"Dump the jerk for good," Ryan advises as he drops me off.

"Look, can we talk?" Scott asks.

"About what?"

"About us. About you and me."

I shake my head. "What's the point? There is no you and me."

"Don't say that."

"Why? It's the truth. Scott, you lied to me and cheated on me. I've had enough."

"Yeah. I did cheat. I know that . . . and I'm sorry." He looks at me, his round blue eyes full of remorse. "But that was the old me. I've learned from my mistake. I'm not like that—not anymore."

I shake my head and smile bemusedly. I used to fall for this stuff. "Scott—it's over."

He runs his hands through his hair. "Well, what about you? You lied too."

"What are you talking about?"

"You said you guys were only friends—you and Ryan. But I knew it wasn't like that . . . I knew you wanted to be more."

I look away from him. What he says, it's kind of true. But the feelings I have for Ryan are foolish—

the guy has Kelly Bakers clawing each other to get to him.

I can feel Scott's eyes studying me for a reaction. "And what happens as soon as we break up?" he asks. "You two get together so fast it makes my head spin."

"We aren't together. We're just friends."

"Yeah, right. The guy dumped Kelly Baker so he could take you to the dance—you're telling me he did that out of friendship?"

I look up at him, stunned. "He dumped Kelly?"

"Yeah. Right after he asked you to the dance."

I bite my lip. That's weird. It almost sounds like . . . My heart gives a gigantic thump. "Scott, I need to go."

I run all the way to Ryan's. When I get there, he comes to the door still in his suit, but his tie is off, and his hair is all rumpled as though he's been asleep.

He yawns. "Robin? What are you doing here?"

Without thinking, I blurt out, "Scott said you like me."

"I think I'm ready to write that love song."

Ryan gives a little laugh. "Don't be shy, Robin—get to the point." He pauses. "So, Scott told you that, huh? I guess the guy's not such an idiot after all."

I furrow my brow. "So, it's true? But why didn't you ever say anything?"

"What was I supposed to say? You go around talking about Scott all the time—it's not like you've been available."

I guess what he says is true. For the past couple of months I've pretty much had a one-track mind.

We stare at each other a moment. "Can I come  in for a while?" I finally ask. "I think I'm ready to write that love song."

Teen
12–19 years
1,884 words

Lightening Up Jackie

By Shirley Byers Lalonde

I used to think I hadn't done too bad in the sibling department—until my little sister, Jackie, hit ninth grade and Northumberland High.

We hadn't been in the same school for a couple of years so you might think, isn't that nice the Michaels kids can support each other, be there for each other, maybe hang together occasionally?

Well, that's what I thought. But, oh no. All of a sudden big brother, Alex, was "crass and barbaric" and Jackie was like, Captain of the Fun Police. I didn't know what had happened to her head but I figured my little sis was way too tense.

Case in point. She was all over my face about how "inappropriately" I had teased her friend, Amanda. All the way, all the *long* way, to school Friday morning, she whined about it.

"You shouldn't have made fun of Amanda's name, Alex. You really hurt her feelings, you know."

"Aw, c'mon, Jackie, lighten up! You know, you used to have a real neat sense of humor, but lately you're about as much fun as double physics on a Monday morning."

"Oh, *so* funny!" Jackie rolled her eyes. "You think you're so smart, Alex Michaels, just because all your dorky friends laugh at your sick humor. Like they know everything!"

And what was all the fuss about? A minor incident yesterday at drama tryouts.

Amanda's last name is Marienhoff. Somehow it had gotten gibbled on Mrs. Hughes' list and the drama teacher had stood on center stage, calling, "Hoff! Marian Hoff! Reading the part of Lana. Enter stage right please. Ms. Hoff! Are you in the building?"

It was a hoot. So later, I kind of kept it up, referring to Amanda as Marian or Ms. Hoff. Everyone laughed and it was all in good fun. But try telling that to my serious little sister.

"What," I said, "is the big deal? I mean it's not as if I called her something *bad*."

Right then and before Jackie could reply, Chris Colby whooshed by on his bike.

"Hey, Mikey! How's it going?" he stuck out an arm in greeting.

"Hey Chris!" I resounded automatically. Then it hit me.

"Did you hear that, Jackie?" I kept my voice casual.

"Hear what?"

Jackie's mind was totally polluted to me these days.

"Chris called me Mikey. A variation of my last name, *our* last name, Michaels. Didn't see me getting all chewed up about it, did you? No. 'Cause it was *all in fun* and maybe just a little reference to the three shots I sank so sweetly at our last basketball game. No big deal."

For a minute there, I had her. She was silent. Then she shook her head and sputtered out something about how it wasn't the same thing at all. Yeah, right.

No doubt about it. The kid would have to mellow out big time if she was ever going to survive at Northumberland.

So how could I help her? Well, I could tease her more, toughen her up, so to speak. But no, the kid was convinced I was a barbarian. That probably wouldn't work. How about if I made a point of teasing her friends? Then she could see that *they* didn't mind and she might relax a little. Now, that might do it.

Nah. Nah, it wouldn't. Jackie's mind was totally polluted to me these days. I could have stood on my head and spit quarters. And all her friends could have started an Alex Michaels fan club and it still wouldn't have impressed her. But, Greg Reimer . . . now there was a guy my little sister *could* relate to. She thought my buddy Greg was just so cool.

After supper and dishes, like always we did our homework in the family room. I only had a little algebra and I was finished in half an hour. I glanced over at Jackie. She'd abandoned the books and was curled up on the sofa with a novel. Time to go into action.

"Hey, Sis!" I threw the words over my shoulder as I exited the family room. "A friend of mine is coming over later to run some lines from the play. Wanna hang around and help out?"

She shrugged, not bothering to look up from her book. "I don't think so. I'm kinda tired and we won't even know until Monday if we got the parts."

"Suit yourself. Maybe Greg can bring someone else or maybe we can just work around the other parts or . . . whatever . . . ."

"Greg? Did you say Greg? Greg Reimer?" She was off the couch, leaping towards the nearest mirror. "I guess I could do a little practicing with you guys. I mean, it can't hurt and it might help, right? What time will he get here?"

I had to bite my lips to keep from smiling. *Alex*, I said to myself, *you are so good.*

The three of us worked hard for about an hour, mostly drilling the lines, getting the right inflections, trying to understand our characters. At about nine we stopped for a Pepsi break.

She lapped it up like a puppy laps up milk.

Greg walked over to the piano. "Hey, Jackie, how about a song?" he said, picking out a melody on the keys"—"Beauty and the Beast," a Celine Dion tune.

My little sister loves to sing so it didn't take much coaxing. She sang "Beauty and the Beast" and a couple more Dion songs with Greg doing the accompaniment.

Greg gave her a big grin. "Not too shabby, Celine!" he said. He called her Celine the rest of the evening and a couple of times he said he wanted to be the first to apply to be her piano man now before she was rich and famous and forgot all about him.

And Jackie? My sober, serious sister? She *loved* it. She lapped it up like a puppy laps up milk and she even gave him some back. "I'll keep you in mind," she said airily, the second time he teased her about being her piano man. "But you do understand Elton John will be *very* disappointed."

I was so pleased with my plan it was all I could do to keep from telling her about it, even doing a little bragging after Greg had gone. But, I knew that would be a mistake. It couldn't hurt to bounce a few wisecracks off the new and improved Jackie though.

"Say, Celine!" I nudged her as we picked up

"You never know when to leave it alone, do you Alex?"

---

glasses and Pepsi cans. "We'll have to cut back on the Pepsi and chips before the big tour. Gotta ditch that baby fat!"

Jackie didn't say anything. I reached to give her hair a little yank. "Hey! Didn't you hear me, Jack? I said . . . ."

"I heard you, Alex!" she spat out the words as she slammed a couple of glasses down on the coffee table. "You always have to spoil everything, don't you?"

"Whaaat? Hey c'mon! I was just having some fun with you. You didn't mind when Greg teased you! It's all the same. I mean you didn't really think *he* meant any of that stuff he was saying, did you?"

She sighed and gave me that look like how could *anybody* be so thick? "No Alex, I don't think he meant it. I knew he was just teasing me. But it was a *good* kind of teasing. It made me feel good. When you tease, it's . . . it's like being picked on!"

"Oh, yeah? Well from where I sit, Jackie, it seems that your so-called good teasing is whatever Greg does but whenever I try to kid around with you, I'm bad old Alex, the jerk who picks on you."

Jackie looked at me for a long minute. Then she sighed. "You just don't get it, do you Alex?" she said quietly. "Greg teases people about things they feel good about, and they can tell he means it as a compliment. You tease about things people feel self-conscious about, so it comes across as a put-down." Then she turned and went up the stairs.

Well, I'd tried. I'd tried my best to help the kid and what did I get? A lot of grief. From here on in, Jackie would be on her own.

By Monday morning she was speaking to me. Barely. I stood behind her and Amanda at the bulletin board where Mrs. Hughes had posted the try-out results. The three of us had all gotten the parts we wanted. I tried to congratulate Amanda. "Way to go Ms. Hoff!" A couple people chuckled. Jackie gave me a look. Amanda was not amused.

"You never know when to leave it alone, do you Alex?" she muttered as she walked away.

"Whoa! What a nasty temper we have!"

"Ms. Hoff has issues," an unfamiliar voice said from behind me. I turned to face Tim Epp, a tenth grader.

Ruthie Duncan spoke in a low voice. "Why can't you guys just let it go? Obviously, Amanda is sensitive about her name."

Tim let a lot of air out of his mouth in a snort. "Aw Ruthie, that is *so* lame. Trouble with people like you and 'Marian' is that you just don't know how to have fun."

"Exactly!" I grinned at Tim. He grinned back. We began to walk down the hall together.

"Hey, Tim. How come you didn't come out for drama? We're doing a comedy. You'd have been great in it."

"Well, thanks. But I haven't given up on a dramatic career." He threw an arm around my shoulders, looked hard into my face. "I figure I'll get my start as your stand-in."

I shook my head. "Uh uh, Buddy. It isn't going to happen. I worked too hard to get that part to give it up and I am very, very healthy."

"Oh, is that so? But won't you be going in for your surgery any day now?"

"Surgery? What are you talking about?"

"Your face, Bud. You've got a loaded pizza happening there. Plastic surgery's the only thing that can help that volume of zits." And Tim let go with a gale of laughter.

I forced my lips into a grin. I had to shove my hands into my pockets to keep them from going to my face.

The zits had come with puberty and they hadn't shown any signs of letting up real soon. But I faithfully used the ointment the doctor prescribed and most of the time I thought my skin didn't look so bad. Not great, not totally clear, but not bad. But maybe I'd just been kidding myself . . . .

Tim punched my shoulder. "C'mon Alex! I was only *teasing*. Hey man, lighten up! You and I, we know how to laugh don't we?"

I made myself laugh. I couldn't understand why I was being such a wuss. It was crazy. Tim was only teasing. It was all in fun, like when the guys called me Mikey. So why was I feeling like I wanted to run away or maybe pull a bag over my head?

I punched him back, maybe a little harder than I needed to.

"You got that right, Tim. The trouble with most people is they just don't know how to take a little harmless teasing."

With
15–18 years
1,829 words

From the Author

Writing to a theme is, for a writer, the best of all times and the worst of all times. I'm a contributing editor for *With* magazine, and every issue is themed. I wrote "Lightening Up Jackie" to fit in with an issue on "play." Sometimes I find it excruciatingly difficult to write to a theme, but I know that the discipline has improved my writing.

In this story I decided to address the issue of teasing because it's such a common issue in the lives of teens. For teen stories, I almost always write in the first person. Teens like first person because it feels "real." I listen to my teenage son and his friends to get a sense of how they talk, but I use slang very sparingly—it dates so quickly.

The "takeaway" of this story was knowing the difference between "good" and "bad" teasing. Inserting that message into the fabric of this story in a believable way wasn't easy, and I didn't get it quite right the first time. Accepting that a story needs revisions and working with your editor to make it all it can be is another exercise in discipline, but for me, it's always been worth it.

The Drive-By

By Heather Klassen

I don't want to hear about it anymore. So I press my hands over my ears, hard. But my friends' mouths keep on moving. I'm surprised to find that I can read lips. Still, I'm not surprised by the words I'm reading.

The drive-by. The drive-by. The drive-by.

All conversation has changed since the drive-by.

I squeeze my eyes shut so I don't have to watch my friends' lips in motion. And I think about how sick it is that there's even a word for this event. A word for something that at one time didn't happen at all. At least not in high school. At least not at *our* school.

Fingers pry at one of my hands, loosening my grip on my ear.

"Sarah, what are you doing?" Amanda asks me.

I open my eyes. I see that everyone at the table is staring at me.

"Can't we just talk about something else?" I plead. My head pounds with the chant. *The drive-by. The drive-by. The drive-by.*

"You can't pretend it didn't happen, Sarah," Marissa says. "Not talking about it won't make it go away."

And Kate, who saw it happen; Kate, who watched Richard crumple to the ground, clasping his chest

---

"Sarah's going around the bend again."

---

where the blood spurted out, nods.

The rest of us only heard it. Only heard the shots. *Pow. Pow. Pow.* Only heard the screams. Only can't stop talking about it. *The drive-by. The drive-by. The drive-by.*

I stand up, gather my books, and clasp them to my chest.

"But you talk about it too much," I say. "You're turning it into another event, like another sock hop, like something normal. You chatter about it, you re-hash it over and over. But what do you do? What does anyone actually do?"

Marissa and Kate glance at each other. I can read that glance. It's the one that says "Sarah's going around the bend again." "Sarah takes everything too seriously, too personally." "Life goes on, Sarah."

"It happened," Amanda retorts. "What can we do about it now?"

Will there be more funerals featuring 16-year-old pallbearers?

I leave my friends at the table, leave them to the endless discussion. Yet I don't know what we can do. What anyone can do.

Morning announcement at school: all students are barred from the front courtyard by the main road, at all times.

That doesn't sound like the answer to me. Sounds like withdraw, hide, keep away. We can't let the guys with the guns have the right of way.

The killer is 16. Our age. Richard hadn't even been the target. The killer missed. Maybe the driver, the girl, took the corner too fast. It might have been a gang thing. It might not have. Rumors fly; rumors spread; rumors keep the cafeteria buzzing.

Maybe parents descending upon the school board will change something. Maybe not. No one spoke up when the drive-bys happened only across town. Now the outrage begins. Now we have our own drive-by.

Or will it be drive-bys? Will we have another and another? Will there be more funerals featuring 16-year-old pallbearers?

A locker slams and I jump. I'm not the only one on edge, I know. Nervous laughter spreads through the hallway. We're laughing at ourselves for being frightened of a slamming door.

But I don't get beyond a wry smile. My head pounds; my fingers feel numb. Not sleeping, not eating, will do it to you, I guess. Dreading fourth period will do it to me, I know.

Richard won't be there. My lab partner was gunned down during lunch break last Wednesday. Now I do the experiments alone. I didn't know Richard well, but huddling over beakers and test tubes together, I became accustomed to the smell of his hair and the sight of the freckles dotting the bridge of his nose.

I wonder if his mother used to play connect-the-dots with his freckles, as my mom did with mine.

"Stop it," I say out loud, too loud. Heads swivel to stare at me. I'm talking to myself to stop thinking

---

The gun's lying on top of the world history textbook.

---

about it. I may be the only person in school who can't talk about it. But I can't stop thinking about it. About the drive-by. About Richard. I have to stop thinking. After all, life goes on, everyone says.

Maybe it does for some of us.

I reach my locker and rummage around inside, not knowing what I'm searching for.

"How's it going, Sarah?" Justin appears at his locker, next to mine. We have been alphabetically assigned to each other forever, since kindergarten, only one letter separating us. No, it's been since preschool. Justin and I sat next to each other at snack time. He used to blow into his straw to make milk bubbles.

"It's not going," I want to answer. But I say nothing. I cannot explain my reaction to being hurled into a reality that makes me unable to function.

Justin pulls out book after book. He's looking for something too. One arm dangerously overloaded, Justin hands a stack of books to me.

"Here, hold this," he says.

I take the stack. Something on top slides toward me, unbalanced. Something shiny and black and heavy. I have only glanced at it. Now I stare.

I'm holding a gun.

No, not holding, precisely, I tell myself. The gun's lying on top of the world history textbook. So I'm one step removed from holding it.

"Here, hold this," Justin says. Like it's just another item pulled out of a locker. "Here, hold this," my classmate says, as if it's normal.

"Why?" I ask. Justin doesn't hear me. "Why?" I ask louder.

Justin looks up, realizing what he has handed me. He puts a finger to his lips, shushing me. "I didn't mean to give that to you. I wasn't thinking. I usually keep it hidden," he whispers. "It's just for protection. You never know."

"Take the bullets out," I say.

"Sarah, I'm not planning on shooting anyone. It's for just in case."

"Take the bullets out," I repeat.

Justin stares at me, realization spreading across his face. "Sarah, you can't tell. I'd be expelled. Or even arrested. I'm not going to use it, I swear."

"Then take the bullets out."

"If you tell, my life will be ruined," Justin pleads. "We've been friends forever, Sarah. Please don't turn me in. Promise?"

I nod. If I turn him in, Justin will hate me. Maybe he even belongs to a gang, and the gang will retaliate against me. For all I know, he does. I feel as if I don't really know anyone anymore.

Justin lifts the gun from the book, clicks something open and empties six shiny bullets into his hand. He starts to slip the gun into his jacket pocket.

"Let me see it," I say.

Justin, a little surprised, maybe a little proud, in the mood for showing off, hands it to me.

"You're ruining my life, Sarah!"

I slide the gun into the space between my books and my chest, slam my locker shut, and start walking. Toward the office. Toward the principal and the ever-present police officer or two. Ever-present since the drive-by. I know they'll believe me. I'm betting that the serial numbers will match up with Justin's father's gun, missing from the desk drawer at home. Justin's fear confirms this for me.

"Wait, Sarah," Justin yells, following me. "You can't do it. You'll destroy my life!"

I walk faster, then start to run. School rule is "no running in the halls." Today I'm breaking it. Justin won't catch me. I'll reach that door. I'll hand over the gun. I'll do something.

Enough? No. Enough to untwist my stomach and stop the pounding in my head and let me sleep at night? Probably not.

Justin screams at me, "You're ruining my life, Sarah!"

The hall is lined with spectators, watching the chase. The gun digs into my chest.

I want to shout back at Justin. I want to yell, "Maybe I am ruining your life, Justin, but maybe not. Maybe I'm saving your life for you. Or someone else's for them." But I don't.

I'm almost out of breath. Besides, maybe this won't make one bit of difference anyway.

Maybe more shots will ring out at my school. Maybe drive-bys will become a normal event. Maybe more of us will be gunned down.

But not by Justin's gun.

Listen
12–18 years
1,416 words

From the Author

Real-life events that keep me awake at night inspire the stories I'm compelled to write. Several years ago, a student was killed in a drive-by shooting at a local high school. She was not even the intended target. Writing "The Drive-by" was my way of dealing with my intense feelings about the event. I hoped the story would help teenagers think about the senselessness of that kind of violence.

I originally wrote the story for *With,* a magazine I'd regularly written fiction for. It did not fit their needs, so I sent it to *Listen,* which had bought several of my stories. Due to the subject matter, the story was obviously intended for teenagers, and the length was determined by the word limits set by the magazines I'd targeted. Over the years, I've learned to write within word limits by getting right into the story, letting any necessary background information and description be revealed during the story.

I always use first-person point of view for teenage stories, since it makes the stories feel personal and immediate. As I write, I don't really decide between using narration and dialogue to tell my story. I become the character, feeling what she is feeling, and the story flows out just the way she is living it. I usually have a story running through my mind before I sit down to write it. I revise by reading the story over several times, making sure that it makes sense and that I've made the best word choices.

I've been writing for children and teenagers since I finished the Institute's course in 1985, and I recently celebrated my 100th sale (two picture books, the rest magazine pieces). I write as often as I can, in between my part-time jobs as a substitute preschool teacher and as a child-care coordinator for an au pair agency and two churches. My two children and their friends help inspire story ideas. My son will soon be a teenager, and I'm looking forward to more ideas springing from his experiences, as well as the opportunity to gather realistic dialogue by listening to him and his friends.

Swimming in the Shallow End

By Nancy N. Rue

"Yeah, the blue outfit's fine," I said into the phone. "You look good in that."

"I don't want to look 'good,' Andy," Kathryn said. "I want to look fabulous."

"Okay, you look fabulous in it. What time do you want to go?"

"You don't think it makes me look fat?" she said.

"You couldn't look fat if you wore inflatable jeans. Gumby weighed more than you do."

"I don't want to look like Gumby!"

"I didn't say you looked like Gumby . . . ."

Across my room Nathan rolled his eyes.

"Kath," I said, "you'd be incredible if you wore a Macy's bag, okay? I'm gonna have to fight off every guy at WinterFaire."

Nathan stuck his finger down his throat.

"You're so sweet," Kathryn said.

I told her I'd pick her up at four o'clock and then got off the phone.

"She's got you trained. You told her three times she looked terrific, and she was still whining for more."

"What was that all about?" he said.

"We're going to that WinterFaire carnival they've got going downtown tomorrow," I said. "We're gonna do the whole shoot-wooden-ducks-for-teddy-bears-eat-cotton-candy thing."

"No, I'm talking about the whole oh-Andy-tell-me-I-look-like-Cindy-Crawford thing," Nathan said.

"You're hallucinating," I said.

"Bet me." Nathan made a stupid voice. "'You'd be incredible in a Macy's bag,'" he groaned. "You're

messed up, man."

I didn't say anything. I don't normally. I've always been more of a listener, and Nathan had me intrigued.

"She's got you trained," he said. "You told her three times she looked terrific, and she was still whining for more. If she were my girlfriend, she and I would have a talk."

"About what?"

I just figured she was out of my league.

"About she goes her way, I go mine," Nathan said.

"Why?"

"Shallow," Nathan said. "She's about as deep as a puddle."

There was a tap on the door—my mom telling us our pizza had arrived.

And that, of course, was the end of the conversation. Nathan being the "deep" type.

Besides, he didn't know Kathryn.

Two of a Kind

I'd never noticed her before I saw "Grease" at school. The girl could sing—LeAnn Rimes, eat your heart out. When everybody took their bows at the end, I was surprised at how many other people were in the show. I'd been looking at her the whole time.

I checked her name in the program—Kathryn Gates—but I totally ruled her out as a possible date. Not that she didn't blow me away with her petite figure, blond hair, enormous blue eyes, and a smile that lit up the stage. I just figured she was out of my league.

Until one of the ushers invited me to a cast party.

"I know how you are about drinking and stuff, Andy," she said, with innocent eyes. "It's all gonna be soda and chips."

So what's the first thing I see when I get there? The stage manager shoving a Budweiser in Kathryn Gates's face.

"I don't drink," she was telling him. She was trying to be cool about it, but her huge blue eyes were darting everywhere like she was scared to death.

"I bet you never even tried it," the guy said.

"She says she doesn't want to," I said. "Why don't you back off?"

No big deal, I decided. I'd just quit reassuring her every 10 seconds. End of problem.

"What are you doing here?" Mr. Budweiser said. "You're not in the cast."

"I'm *not* here," I said. "I'm gone."

I didn't even get off the front porch before Kathryn was out the door after me.

When I dropped her off at her house about two hours later, I felt like she'd shot me full of adrenaline.

I found out she was not only good-looking, but she was a Christian like me. She felt the same way I did about a lot of things: drinking, sex, stuff like that. Since the cast party two months ago, she'd been giving my life a kick it hadn't had before.

It was weird, though. Lately, I felt as if I was the one doling out the energy. Even right now, after a 10-minute conversation, I felt more tired than I did after two hours of basketball.

I hadn't focused on it until tonight, but maybe Nathan was right. Maybe Kathryn did want me telling her too much that she was drop-dead gorgeous.

No big deal, I decided. I'd just quit reassuring her every 10 seconds. End of problem.

Unfair Faire

At first it didn't look like it was going to be that hard. She slid into the front seat when I picked her up the next afternoon and instead of saying, "Does

my hair look stupid like this?" she said, "Did you get your schedule in the mail today?"

"Yeah," I said. "I can't believe we only have two days of Christmas break left. Who'd you get for English?"

"Toti, first hour," she said. "Then math, environmental science, computer typing fourth, study hall, history. And I got Caxton for that—everybody says he's easy."

"When do you have chorus?" I said.

"I'm not taking it this semester."

I took my eyes off the road long enough to stare at her.

"Why not?" I said. "Chorus is your big thing!"

"I don't need it," she said. "I'm gonna be way too busy."

"Doing what?"

"Going to your basketball games. If I'm in chorus, I'll have to miss half of them because of rehearsals. Besides, you might need me to help you study. You have to keep your grades up to get a scholarship. You said that."

"What about *your* grades?" I said.

"I don't need a four-o."

I didn't answer. This conversation was turning lame. I was tired already, and I wasn't even pumping her up.

But things looked up when we got to the Faire. Who can feel tired when you're surrounded by 8-foot-tall snowmen coaxing you to ice skate and barkers luring you to win big, stuffed Tweety Birds? Plus, your girlfriend looks like a shiny-eyed little girl smiling at you over her blue cotton candy.

I was jazzed again, and I got Kathryn into the ice palace, on the Eskimo slide, and even took her on a carriage ride where we had to bundle up in a blanket to keep warm. She laughed her song of a laugh and cuddled up next to me. I thought about Nathan being enough of a jerk to give this up just because he didn't understand women.

I'd told myself to be afraid if I ever started taking advice from Nathan.

Then we walked past the guy who shouted, "IF I CAN'T GUESS YOUR WEIGHT WITHIN TWO POUNDS, YOU WIN A FREE PRIZE!"

"Forget that," Kathryn groaned. "I'm not telling

my weight in front of *anybody!*"

"Knock that off, Kath," I said. "Half the girls at school would kill to look like you, and you know it."

Her eyes immediately swam with tears. You'd have thought I'd slapped her. I felt like some kind of brute.

"I'm going to the bathroom," she said, voice quavery. "I'll be right back."

I was glad for her to be gone. Man, she was even more sensitive than I thought.

Or was it sensitive? What had Nathan called her? Shallow?

I'd told myself to be afraid if I ever started taking advice from Nathan, but it was almost as if he had a point this time. Was it really all Kathryn cared about: looking perfect—making sure every eyelash was in place?

"Man," I muttered to myself. "How have I gone out with her for this long and not seen that?"

The Power of Song

She came out of the bathroom then, lips all slick and hair done into a braid. She'd apparently decided not to cry. She put her hand in mine, tilted her chin up and said, "Let's walk on the boulevard."

"Whatever," I said.

I felt less like talking than ever. As we dodged the old guys pushing even older couples bundled into rickshaws and the hordes of people shoving their way into coffee shops, I looked around for something to do.

I scanned past the boulevard, and my eyes lit on a good possibility.

She looked like she was slipping into shock.

"Come on," I said. "Let's go do that."

"What?" Kathryn said. Her face brightened like she was glad I'd said something—anything.

"Karaoke," I said.

Kathryn giggled as I dragged her across the street. "You're gonna sing?"

"No," I said. "You are."

It was 10 bucks a song, and you got to keep the tape.

"Andy, no!" Kathryn said as I forked over the money. "I'll be embarrassed!"

"Why?" I said. "You have a great voice."

Man, I was doing it again. It was like she was manipulating me into giving her compliments. I gave her a little shove.

"Pick a song," I said.

She actually looked a little freaked-out as she blinked at the selection of songs.

"Do something by Celine Dion," I said. "What about 'Because You Love Me'? Do that."

At that point I think she'd have done Pearl Jam if I'd suggested it. She looked like she was slipping into shock.

The guy got her set up with the microphone and a TV screen showing the lyrics. She stared at both of them as if they were gonna whip out fangs and bite her.

"What's the big deal?" I said. "Just sing."

The music started, and then the letters on the screen flashed red. Her mouth automatically flew open.

At first her voice sounded like somebody was holding a gun to her head, and I thought, *Give me a break. Enough with the act already.* If I hadn't been so annoyed—and maybe even a bit smug—I would have been disappointed. I really thought there was more to her.

And then, slowly, she started to sing. Not just sing and sound really good, but sing like she meant it . . . like she felt it. The song didn't just flow from her—it worked its way out like a deep-felt emotion. It almost hurt to see her sing, yet I couldn't take my eyes off of her.

A crowd gathered around the booth by the time she finished the song, and everybody clapped. Her blue eyes startled, until she saw me. And then she lit up the boulevard with her smile. She wasn't shallow. She just hadn't discovered her own depth yet. But she had to see it now. There was no way she could miss it.

A Sour Note

I grabbed her when she stepped out of the booth, tape in hand,

"That was incredible," I said. "Kath, you can't quit chorus. You have to keep singing."

She laughed and dropped the tape in her purse. "Why?"

"Get away from me with that dog food," I said. "You *know* why. You love it. It's in you."

"Yeah," she said, "but there are about a million

other girls with voices just as good as mine."

It was like I'd handed her a soda and she'd thrown it in my face. I couldn't believe it.

"Would you stop it!" I snapped at her.

Several people turned around and looked at us. I stomped off down the sidewalk to the old courthouse and took the steps three at a time. She caught up to me when I'd hurled myself down onto the top one.

"What's wrong?" she said.

I gave her a jerky shrug. Inside, I was seething.

"Come on, Andy," she said. "I hate it when you clam up."

That did it. I exploded, right there under the sculpture of Lady Justice.

"The only reason you want me to talk is so you can hear about how wonderful *you* are every 10 seconds," I shouted. "That's *all* you want!"

Her eyes overflowed, and she wasn't trying to stop them this time. The hurt twisted her face, and I felt bad about it. But I also felt trapped and squeezed and pushed and tired. I just shoved my hands in my pockets and chewed my cheek.

"I don't *want* you to reassure me, Andy," she said with tears in her throat, "I *need* you to. I just feel ugly and ordinary. I keep thinking if you tell me enough that I'm pretty and special, I might start to believe it."

One minute I thought she was shallow and the next I thought she was a basket case.

Suddenly, it all came together for me. Why being with her was giving me chronic fatigue syndrome. Why one minute I thought she was shallow and the next I thought she was a basket case.

"What?" Kathryn said. There was desperation in her voice. "Talk to me, Andy. Is it the chorus thing? I can still change my schedule."

I looked down at her. Man, she really was gorgeous, and talented, and full of feelings I'd probably never have. She was deeper than me and Nathan put together.

"Would you be doing it for you or for me?" I said.

"I don't care!" Her face white-scared. "I just want you to be happy. If it will make you proud of me, then I'll do it . . ."

I grabbed her by the shoulders. "Kathryn!" I said. "Your self-esteem can't be my responsibility."

"What do you mean?" she said. "I don't get it."

I could have told her. Maybe as a good Christian kid I should have. Except it wouldn't have been enough. Ever. And it still would have been me telling her—not Kathryn exploring the depths for herself.

And I was tired of swimming in the shallow end.

"Come on, Kath," I said. "I'll drive you home."

Breakaway
12–18 years
2,224 words

From the Author

I've written novels, nonfiction books, and short stories for teens, probably because I spent 16 years teaching high school. All kids have their own stories, and it's important to me to tell teenagers' stories from their own realistic points of view, in their own language. I love the way teenagers talk—there is so much rhythm, imagery, and humor in the way they express themselves, which hasn't changed much in the last 25 years.

My own daughter (who just turned 20) and her boyfriend helped me with the dialogue and realism of "Swimming in the Shallow End" on a trip to the Atlantic City boardwalk one summer. But they weren't the models for my characters. A young man I met at a writer's workshop, in a conversation about relationships, said, "What I hate is a high-maintenance girl I constantly have to be reassuring—I become her self-esteem. It drains me. That's not what I want." I could see a great story idea there.

When I submitted the story to *Breakaway*, they wanted me to change it from a summer story to a winter story, so I had to revise by changing the setting and a few of the characters' background details. But that kind of revision is unusual for me. Since I write from very detailed story outlines, I usually write my stories in one draft, and the only thing left to do is cut them to the right length. I'm a big one for really running on!

The Survivor

By Donald Silverman

Laura Sandler walked past the aging Kings Hotel on King George Street in Jerusalem. Her mind was on Hebrew grammar, which was giving her a dreadful time, when her thoughts were interrupted by the sound of uncontrollable coughing. She turned to see an old man doubled over trying to catch his breath. Laura rushed to him but wasn't sure what to do.

When the spell passed, the old man looked up and inquired in broken Hebrew where he could find a drugstore.

"Excuse me, do you speak English?" Laura asked.

"Oh, you speak English," the man replied. "Oh, thank God." The coughing started again, but it was not quite as severe.

"Yes," Laura said. "It's much better than my Hebrew. Can I help you?"

"Please, could you tell me where is there a drugstore? I need something for my cough."

"Can I go and bring it to you?" she asked, worried about the old man's apparent weakness. "Where are you living?"

"I'm staying right here at the Kings Hotel. But no, don't bother. I couldn't trouble you."

"I'd be happy to. I'll get you some cough syrup and bring it to your room. It won't take me long. It's just down the street."

"You wouldn't mind?"

"No. What's your name and room number?"

"Room 306. My name," he replied, as if he had to recall it. "Name is Turk, Joseph Turk."

"Mr. Turk, I'll be right back."

"Let me give you money."

"You can pay me when I return."

"Thank you, thank you so much," he responded between hacks.

Laura watched Mr. Turk as he headed toward the hotel. Joseph Turk was short and slight. His blue flannel pants were baggy. Over his shirt and tie he wore a worn maroon sweater, which should have been enough to bring out a sweat on this warm spring afternoon, but he had topped the sweater

---

"I'm studying to be a rabbi."

---

with a shabby grey sport jacket. A brown shapeless fedora completed the unmatched ensemble.

Laura went to the drugstore and bought syrup and a package of cough drops, and returned to the hotel. As she walked down the hall of the third floor, she could hear Mr. Turk coughing. She knocked on his door.

Mr. Turk ushered her into a room so small it looked cluttered with only his suitcase and meager clothing. Laura was aware of a musty smell. She handed him the package and he gave her some shekels.

"You're a good girl. Thank you."

"You're welcome," she replied. Laura worried about leaving Mr. Turk alone in his condition. "Are you visiting someone in Israel?"

"No. I don't know anyone. Don't worry. I'm all right."

"Can I check in on you tomorrow? I finish classes at three."

"You're a student?"

"Yes, I'm studying to be a rabbi."

"Oy, a pretty girl like you, a rabbi. It's a different world from when I was young. You're one rabbi who will never grow a beard."

A wide smile spread across Laura's face as she repeated her request. "Can I check on you tomorrow?"

"I don't know if I'll be here. I hope, if I'm better, to take a tour."

"I'll check. If you're gone I'll know you're okay."

Laura didn't make it to the Kings Hotel until four-fifteen the next day. Rabbi Forgosh had wanted to speak to her about her Hebrew grammar. She should have paid more attention in religious school when she was a kid. But who knew?

She ran all the way to the hotel. Mr. Turk responded at once to her knock.

"It's a sin against God for a girl to wear a kipah."

"How're you feeling?" she asked breathlessly.

"How I am feeling? Much better, thank you."

He looked better. There was color in his face and a sparkle in his eyes as he smiled at her. Laura was pleased at his recovery but felt a bit uncomfortable, not knowing if she was imposing on him or not.

"I want to thank you again. You're a good girl."

"That's okay," she replied shyly.

"I was going to take a walk before my supper. Would you like to join me?" Mr. Turk asked.

"Sure! That would be nice."

"Are you dressed warm enough?" he asked.

It was a mild evening. Laura smiled both at his concern and his own multi-layered wool clothing. "I'll be fine," she responded.

They wandered aimlessly through the ancient streets of Jerusalem. Laura wanted Mr. Turk to know he was no longer alone in Israel and so put her arm through his, hoping she wasn't being too bold.

"Where are you from?" she asked.

"The Bronx. I work in a doll factory. I put the wigs on the dolls. I've been working there since 1947. A long time, huh? Let me see, forty-six years."

"Have you been to Israel before?"

"No. This is a dream come true, a month in Israel. I'm not a rich man. I've saved a long time."

A Hasidic Jew, dressed in a long black coat and a wide-brimmed hat passed them before turning and shouting, "It's a sin against God for a girl to wear a kipah."

Laura removed her yarmulke. "I'm afraid I forgot. I was wearing it at school. I take it off when I'm on the streets. I don't want to offend the Orthodox . . . and I don't want to get beat up either," she said and smiled.

"A girl wearing a yarmulke. To tell you the truth, it looks strange to me, too."

Laura wondered why he was in Israel alone. Was he married? She hoped he was. Maybe his wife just couldn't come. Did he have children? Again, she hoped the answer was yes. She didn't want Mr. Turk to be alone in this world.

"Are you married?" she asked, quickly adding, "I'm sorry, that's none of my business."

"It's okay. No, no I'm not married. Why? Are you looking?" They both laughed at his attempt to be funny.

They were on Ben Yehuda Street. Vendors' voices filled the air with Hebrew. Gaily lit shops teemed with customers.

"I'm pooped," Mr. Turk said. "I need a cup of hot tea."

They sat at an outside cafe.

"You have a beautiful smile, Laura. It makes me happy. You know, I had a wife once, and two children." His face changed. "We got sent to a camp. To Buchenwald. They died. You know Buchenwald?"

Laura nodded, stunned. She had been to Yad Vashem, the memorial to the Jews who had died in the Holocaust. Six million. She had glared at the pictures of the Nazis, Hitler, the guards, the mass rallies, trying to understand such evil. It had been impossible.

But when Laura looked at the pictures of the emaciated victims, she could feel their hunger. When she had looked at a hand sticking out of a barred window of a cattle car, she could feel its desperation. Laura could not grasp the magnitude of the evil of the Nazis, but she was able to feel the pain of the victims. And now she was sitting at a cafe in Israel with a survivor. Six million was an incomprehensible number. Mr. Turk's loss was comprehensible. At that moment, Laura remembered again why she was a Zionist, understood again the law of return and the importance of Israel to her people.

Mr. Turk reached into his wallet and handed her an old photograph of a woman and two young boys. "My wife and two sons," was all he said.

As Laura looked at the crumpled picture, tears began to slide down her face. Mr. Turk jumped to his feet. "I'm sorry. I'm sorry," he blurted out. "I didn't mean to make you cry. It's okay. It was so long ago."

Two soldiers, passing by with Uzis on their shoulders, stopped for a moment to look at the weeping young woman and the flustered old man.

With studies and other activities, Laura didn't get to spend much time with Mr. Turk. She made promises to herself but just couldn't keep them. Not that she didn't see him sometimes. They spent an afternoon at the Diaspora Museum in Tel Aviv, and Mr. Turk was there once when Laura led Sabbath services at Hebrew Union College. He beamed so broadly, you would have thought he was her father. Toward the middle of April, she called him.

"Turk here," he answered his phone.

"Mr. Turk, it's Laura."

"Ah, Laura. I'm glad you called. I leave for America in a few days. My stay's nearly over. I wanted to say good-bye."

"When? When do you leave?" Laura felt a rush of sadness. Could it be a month already?

"After Passover. Sunday morning."

"Oh good." There was relief in her voice. "I want you to join us for the seder. I've invited a few students to share Passover with us."

"You don't need an old man."

"Please, we want you to lead the seder."

"All the young rabbinical students? You should lead the service. You don't need me."

"Mr. Turk, we do need you. We want you to join us, very much."

"So, I'll be there."

Laura had invited three cantorial and four rabbinical students to join Mr. Turk. The old man arrived with a bouquet of roses and carnations, which Laura put in an empty juice bottle. She led Mr. Turk to the seat of honor, where a pillow had been placed for his comfort. After he sat, she handed out the Haggadahs to all the guests. The nine of them sat squashed around her small table.

"Mr. Turk, will you lead us?" Laura asked.

The old man nodded gravely. He was dressed in a dark blue suit, newer than any of the other clothes she had seen him in. He looked distinguished, wearing the richly colored kipah, embroidered by Ethiopian Jews, that Laura had given him.

He seemed radiant.

Mr. Turk had heard the voice of the cantor many times at temple, but this was different. The three students sang the songs and chanted the prayers with voices in a rich harmony that could never be achieved by a single cantor. Mr. Turk led the young people through the Haggadah, retelling the exodus of the Jews from slavery in Egypt to freedom in the promised land. When the time came for the four questions, it turned out that Laura was the youngest at the table, so she asked each question and Mr. Turk answered.

Laura arrived at the Kings Hotel an hour before Mr. Turk was to leave for Ben Gurion Airport. As they waited, they exchanged addresses to disguise what Laura knew in her heart. This was really a permanent good-bye. The taxi arrived and they carried out his bags.

The two of them hugged, holding each other tightly while she kissed him on the cheek, surprised by the tear that met her lips. He was crying. Oh, God.

"You are a shana maidel, a beautiful girl. I wish I had a grandson for you."

She watched as the taxi took Mr. Turk out of her life. What had he said? "I wish I had a grandson for you." He meant no more than he said, yet Laura realized the full implication of his words. She wiped a tear from her own cheek.

"It will not happen again, Mr. Turk. I promise you, never again," she whispered to the wind.

SHOFAR
9–13 years
1,880 words

From the Author

"The Survivor" was based on an experience my daughter had as a rabbinical student in Israel. I like to play with the facts to suit me, so it became a work of fiction.

When I write, I just let the first draft tumble out with no regard to art. I don't worry about quality, as I know I will be rewriting many times. Although I have the entire story in my mind, it often takes on a life of its own and I end up with a different story than I intended. For me, that's the fun of writing.

Black-Cherry Eyes

By Kezi Matthews

Izetta was a brilliant liar. You know how they say water finds its own level? Well, Izetta certainly married into the right family when she married my father, Jack.

I come from a family of great liars. Cover-up liars. We think fast on our feet. Before Izetta, my aunt Delia was probably the champ. She could build a scenario to cover her butt so fast you got giddy just listening. She'd live her lie, you know, and probably would have died defending it—that is, if these people were inclined to die defending anything. I know them well now and I don't turn my back on them. But they met their match with Izetta; she was without peer.

Her power was in her voice. It was low and measured, with the soft, mournful sound of a dove. If you closed your eyes, you could see her in robes

---

I was ten years old and knew I was looking at an enemy.

---

and a crown. She was from Heaven's End, a small island of inbreeding set jewel-like in the Santee River; a culmination, a fulfillment of her skewed gene pool. Even when you knew she was hitching her imagination to the dark star of her needs, you couldn't help yourself.

It's funny, the things you decide to remember; they make you who you are, and you grow yourself a certain way because of these things you hang on to. The first time I saw Izetta, my stomach gave a surprised start as though it had lurched and stumbled. I was ten years old and knew I was looking at an enemy. Her breasts shimmied when she walked, and her eyes were so Indian-dark they glittered. She had a big, rosy smile full of big, white teeth and she hung on to Jack's arm like a kid scared of being lost. She was seventeen and had been the second Mrs. Jack O'Brien all of six months when they came to pick me up at St. Joseph's Home for Girls. I'd been stashed there since my mother, Janelle, ran off when I was four.

Jack blew his top, stirring up a sudden hornet's nest of memories.

Down at gut level, I've always wondered why Jack reached back for a kid he didn't want. When it came time to leave, I had a sudden sinking feeling. I knew shadowed eyes silently watched my every step. Before climbing into the backseat of the car next to my cardboard suitcase, I glanced around. Sister Paul was standing on the gray stone porch. She gave me a little wave. Just before we turned onto the main highway, I looked out the back window. St. Joseph's stood on the hill, still and dark as a tomb against the radiant spring sky.

When we stopped at a filling station to gas up, Jack bought me an orange soda and a box of cheese crackers that were stale but so thrilling I pigged them down. A half-hour later, I spewed them out all over the backseat. Jack blew his top, stirring up a sudden hornet's nest of memories—of fighting and screaming and a silent child huddled in a corner. All the while he was cleaning up my mess in the car, shoving me out of the way, cursing under his breath, Izetta sat frozen like one of those little green lizards trying to blend in. When we were on the road again, I caught him looking at me in the rearview mirror. "How you doing, Garnette?" he asked, real fakey.

"O.K.," I said and I smiled up at the mirror. Staring at the back of his head, I felt an odd impulse to reach out and touch his sandy red hair. But I didn't. Every once in a while, Izetta glanced over her shoulder at me. I closed my eyes so I wouldn't have to look at her and made up a song to myself about being on my way to a place I couldn't remember with people I didn't know. After a while the reedy wind music sneaking in around the windows lulled me to sleep.

The first month with them in Charleston I was sleepwalking, trying to keep up with do this, don't do that—trying to fit in and not knowing how. The food tasted different; the bed felt funny. Instead of my uniform and brown oxfords, I had odd little sandals and tennis shoes with someone else's footprints inside and hand-me-down shorts, shirts, and sundresses.

I began to catch Izetta staring at me, and finally one day she said, "Why, you don't look anything like your daddy, do you? I mean, your hair's red and all, but you don't look like an O'Brien." Then I began to notice that whenever Jack was home, she'd watch him to see if he was looking at me. She never left us alone together.

Jack's family couldn't get over him up and marrying this ignorant country girl from Heaven's End without telling them.

Miss Alva—Jack's mother and my grandmother—my aunt Delia, and her daughter, Amy, started showing up on Sundays sometimes. They always came together and left just as soon after the two o'clock dinner as decency allowed. And they always left a trail of frost behind them—Izetta, distant and wounded, with tears trembling on her long, black lashes; Jack, slammed shut and locked up tighter than a meat freezer. Jack's family couldn't get over him up and marrying this ignorant country girl from Heaven's End without telling them. Just showing up one morning with his bride, Izetta LaValien, in tow as though he'd caught a bigger trout than usual, is the way Miss Alva put it.

Izetta could never let it be. After each visit, her mournful voice wrapped itself around Jack relentlessly until, at last, he stalked from the house. Of course, they made up later. All she had to do was stand next to him. You could see the heat coming off her in waves like it does on Folly Beach Road in August.

Izetta's family was unpredictable, showing up at random, usually when Jack was off on the dredge. You could hear them a block away in their old gray Chevy. Like some weary old bones grabbing its chest and wheezing, it always staggered to a near stop as it tried to make it up the driveway. A back-

---

They bulked up around the kitchen table, grunting softly and murmuring to each other like a small herd of exotic beasts.

---

fire followed by squealing hinges and doors opening and slamming said they'd made it. They piled out of the car, short, big-breasted women with skin glowing like summer peaches and long, dark hair, slick as beaver pelts, tied back with bright ribbons. They bulked up around the kitchen table, grunting softly and murmuring to each other like a small herd of exotic beasts—her mother, Marcella LaValien, and her older sisters, Marquita, Lavonna, and Suzanna. Izetta always sent me outside to play. I sat quietly beneath the kitchen window, tucked inside the fragrant shadows of a honeysuckle bush, trying to decode the mournful ebb and flow of their words. Izetta lost no time in mocking Miss Alva with deadly skill, usually adding about two yards of embroidery. Every once in a while, I'd hear my name, along with the creaking of chairs and coffee cups moving restlessly on the Formica tabletop. And always, "She sure doesn't look nothin' like that man. Lord, how do you *stand* it!"

I could imagine Izetta's expression. Each time the O'Briens came around, they went to great lengths to comment, as though in great surprise, "Why, she's the spittin' image of Janelle." Every time those terrible words came out of their mouths, Izetta's black-cherry eyes went flat.

She was forever telling Jack cockamamie stuff, like the time she had him almost crazy with a long story about a man lurking around the back fence all day. "But the dogs . . . " he said.

"Oh, those dogs," she shook her head, "they're

just like old rags when you're not here." I sat at the kitchen window, watching Jack walk up and down behind the back fence, looking for tracks or whatever. Of course there were none. I started steering clear of Izetta when I could. Some kind of warning system told me to watch out.

Before long, I was looking forward to Sundays, hoping to see my cousin, Amy. She was a year older than me, and for all her prissiness, there was a vanilla-pudding sweetness about her that was hard to resist. She always made a point of sitting next to me, smiling, expectant, waiting for some sign from me that we could be friends. I hated her in a way; all the accidental, unearned love heaped upon her by Miss Alva and Aunt Delia sometimes stung my envious soul to its quick. Yet I desperately wanted to be just like her, pretty and at ease.

After her terrier, Bitsy, had puppies, Amy showed up one Sunday with a fat, black-eyed ball of white fur, a red ribbon tied around its neck. Jack looked at it like it was a turd. Dogs were for hunting or police work, he said. Dogs like this were yappers, freeloaders, one step up from rats. Izetta rolled her eyes toward the ceiling. "Who's going to take care of it?" she asked.

Clutching the puppy to my chest, I blurted out, "I will . . . I will . . . I'll take care of her."

"That dog died, because you handled it too much."

Aunt Delia said, "My God, that child has a voice after all." Then she added quickly, "Heavens, Jack, these little things housebreak real easy." She had no intention of taking that puppy back home.

I named the dog Trudy after my best friend at St. Joseph's. I had her for three days, Monday, Tuesday, and Wednesday. When I got up Thursday morning, both Jack and Trudy were gone, Jack up the Santee River, Trudy to heaven.

"That dog died," said Izetta, "because you handled it too much." I cried all morning, then thought to ask for Trudy, dead and all, so I could bury her.

"Jack did that before he left this morning."

When I asked her where, she just gave me a look and walked away. I found Trudy's red ribbon on the back steps and felt something hard and unforgiving settle in my throat. I searched every inch of the yard and beyond. I knew what graves looked like; I'd seen them at St. Joseph's. Trudy wasn't buried in the backyard.

Jack got in late that night. I awoke hearing the soft rise and fall of their voices coming from their bedroom, so I got up and put my ear to the wall. I thought I heard her say she found Trudy dead on the back porch and, "You don't suppose she killed it?" When I strained to remember her exact words the next morning, they just fishtailed away. Finally I

The birds were quiet, tucked away inside the shadowed shelter of the trees.

---

thought it was a dream. Jack never said one word to me about Trudy. It was like she'd never been there. A couple of nights later, they seemed to be arguing for a long time. I tried to imagine them lying in bed in the dark. Jack finally said, "Well, try a little harder, dammit!" followed by Izetta's muffled sobbing. I knew it was about me. I didn't feel sorry for her at all.

I slept with Trudy's red ribbon under my pillow for weeks, hiding it behind the dresser mirror during the day. I still have it.

I've noticed when some awful, unexpected thing happens, people have this wishful way of saying, "It was a day like any other." Well, the day I came face to face with Izetta's genius felt different right from the beginning. The sun seemed to rise earlier than usual, spreading a blinding glare over the cloudless sky with a vengeance. The birds were quiet, tucked away inside the shadowed shelter of the trees. The milkman passed right on by our porch without stopping, and Izetta said, "Well, too bad. I was going to

---

As I walked round back, the dizzying aromas of fried porkchops and apple pie mingled and rushed out through the screen door.

---

make us some blueberry pancakes." Instead she made me a bologna sandwich. I was getting sick of bologna. That's all we had whenever Jack was out of town. I ate a couple of bites and took the rest out to the dogs. They were sprawled in the skimpy shade of their shed. I hosed some fresh water into their bucket and threw down the bologna sandwich. Mike, Jack's prize liver-tick, lifted his head, sniffed the air, then flopped back down.

At eight-thirty, Jack called and said he wouldn't be going up to Wilmington after all—he'd be home by five or five-thirty.

A little after noon, Aunt Delia's car pulled up in the driveway. She kept the motor running while Amy came in asking if I could go to the pool downtown, her treat. My heart soared.

"She doesn't have a bathing suit," said Izetta. On really hot days, I'd been running under the sprinkler in a pair of old shorts.

I could hear Izetta sobbing inside the house as I walked to the screen door.

"I've got one that'd fit," said Amy, smiling at me.

I could see *no* written all over Izetta's face, then a smile spreading like sunlight on a country rose turned her incredibly beautiful. For a moment, I think I saw her through Jack's eyes. "Well, O.K.," she said.

While I raced to put on clean shorts and grab a towel, Izetta walked out to Aunt Delia's car. "Had my hands full with her this week..." Her soft words fluttered off into the air like vagrant butterflies as Amy and I walked up. "Be sure to bring her back 'bout four, O.K.? You have a good time now, Garnette."

To this day I still can't decide if she planned what happened, waiting for the right moment, or if it was just a sudden inspiration.

Aunt Delia and Amy dropped me off at the house somewhere around four-thirty. The screaming, splashing world of the pool had let me loose, free of the anxiety I'd carried around in the pit of my stomach all summer. As I walked round back, the dizzying aromas of fried porkchops and apple pie mingled and rushed out through the screen door. Izetta didn't hear me come in. She was in a world of her own, humming softly to herself like little girls do when they're playing house. She sensed my presence and lifted her head, listening, and then looked over her shoulder at me.

"Oh," she said, "come here, taste this." She held out a saucer of apple-pie filling. I could hardly wait to get it to my mouth. She turned suddenly, bumping my arm, sending the filling down the front of

my blouse and splattering onto my sandals. She grabbed a damp dishtowel and wiped me down. "That's O.K. for now," she said. "You can shower when you get back." She quickly wrapped wax paper over one of the three pies on the counter. "Here, take this up to Miss Cooley. Right quick now." The bottom of the pie tin was still too warm, but she pushed me toward the screen door. "Don't be such a baby. Hurry now. Jack'll be home real soon."

Miss Cooley was a distant relative of Izetta's, an old woman in her nineties who lived by herself in a ramshackle old house up by Henderson's Grocery. I had to bang on the front door pretty hard before a bony finger with a long, waxy fingernail scrabbled at one side of a frayed window shade, and a milky eye peered out at me.

"I've got a pie for you, Miss Cooley," I hollered, holding it up for her to see.

"Just leave it by the door." Her voice barely carried through the window.

I set the pie down and cut back for home as fast I could. The sugary, spicy smell of apples and cinnamon on my clothes had my stomach crazy for food. Turning the last corner, I could hear the dogs barking, Mike's voice rising above the others, piercing and frantic with happiness. Jack was home. Then they fell silent, all at once. I raced around the side of the house expecting to see Jack feeding them.

The frying pan was in the middle of the floor, a big, black lollipop sprinkled with cucumber slices.

Instead they were cowering by their shed. One of the heavy, chrome-legged kitchen chairs was up-ended next to them. I could hear Izetta sobbing inside the house as I walked to the screen door.

They were standing in the middle of the kitchen. Jack had his arms around her, petting her, stroking her hair. At first, I couldn't understand why the kitchen looked so upside down. Then slowly, I saw the mashed potatoes and gravy smeared on the walls, the apple pies upended, crushed, oozing off the countertop and down the cupboard doors. The frying pan was in the middle of the floor, a big, black lollipop sprinkled with cucumber slices. The porkchops, splayed across the floor, led right to me. Something had happened. Something sudden and frightening.

"I was trying to clean it up before you got home, Jack." Izetta's voice trembled as she choked back the sobs. "I got out of the shower and found . . . this. Why does she hate me so much?" She burst into fresh tears.

For as long as I can remember, there's been a place I go inside when there's no place to run.

Jack stiffened, turned his head, and looked toward the door. A long shaft of fading sun, slicing through the sink window, cut across his stunned face.

"Why would you *do* such a thing?" His voice rolled at me like a ball of thunder. "Are you *crazy?*"

For as long as I can remember, there's been a place I go inside when there's no place to run. It's a place of absolute silence, and I don't so much run to it as it overtakes and swallows me. I could feel myself sinking, falling away.

Within seconds he had me inside, screaming at me, shaking me. I couldn't hear a word he was saying. I was weightless in a sea of silence.

Izetta was standing back by the refrigerator. She seemed to be glowing, an eerie halo all around her. I thought for an instant I saw a snake curling around her ankle, and I fainted.

When I awoke later in my room, it was dark, and only a slit of light edged the bottom of the closed door. The air was stifling. I felt feverish, my skin wet and itching with sweat. Up near the ceiling a fly droned. I lay on the bed, listening to Jack and Izetta moving about and knew they were cleaning the kitchen. Gradually, the house grew quiet. From the end of a long tunnel, I heard Izetta's voice. "Miss Alva said all right?"

He looked at me—really looked at me—for the first time that summer.

In a reverie, I saw my mother, Janelle. She was sitting on the edge of a silver crescent moon, swinging her legs back and forth. She looked right at me, cocked her head to one side, and smiled. "Love you," she crooned.

In the morning, the merciless sunlight that flooded the room woke me. Squinting against the brightness, my sleep-swollen eyes saw the difference immediately. My bedroom seemed bare, stripped like a hospital room in that small breathing space between patients. Then I saw my cardboard suitcase standing just outside the open door. A clean dress and underwear were waiting for me at the foot of the bed. Just as I sat up, Jack stuck his head in the doorway. "Get up and get dressed," he said.

"I didn't do it," I said, looking him dead in the eye.

He looked at me—really looked at me—for the first time that summer. Some fleeting, puzzled thing crossed his face. "I'm taking you to Mama's for a while." He glanced at his wrist watch and went down the hall to the kitchen.

Mama's. Miss Alva. I eased off the bed and got Trudy's red ribbon from behind the mirror, folded it, and stuck it in the toe of my tennis shoe.

When she was sure Jack was looking, Izetta tried to hug me.

The kitchen was spotless. Izetta had made a big stack of blueberry pancakes. I sat with my hands folded in my lap, sullen, deliberately studying her face. She didn't seem to mind. She just looked over at Jack, shook her head sadly, and sighed. Jack said I couldn't leave the table until I ate at least one pancake. I outlasted him; no food was going to get past the knot in my throat. That was about all he said except, "Come on," when he picked up my suitcase and headed for the front door. When she was sure Jack was looking, Izetta tried to hug me. I pulled away, but not before I felt the furious pounding of her heart.

Inside the car, Jack didn't look at me. He leaned back against the seat for a moment, staring out through the windshield, then sighed and put the key in the ignition. The motor roared, churning up lazy dust motes in the hot air. As the car backed down the driveway, I glanced toward the house. Izetta was standing in the doorway—smiling and waving.

Cicada
14–21 years
3,464 words

From the Author

The idea for "Black-Cherry Eyes" came out of my Southern background, which overflows with complex characters, events, and situations. There was no signal moment for its arrival; it just bubbled to the surface. Its theme—the emotional abandonment of children—is one that haunts me and one that young readers immediately understand and often identify with. The immediacy of first-person point of view was the purest way to convey the tension and vulnerability of Garnette's situation.

Television has made today's young readers visually oriented to an extraordinary degree. Keeping this in mind, I write what I "see" through my mental camera, frame by frame. If I can't see the action taking place, then I'm not moving the story forward.

I use dialogue to move the story forward and give the reader a breather from too much page density. A charismatic first-person voice can easily propel the reader through longer passages.

After I got the first draft on paper, "Black-Cherry Eyes" underwent a merciless second draft where entire paragraphs, interesting but irrelevant, hit the wastebasket. I then put the manuscript away to incubate for several weeks. When I took it up again, I read it aloud and marked sections to rewrite.

"Black-Cherry Eyes" went through several more polishing and tightening drafts, each two to three weeks apart. I never rush my work and I've learned not to rush sending it out.

Who Eats the Fish Head?
Tips on Table Manners in Hong Kong

By Gigi Orlowski

Nothing brings a group of people together like a good meal. The Chinese understand that better than just about anyone, and much thought goes into hosting their famed banquets. But a guest who is unfamiliar with Chinese culture may quickly realize there is more to table manners in Hong Kong than mastering the use of chopsticks.

For example, how do you know where to sit? Why is great care taken never to turn over a fish? What does it mean when a fish head points toward you? What do you never want to do with your chopsticks? And how do you know when a meal is over?

Most Chinese dining tables are round, and seating order is very important. Generally, the guest of honor sits opposite the entry door, so he or she faces the host. Other guests are then seated to the left and right of the head guest according to such factors as their age and rank. If in doubt, wait for the host to indicate your seat. Hosts generally sit closest to the door, where they can better instruct the serving staff.

Never start to eat any course until some gesture is made by the host. At a formal banquet, the host will often serve guests the first portions of food, assuming guests are too polite to help themselves.

The many courses are served, one at a time, from large common platters. Even if you are very hungry, it is polite to take small portions and pace your eating with the host and other guests. Don't worry about not having enough to eat. A single banquet often includes eight courses or more.

When a whole fish platter is placed on a table, the fish head will usually be pointed toward the guest of honor. That is because the fish head is considered the most nourishing part. The fish eyes and lips, especially, are regarded as delicacies. What should you do if you are the guest of honor and do not care to eat the fish head? Very generously offer this privilege to the next most important guest on your left. Another solution is to politely turn the platter around and allow the fish to face the host.

The top half of the fish is always eaten first. But when the bones are exposed, the fish must never be flipped over to eat the rest. It is considered very bad luck. According to superstition, it signifies that a fishing boat will capsize. Usually, the host or waiter will remove the bones, allowing guests to enjoy the fish with peace of mind, knowing no fishing family suffered grave misfortune.

It is also believed that bad luck will result if chopsticks are dropped or crossed. An uneven pair of chopsticks means you are likely to miss your plane, train, or boat. Worst of all, never poke your chopsticks upright in a bowl of rice. That conjures up images of incense sticks in an urn of ashes—an omen of death.

Traditionally, a banquet ends when the guest of honor rises from the table after everyone appears to have had enough of the final ceremonial tea or drinks. If a banquet is held at a restaurant, the waiter will stop refilling the teapot and place a bowl of fruit or flowers in the center of the table.

In Hong Kong, it is easy to impress Chinese friends with understanding and appreciation of their culture, and good manners at their table.

Faces
8–14 years
581 words

The Spin Doctor

By Jeff Piasky

Reuel Erickson wipes the sweat from his eyes as he glances up at the blistering Nevada sun. *Another scorcher,* he thinks, *but a great day for jumping.*

In a flash, the 18-year-old is off, pedaling down a steep dirt hill then up a six-foot dirt ramp. Reuel and his BMX bike leave the ground like an airplane taking flight.

With arms and legs outstreched, Reuel glides across the sky some 20 feet up. He grabs at air as his bike floats a few inches below.

In seconds, gravity clips his wings, sending him back to earth. Reuel reaches out for handlebars and pedals before touching down on another dirt ramp five feet from the original launch pad.

Emerging from a cloud of dust, Reuel skids to a stop, takes off his helmet and looks back on a jump well done.

Flying High

Reuel (roo-EL) is a dirt jumper, a bicycle moto-cross—BMX—rider who performs aerial stunts to the amazement of judges, audiences and, sometimes, even himself.

"It's a scary feeling when you go up in the air, like you're on a rollercoaster that's gotten loose," Reuel says with a grin. "It's always a thrill to make it to the other side."

Even though most BMX stunt riders are 22 to 25 years old, Reuel is considered one of the best dirt jumpers in the country. The Eagle Scout from Henderson, Nev., has continued to win national competitions against older, more experienced athletes.

"Reuel's a phenomenal talent," says Brian Gass of GT Bicycles, which made Reuel part of its factory BMX racing team in 1996. "He really thrills the crowds when he goes up—they just never know what he'll do next."

No Playing It Safe

With that high-altitude action comes danger—and pain.

Take his crash landing in November 1996 at the American Bicycling Association (ABA) Grandnationals in Oklahoma.

"I like to mix things up a bit—and go big."

Reuel had just scored high points on two 360-degree spin jumps. One more jump would win him his first "King of Dirt" championship.

But Reuel couldn't play it safe—that's not his style. Instead of making an easier jump that would have clinched the championship, he tried a double back-flip, a stunt never done on dirt.

"A lot of the other [dirt jumpers] are cautious," Reuel says. "I like to mix things up a bit—and go big."

This time, however, he went too big, over-rotating at the end of his second flip. Reuel's 40-pound bike landed on its back wheel instead of the front. Reuel, like a wounded bird, flew over the handlebars.

Slowly, he picked himself off the ground, brushed off the dirt and signaled to the judges with a smile. He had escaped with only bruises but couldn't finish the competition.

Reuel hasn't always been that lucky. Since he started dirt jumping in 1994, he has suffered a pinched nerve, dislocated shoulder, broken collar bone, broken ankle and two busted wrists.

"Whenever I get hurt in competition, I watch a

videotape of the jump," Reuel says. "Studying the tape makes me hungry to hit the jump correctly next time."

Jump Till You Drop

Being a great dirt jumper takes practice. Reuel gets plenty. That's because there's always a place for him to jump—at home, at dirt-racing tracks, even at a local lake.

A few miles from his house, Reuel has attached a small wooden ramp to the edge of a dock. With some serious pedaling and a little luck, he and his bike take off and *splash!* right into the water.

Jumping into the lake lets Reuel focus on the stunt and not the landing. "It's great because I can land anywhere I want," Reuel says.

At home, Reuel will sometimes spend hours twisting and turning on a trampoline (without the bike, of course) to see if his body can move in certain ways.

He also practices on a 10-foot-high ramp in the backyard. His parents built the wooden ramp as a way to keep Reuel and his seven brothers and sisters close to home. Kids from the neighborhood often come over to join in the fun. Some ride, but most just want to watch Reuel catch air.

Fast Track to Success

Dirt jumping is not all Reuel does with bikes. He designs them too.

When GT gave him his first bike in the spring of 1996, Reuel saw problems.

"It was all wrong," Reuel says. "The bike's design was too old and weak for dirt jumping."

Instead of complaining, he decided to fix it. With some help from a local bike shop mechanic, he lengthened the front end and shortened the back. Then he replaced the tubing and wheel bolts with strong materials. A super dirt-jumping bike was born.

GT officials let Reuel design his next bike. They were so impressed, they gave Reuel a job.

When Reuel wasn't riding for GT, he helped design and test their latest bikes. He's also been featured in television commercials for GT and the ABA.

His career took off in another way too. In late 1996, Reuel started performing his acrobatics at "air shows." These BMX demonstrations dazzle audiences at high schools and National Basketball Association games across the country.

"In the future, I'd like to design my own bikes and do stunt work for TV and movies," Reuel says.

"But for now, I'm happy just riding and competing."

One of Reuel's most difficult bicycle stunts is the back-flip. He practiced every day for months to master the upside-down move.

"A lot of the jump is setting up beforehand, both mentally and physically," Reuel says. "You need to find out how fast to go, when to pull up and how hard."

For the stunt, Reuel starts a dead sprint toward the ramp. As he approaches it, he crouches low on the bike to avoid wind resistance.

Then, as he clears the dirt ramp, Reuel pulls the bike backward with his arms. Leaning back his head, he arches his back and flips around as fast as he can.

"I try to keep my body as straight as possible," Reuel says. "If you're off a little bit, you'll miss the ramp."

As he rotates, Reuel looks for the ramp on the other side. To brace for the landing, he bends his knees to absorb the shock.

"It feels like you have no control," Reuel says. "But you still just hang on tight and finish the jump."

CAUTION: Reuel warns beginning riders not to just pick up a bike and start dirt jumping. Start with small jumps under the guidance of an experienced  adult rider, Reuel says.

"And of course, always wear a helmet and safety pads."

Boys' Life
7–18 years
1,110 words

From the Author

This was only my second try at a feature article after about a year as a copyeditor at *Boys' Life*. Since most of my experience was in writing college essays on literature, I initially resisted writing simple sentences with easy-to-understand words. Plus, I hadn't fully grasped how to paint a picture with words (showing, not telling).

In writing the piece, I thought about what kids would want to know, like exactly how Reuel does those incredible tricks on his bike. With the help of another editor and after two revisions, I showed my draft to my managing editor, who edited it more. The more people who look at your work, the better.

Shaking the Jitters

By Barbara Marquand

It had been twenty-five years since Sherry Snyder struggled through high school math classes, yet the same stomach-turning anxiety returned when she watched her college statistics professor write a problem on the chalkboard. She felt so anxious, she says, "I literally had to excuse myself from the room."

The statistics course was the only thing standing in her way of getting her doctoral degree, yet Snyder felt so insecure about her math ability, she wondered how she'd ever pass the mid-term and final exams.

Snyder, however, not only passed both semesters of statistics, she aced them. Now in her job that involves lending academic support to college students at the University of Colorado at Boulder, she works in none other than the math-intensive College of Engineering.

She succeeded in her bout with test anxiety, which can stem from a variety of sources and happen to some of the brightest people. It can vary from mild nervousness to a full-blown block about a subject or test-taking in general. But whatever its causes, test anxiety can be overcome.

"Test anxiety is something everyone faces at some time," says Norman Tognazzini, president of Energeia Publishing Inc., which publishes educational materials, including guides for developing good study habits and overcoming test anxiety. "It's a stressful situation when you come up against anything challenging that you're not familiar with."

Students vary widely in how they respond to exams. "Some are extremely relaxed and kicked back, and others, you can tell, are extremely uptight and worried," says Tognazzini, a former college teacher.

If you're among the jittery crowd at test-taking time, the first step to overcoming such a psychological roadblock is to figure out why. Do all tests make you nervous or just tests in certain subjects?

"It depends on what kind of test it is," says Katie Wood, a sophomore at Placer High School in Auburn, California. "Like a math test—no problem. I'm good at math."

Most test anxiety is related to study habits.

English vocabulary tests, though, are a different story. Though Wood says she doesn't get uptight about tests, she's more likely to get nervous about English exams than those in other subjects—especially if she's not prepared.

Does anxiety get the best of you when you're trying to pick your brain at exam time? Here are some tips to help you overcome anxiousness and experience test-taking success:

Study hard, and study smart. Most test anxiety is related to study habits, Snyder says. Sometimes students don't study enough, or they may spend a lot of time studying but don't focus on the right areas.

"They say, 'I studied a lot, but the material I studied didn't appear on the test,'" Snyder says. The key, then, is not just studying hard, but studying smart. Students have to learn to think like their teachers. What do instructors think is important? From where do they draw material for tests?

"Students should ask a lot of questions to make sure they know where their teacher is coming from," Tognazzini advises.

Some teachers may come right out and tell students what will be on the test. But others are more cagey, so students have to look for clues, such as in notes taken in class, textbooks, and assignments. And of course, the more time a teacher spends on a topic, the more likely that subject will appear on a test.

Knowing how the teacher operates is critical, according to Tognazzini. He recalls a college political science professor who included on tests everything he wrote on the blackboard during lectures.

"I aced his classes because I took copious notes," he recalls. "He just spelled it out for you."

If your teacher doesn't provide a practice test, prepare and complete your own. In addition, study with friends and quiz each other—but stick to the subject. "Study groups are good," Tognazzini says, "as long as you're studying and not socializing."

Sometimes, however, it's not just about studying. Though tuning up study skills usually can help curb test anxiety, the problem sometimes is rooted in an emotional issue. Snyder, for instance, worked with a student who otherwise was successful academically but had failed college anatomy three times. She went to Snyder for help after she enrolled in the same class for the fourth time.

Together they retraced when the student's difficulties with the class began, and the student realized it was related to traumatic memories of her mother dying the first time she took anatomy. Each time she took the course, it threatened to bring up those memories, so she blocked out the subject. With counseling and tutoring, the young woman was able to pass anatomy with a "C+."

If the course problem doesn't seem to lie in study skills, ask yourself when it surfaced and with what events it may be connected. Ask a counselor at school for assistance in identifying the problem.

While good study habits lay a firm foundation for excelling on exams, savvy test-taking strategies also can boost performance. Before beginning an exam, for instance, read over the entire test first whenever possible.

"Reading the whole exam will give you the gist of what it's all about," Tognazzini says. "If you don't know an answer to a question, it may appear somewhere else in the test, or something may jog your memory."

Pace yourself during a test. After you've read the exam, roughly estimate how much time you should spend on each part. If you have forty-five minutes to complete the test, and there are five essay ques-

tions worth twenty points apiece, for instance, don't spend thirty minutes on the first question. Establish a time limit for each one.

After you've completed the test, look over your answers and evaluate what you've written. You may catch something you overlooked or find spelling errors. Don't, however, second-guess yourself. Advises Tognazzini: "Your first answer is almost always the best answer because you're going on instinct."

And after a test is finished, let it go. Agonizing over an exam after the fact won't change your grade, and it might interfere with your performance if you have to take or study for other tests that day.

Finally, seek help if test anxiety continues. It's normal to be a little nervous about taking tests. But if anxiety is threatening your grades, talk to a teacher for help or contact a tutor. Snyder did both during her statistics course, and it paid off. She still felt nervous about the mid-term and final exams—even experiencing a nightmare in which she was a high school freshman again, taking an algebra test—but she was able to learn the material and conquer the anxiety.

"(In high school) I had a lot of fear about math and a lot of poor experiences with math," she says. "But I was able to work through it almost thirty years later."

You don't need to wait thirty years. Whether you want to shake mild nervousness during finals week

or tortuous anxiety about learning a subject, you can begin conquering classroom anxiety now.

Keynoter
14–18 years
1,178 words

From the Author

I like to brainstorm ideas with a particular publication in mind, concentrating on the audience for that magazine. For this piece, I tried to remember what concerned me in high school. I recalled some friends who would get so anxious about taking tests that they'd forget much of what they'd studied.

After I queried the editor and got the assignment, I contacted universities to find specialists who counsel students in study skills. I also found a student to interview through the local high school. This article was fairly easy to write because I found a compelling anecdote for the opening paragraph.

The Last Years of Good Queen Bess

By Gloria W. Lannom

E lizabeth loved to be loved by her subjects and she remained popular throughout most of her long reign of 44 years and 127 days. On November 30, 1601, in the "Golden Speech," her last appearance in the House of Commons, she expressed her great joy at being their queen.

Just days earlier, on November 17, festivities celebrating Accession Day had featured prayers, bonfires, fireworks, and feasting. The purpose of this annual crowd-pleasing holiday was to replace the Catholic veneration of the Virgin Mary with the cult of Gloriana that praised the Protestant Elizabeth I and her rule over England.

An expert at public relations, the Queen made herself accessible during summer travels throughout her realm. These trips, called "progresses," allowed people to see their sovereign in person riding majestically on horseback with her attendants and assistants. She made spur-of-the-moment speeches, thanking the crowds for their loyalty and good-humoredly accepting even the simplest praise. Lasting a month or two, these excursions also served her politically and saved

Extra quantities of candles were also required because the queen often stayed up late.

the frugal monarch money as her hosts now paid many of her living expenses. "Progresses," however, were a terrible strain on the attendants making the travel arrangements, especially since Elizabeth's massive carved and gilded Great Bed of Ware always went along. In addition, they placed enormous pressure on those entertaining her.

Some of England's great country estates were built because the nobles and gentry were obliged to offer Elizabeth splendid accommodations. On occasion, prospective hosts viewed the announcement of a royal visit as a threat rather than a privilege. It was very expensive to provide the food she and her attendants favored (such as swans, pigs, geese, deer, wild birds, crayfish, herring, and oysters), the drink (measured in 54-gallon hogsheads), the entertainment (plays, acrobats, and fireworks), and the gifts of jewelry and textiles. Extra quantities of candles were also required because the queen often stayed up late.

Her favorite fruits were apricots and cherries.

In public, the queen dressed in elaborate multilayered clothing. Precious gems sparkled on her robes, neck, hair, and hands. In private, she usually dressed far more simply. In her youth, she favored yellow, ginger, orange, and russet, all tones that complemented her white skin and red hair. In her sixties, however, she preferred to clothe her still youthful figure in black, white, and silver, with gold trimmings. After her own hair faded, the Queen wore startling red wigs of "a shade that nature never made," one contemporary noted.

She used musk and rose-water scents, and employed beauty creams and oils lavishly. She concealed her many wrinkles under heavy white makeup. Bright rouge colored her cheeks.

To help mask offensive plumbing odors unwelcome to the royal nose, attendants liberally sprinkled rose water wherever she was to be. Her fondness for flowers was well-known. In winter, artificial flowers replaced fresh blooms indoors.

Her favorite fruits were apricots and cherries, but she also enjoyed a lifelong love of sweets that caused her remaining teeth to turn black with decay. To the end, the queen remained a woman of great determination, energy, intelligence, and incredible memory. On the negative side, however, she was prone to jealousy and temper tantrums. In 1593, when the French ambassador witnessed Her Majesty in a terrible rage, he said he wished he were in Calcutta, India!

A stubborn woman, she refused to go to bed and instead sat listlessly on cushions, with one finger in her mouth, refusing to eat.

Elizabeth I enjoyed playing and listening to the virginal (a type of harpsichord) and lute music. She liked to "dance high in the Italian style" and once in old age, she was glimpsed dancing vigorously by herself to music called the "Spanish Panic."

Eventually, she began showing her age. In January of 1603, after moving from her palace at Whitehall to Richmond Palace, she became ill. Elizabeth had always distrusted her doctors, and now, contrary as ever, she would not take the medicines they prescribed. A stubborn woman, she refused to go to bed and instead sat listlessly on cushions, with one finger in her mouth, refusing to eat.

Finally, she agreed to go to bed and, on the evening of March 23, John Whitgift, the Archbishop of Canterbury, prayed at her bedside for hours. When he turned to leave, she indicated, in a final display of strong will, that he must continue praying.

Hours later, Elizabeth I died in her sleep. Across the land went the report: "This morning about three o'clock hir Majestie departed this lyfe, mildly like a lambe, easily like a ripe apple from the tree . . . ."

Calliope
8–14 years
730 words

From the Author

My interest in writing began in the fourth grade. I bought a small, lined notebook and wrote poems in it. It disappeared somewhere along the way, but my recollection of the poetry is that it wasn't very good. Its value lay in *practice,* the practice of writing. You can't do much of anything right off, especially in the field of writing. You need practice.

Right now I'm writing a lot of nonfiction for young readers and adults, but I also write fiction and, yes, some poetry. My educational and life experiences involve art history. I like foreign topics because I lived outside of the United States for many years.

I had just returned from London, where I visited the Tower of London and took a boat ride on the Thames River, when I noted that *Calliope* planned an issue on Queen Elizabeth. I write only about what I find interesting, and this sounded intriguing.

At the library I looked up information on the subject and began taking notes. (I take research very seriously and make a major effort to read the latest publications on a given subject.) When I felt that I had a grip on the subject, I wrote a proposal to the editor.

In this case, the editor assigned something different from my original proposal, which was to write about portraits of the Queen. I liked my new assignment on the Queen's last years better.

The structure of the article was easy because the subject of her last years lent itself to a chronological format. The Queen looks solemn and stiffly historical in her portraits, but the facts I selected show how human and lively she was, even toward the end of her life. She loved make-up, jewelry, dancing, parties, traveling around the country while others paid her expenses, and generally getting her own way.

Before I begin an article, I make a simple outline (based on my notes) to decide what's important. Then I start writing. Usually everything comes together in my first draft. Thanks to my word processor, I do not dread revisions. For me, rewriting is fun. I do five or six drafts before I'm satisfied with my work. My biggest problem is length: I want to tell the reader everything I know about a subject! That makes the article too long, and it can wander away from the main points.

Writing brings me great pleasure. It feels good to complete an article and later to see it in print.

Shoplifting Nearly Trashed My Life

By Candice Gwiaz, as told to Lisa Liebman

I had it all when I was growing up in sunny Carlsbad, California: a loving family, a great house with a white picket fence, three cars in the driveway, and a garden so gorgeous strangers would stop to snap pictures. My parents gave me just about anything I wanted. But somehow this wasn't enough. I felt an emptiness inside and, at 12, I found a way to fill it—with the thrill of shoplifting.

I was terrified of getting busted, but I also got off on this amazing adrenaline rush.

It started when a friend's older sister bragged about her stealing habit. She snatched cheap things, like candy, from the local newsstand and had even ripped off a hamster from a pet store by stuffing it in her pocket and walking out! A week later, when I was at Woolworth's with my dad, I decided to steal something to see how it felt. I crept into the drugstore area alone, saw a $1.50 bottle of Binaca breath spray, and jammed it into my jacket pocket.

I was terrified of getting busted, but I also got off on this amazing adrenaline rush. Once we were out of the store and I knew I'd gotten away with it, I was flying high. I felt like I could nab whatever I wanted, whenever I wanted it.

The next day at school, I spilled what I'd done to my friends. They thought it was cool, and they were itching to try it. A week or two later, several of us went to the mall to score jewelry and make-up. We were too pumped to worry about getting caught.

Inside the first store, one of my friends stood guard by a rack of headbands while another girl loaded her backpack with necklaces and keychains. Then we were on a roll, cruising from store to store and shoplifting in each one. I took lipstick, lipliner, and some candy. Finally, in an accessories store, my friend Debbie* tucked an anklet into her bag, and a saleswoman grabbed her arm.

"What are you doing?" she yelled. Everyone but me blew out of the store—Debbie was such a good friend that I couldn't leave her.

A salesclerk from another store spotted the rest of our friends dumping their loot into the mall's potted plants and called security. The mall cops dragged everyone back to the shop where Debbie and I were.

Getting Hooked

My friends cried hysterically as two security men searched their bags. Somehow, I kept cool—I'd hidden my stuff in my back pocket—but inside, I was feeling really guilty. After a saleswoman called our parents, the store manager told us we were lucky: This was one of the few stores that didn't prosecute shoplifters.

But I sure didn't feel lucky once my mom showed up. When I saw the anguish on her face, I

We hid clothes in the shopping bags we'd brought along.

wanted to die. "I didn't take anything," I lied over and over. She was desperate to believe me, so once the saleswoman told her that I hadn't run away like

Teen Nonfiction

my friends, she assumed I was telling the truth. I was the only one who got off scot-free that day. My dad was surprised when he heard what happened, but my parents trusted me.

Shaken up, I stopped stealing for a couple of months, until my friend Mel came to school in a great outfit she'd lifted from a department store. I'd never thought of taking clothes, but I was dying to try it. I asked my friend Amanda to hit that same department store with me. We hid clothes in the shopping bags we'd brought along, and then innocently browsed the store. A huge part of the thrill was fooling the salesclerks. Nobody suspected a thing because I looked like a nice kid.

Pretty soon, shoplifting grew into a major craving. The more I took, the more I wanted. I nabbed clothes, CDs, makeup—anything to satisfy that hunger. My folks didn't say a word about the things that accumulated in my room, so I began to steal even more.

When they finally started asking where I'd gotten everything, I lied and said I'd borrowed the stuff I'd stolen or that I'd hit a sale. Since I was getting good grades, singing in the school choir, and playing on the volleyball team, they had no reason not to believe me.

Reality Bites

I was 13 years old when I hit my favorite sporting goods store with my friend Penny. She wasn't into stealing, but I took some bikinis and a pair of board shorts and slipped them on under my clothes. After we walked out of the store, two clerks suddenly jumped into our path. "You took some clothes from our store, and we need you to come with us," the guy said. My eyes welled with tears as they took us into the store manager's office.

The clerks said that they were going to call the police, who would call my parents. They told me to remove what I had stolen. I swore I'd never steal again, and I begged them not to call, but they didn't listen. After all, I'd swiped $332 worth of clothes.

When the police arrived, I knew this was for real.

When the police arrived, I knew this was for real. No more getting away with lies and innocent smiles. They charged me under section 490.5 of the California Civil Shoplifting Law, then let Penny go 'cause she hadn't taken anything. They left me alone in the office to wait for my parents. It was the longest hour ever. As I pictured my parents' heartsick faces, I bawled like crazy. My mind started racing about how the charge could ruin my life. How would I get into college if I had to admit to being a criminal on the applications? How would I get a job? Suddenly, a habit that had made me feel sky-high had slammed me into the worst low of my life.

The intense anger on my dad's face when he picked me up is forever etched on my mind. He didn't say a word to me on the drive home. I went straight to my room and cried all night.

This time, my parents were harsh. They grounded me for weeks—including spring break—and checked out my friends, deciding whom I could and couldn't hang with. I had to bring one of my parents along when I shopped, because they didn't trust me alone. I apologized again and again, but it took months for me to admit the times I'd stolen without getting caught. Every time I saw their disappointed faces, I just wanted to vanish.

I'm 16 now, and I feel like I'll never stop paying for those quick thrills.

I pled guilty to shoplifting and was fined over $500 in merchandise and courts costs, $200 of which I paid myself. The court made me go to rehab class with other criminal kids, where we discussed why what we did was wrong.

I also had to perform 50 hours of community service, so I spent my summer break at the local Boys' and Girls' Club, cleaning bathrooms and floors. That was a drag, but the worst part was being told that, because I was a criminal, I couldn't talk to the kids running around the club. I felt humiliated.

I was so relieved when my probation officers said that my criminal record would be sealed when I turn 18, as long as I stay clean till then. But that didn't ease my shame. I'm 16 now, and I feel like I'll never stop paying for those quick thrills.

Why would a kid like me start stealing? I think I did it for attention. I felt that my parents favored my sister, Jenny, who is three years older. While I was the outgoing kid, she was the sweet one who got great grades. Once she started thinking about college, my parents seemed to stop noticing me.

My way out-of-control habits could've ruined my prospects for college, jobs—a happy life. Yeah, my criminal record may fade, but nothing can make me forget what I've done to the people I love. My parents now let me shop solo, but they may never trust me like they did only a few years ago—before they knew my secret. Even though I'm constantly trying to prove how responsible I am, I don't know if I'll ever really win back my mom and dad's respect and faith in me. I wanted their attention—I got it all right.

*All friends' names have been changed to protect their privacy.

YM
14–24 years
1,391 words

From the Author

As a magazine editor, I've worked for publications as diverse as *YM, Marie Claire, Psychology Today, New Woman,* and *American Homestyle and Gardening.* My background also includes a stint as a freelance writer of entertainment, style, and trend stories for the *New York Times, Glamour, Mademoiselle,* and *Self,* among others.

I became aware of Candice's story as executive editor of *YM,* when we received her entry in the magazine's yearly first-person story contest. Her writing wasn't publishable, but we felt her story was compelling. Though her parents were leery, she agreed to be interviewed for a piece written by me. The interviews—and there were several, because I had to pull the information out of her—were conducted on the telephone. I sat at a computer keyboard taking copious notes while we talked.

Because there is somewhat of a formula to *YM's* first-person pieces, and I had edited many of them in the past, I didn't use an outline. After the article was published, *Dateline* (the NBC-TV newsmagazine) contacted me; they were interested in doing a piece about teen shoplifting and using Candice in their story. I put them in touch with *YM.*

Spinning Out of Control

By Susan Smart

It was a beautiful Saturday morning, and I couldn't wait to get up in the air.

I'd always wanted to fly. And now, just a few months after graduating from high school, my dream was coming true. I was taking flying lessons, and this particular day looked especially promising.

I was looking at the plane I'd be flying, a Cessna-150, when someone called my name.

"Hi, Sue," said Jim, my flight instructor. "Ready for your third solo flight?"

"Yeah, I think so," I said, hesitating. Flying without Jim still felt weird, but as a student pilot, sooner or later I had to let go of my insecurity.

"Now remember," Jim said, "I want you to work on your stalls today. And don't be afraid to really stall the bird, Sue. You tend to recover too early, but I want to see you practice those stalls more thoroughly."

Jim was right: Stalls were not my best maneuver. They left me feeling shaky, so I tended to recover much sooner than necessary.

Learning stalls is a critical part of any flight training plan. A stall happens when the plane's air speed drops too low to keep flying. Stalls are an important part of every safe landing. Pilots routinely practice their stalls at 5,000 feet or higher, where there is plenty of room to recover safely.

A few minutes later, I was airborne, and asking God for his protection.

Even though this was only my third solo, Jim's quiet confidence in my ability encouraged me. Still, I missed his reassurance from the other seat.

I was on my own.

At 5,000 feet, high above a small farming community, I looked down at the beautiful view. Taking several deep breaths to relax, I remembered Jim's words of instruction before practicing my stalls.

OK, I thought, *it's time to work.*

I started with a take-off stall, slowly but steadily pulling the nose back, keeping an eye on the airspeed: 65 knots...60...55...53... The warning buzzer began to squeal, so I quickly recovered, dipping the nose down while carefully easing back on the throttle.

You pulled out too quickly, I thought.

I remembered Jim's advice to "really stall the bird." So I set up for another one. *Jim,* I thought, *I'm really going to stall it this time.*

With my left hand, I pulled back on the stick, propelling the plane upward. My right hand grasped the throttle, gradually reducing the engine's power.

"Everything's under control," I told myself.

As the air speed began to drop, the stall-warning buzzer went off as usual, its whine filling the tiny cockpit. Normally, I would recover at the earliest annoying sound of that buzzer, my skittish emotions compelling me to jump the gun. But not this time. No, I decided to let that buzzer screech as loudly as I could stand before pulling out of the stall.

I waited too long.

A slight, dropping lurch from the propeller was my only warning.

A slight, dropping lurch from the propeller was my only warning. Almost instantly, the left wing dipped, then tipped over, pitching the Cessna into a wing-over-wing spin.

Jerking my head around, I glanced out my side window. Instead of seeing the horizon, I gaped in horror at the ground. As the altimeter quickened its pace, unwinding at an alarming rate, headlines raced through my mind: "Student Pilot Killed in Spin."

Precious seconds grew incredibly long as I desperately tried to regain control over the little airplane. My frantic efforts only plunged it—and me—into an ever-tightening death spiral.

As I yanked and fought against the inevitable pull of gravity, words of wisdom somehow popped into my brain.

I covered my face, bracing for impact.

A few weeks back, Jim had said, "If you ever get into a spin in a Cessna-150, just let go of the controls. It's built to fly on its own."

Jim's words now reached into my confused thoughts, much like a life preserver thrown out to a drowning child. But could I trust them?

"Let go!" I screamed three or four times. My hands seemed glued to the controls. I was unable to pry my fingers off.

Pulling hard one last time, I threw my arms up in the air, releasing my stranglehold on the yoke. I covered my face, bracing for impact.

Yawing and pitching wildly to the right, then to the left, the Cessna made grotesquely odd noises, something like the droning of a lawn mower that suddenly stops and then roars to life again. Then shaking, shuddering gyrations gradually stilled. Amazingly, the airplane slowly but faithfully returned to straight-and-level flight. My eyes scanned the instrument panel, resting on the altimeter: 2,100 feet above sea level.

I had fallen more than half a mile.

Jim was sitting at the front desk when I got back. I told him what had happened. And I told him I never wanted to fly again.

His blue eyes twinkling, Jim peered out the window toward the Cessna, now safely tied down.

"The plane looks fine to me, and you do too," he said, smiling. "You obviously remembered my advice. It worked, didn't it?"

Trust in the Lord with all your heart and lean not on your own understanding; in all your ways acknowledge him, and he will make your paths straight.
—Proverbs 3:5-6

I learned an important lesson that day:

When I find myself in situations seemingly spinning out of control, God reminds me to let go of the controls of my life and trust him.

He'll always return me to a straight-and-level course.

That's a promise . . . from on high.

Campus Life
13–19 years
921 words

From the Author

I'm a fairly new writer, and have been writing nonfiction articles for about four years. To date, I've sold about 12 articles. I work in the clerical department in a suburban police department (lots of good ideas pop up in a police department!). My husband and I are currently co-authoring our first novel. We hope to have it completed by the end of the year and are looking for a publisher.

"Spinning Out of Control" is a true story I originally wrote for *Virtue*, a Christian women's magazine. My story appeared in their "One Woman's Journal" column, which showcases first-person, real-life dramas. In that publication, the piece was titled "Finding Safety in a Spin."

Over the years, I recounted the tale of my brush with death to friends and acquaintances (biographers sometimes call this a "set piece"), so I decided it was time to put it down on paper. I conducted a small bit of research for the article, such as looking up the stall speed for the Cessna 150, as well as consulting my pilot's log book to check the written record of that flight.

I decided to query *Campus Life* about my spin story several years after it appeared in *Virtue*. I believed the message could cross over to the teen market, particularly since I was only 19 years old when I was a student pilot. I was familiar with *Campus Life*, having read it on and off over the years. They had a "hip" new appearance, and I thought my article might fit in with the kind of reader they now courted. Within a few weeks of my query, *Campus Life* contacted me, and we negotiated the sale. They made some revisions, but the majority of the article remained the same.

Empress of the Blues

By Lisa Vihos

essie Smith was born in Chattanooga, Tennessee, in 1894 into a very poor family. Both her parents died before she turned 8. Raised by their oldest sister, Bessie and her siblings lived in a tough section of Chattanooga called Tannery Flats. If anyone ever deserved to sing the blues, it was Bessie Smith.

At age 9 Bessie often sang popular tunes on Chattanooga street corners for spare change, but she hadn't yet started singing the blues because,

Bessie had a tough, edgy voice.

like most people, she hadn't heard of it yet. The blues originated in the South around the year 1900, growing out of field hollers, work songs, spirituals, and guitar ballads. Black musicians traveled the countryside and played the gritty, sad-sounding music to earn a living.

In 1912, Bessie's brother Clarence got her an audition with a traveling vaudeville show, a form of theater that included comedy skits, singing, and dancing. Bessie joined the show primarily as a dancer. Soon, the troupe's star singer, Gertrude "Ma" Rainey, befriended Bessie. Ma had heard blues music in her travels, and she began to perform it in her vaudeville act. People often call her the Mother of the Blues because she took this form of music off the backroads and brought it to a wider audience.

With Ma as her inspiration, Bessie began to sing the blues. A natural singer, Bessie had a tough, edgy voice and could stretch out her notes in a wistful way that added to the sad meaning of the lyrics.

Most blues songs describe love's misfortunes, or losing all your friends or possessions. "When it rains five days and the skies turn dark as night, then troubles takin' place in the lowlands at night," Bessie sang in a song called "Backwater Blues." "I can't move no more, there ain't no place for a poor old girl to go." Bessie had plenty to sing about (poverty, losing her parents and her first husband, who died soon after they were married) and she could sing from the heart.

Blues music was popular among Blacks in the South. Northern audiences, both Black and White, were finally introduced to the blues when record companies realized that music like Bessie's would sell if recorded. Although she sang and gathered a following in the South for quite some time, Bessie did not make her first record until 1923.

Her second husband, Jack Gee, pawned his night watchman's uniform and a pocket watch to buy Bessie a dress for her recording session at Columbia. This became a joke between them later, when her record sold 780,000 copies in the first six months and Bessie bought Jack expensive suits.

She'd lived a life of both poverty and glamour, good times and bad times.

By 1924, Bessie had become the highest-paid Black entertainer of her day, earning the title "Empress of the Blues." She toured with her own show, and even bought her own railroad car to carry her troupe around in style.

In 1929, however, her record sales fell and "talkies," movies with sound, replaced vaudeville as a form of entertainment. The country also plunged into the Great Depression, when everyone fell into hard financial times. Columbia dropped Bessie from their label in 1931. For six years she was out of the spotlight. But then in 1937, at the age of 43, she staged a comeback. We'll never know what the next chapter of her life would have been, because she died in a car crash in September of that year. About 10,000 mourners paid their last respects at her funeral in Philadelphia. She'd lived a life of both poverty and glamour, good times and bad times. For us, her music lives on as a reminder of this remarkable woman.

> It's a long old road, but I'm gonna find the end.
> It's a long old road, but I'm gonna find the end.
> And when I get back,
> I'm gonna shake hands with a friend.
> —Bessie Smith

New Moon
8–14 years
631 words

From the Author

In a period of three years, I wrote six short features on famous women for *New Moon*. Some of the pieces were assigned to me, and some I pitched. The editor asked me to write "Empress of the Blues" for the "Music and Entertainment" issue.

I went to my local library and took out the two books they had. One was a short biography with pictures and lyrics to many of Bessie Smith's songs. The other was a longer biography. To help me understand more about the context in which the blues developed, I read portions of a book I happened to own. (*Deep Blues* by Robert Palmer describes the musical and cultural history of the Mississippi Delta.) Most important, I listened to Bessie Smith's recordings. These were a great help to me in understanding and describing her special affinity for singing the blues.

Because the article was basically a short biography, it was very easy to structure. For all my *New Moon* articles, I always tried to begin with details of the woman's childhood that young readers would find interesting. In the case of Bessie Smith, I also had the advantage of being able to include the lyrics to some of her songs to help tell the story of her life.

I feel very fortunate that I got my start writing for children in *New Moon*. Besides the adult editors on staff, the magazine also has a girls' editorial board that makes many significant decisions about what should be included in each issue. The girls give thoughtful feedback on first drafts and ask pertinent questions that always help sharpen the second drafts.

My background is in art history and I've worked as a museum educator for 15 years. During this time, I've written extensively about art for both children and adults. Besides my "non-museum" writing for *New Moon* and several book reviews of art-related books for *Children's Book Review Magazine,* I've recently contributed to a teacher's edition of an art textbook. I continue to write about art in my current position as Manager of Educational Resources at the J. Paul Getty Museum.

The Annual Garage Sale

How to Turn a Fundraising Mainstay into a Truly Fab Source of Funds!

By William F. Stier, Jr., Ed.D.

It's easy to buy into the garage sale fundraiser. What squad wouldn't be sold on benefits like the potential to generate between $2,500 and $4,000 each year with only a moderate amount of work and minimum risk? Other major selling points: The event is simple to plan and implement and can be used year after year to generate the big bucks.

This fundraiser's essential elements revolve around four factors:

1. Securing donated items (both new and used) and services to be sold at a deep discount (50 to 75% of their actual value).

2. Selecting an appropriate venue for the event—forget your parents' garage.

3. Picking a suitable date.

4. Publicizing and promoting the project to the general public.

Donation Do's and Don'ts

When it comes to rounding up donations, get your hands on anything and everything of value. Used furniture, lawn and garden equipment, toys, old records, sports equipment and supplies, clean clothing, baby items, kitchenware, seasonal merchandise, jewelry and small appliances are all possibilities with great resale potential.

Widen your donor pool. Don't limit yourself to asking only friends and supporters for items and services. Try getting donations from a variety of sources, especially local businesses. Owners and managers are often only too happy to donate items and/or services for a worthy, not-for-profit cause such as your cheerleading group. Be sure to hit your local drug stores, gas stations, car washes, movie theaters, restaurants, clothing stores, specialty shops and hardware stores. You might even want to approach local hotels about donating a weekend excursion package. Virtually every type of business can be approached to donate something.

It's crucial to have ample parking space.

For best results, plan ahead. Since it's wise to solicit and collect items for the sale all year long, your group will need a place to store everything until the day of the event. Consider having volunteers move the items from the storage place to the sale site several days before the event so that you have ample time to set up.

Siting for Success

Location is probably the prime element for your event's success. The sale site needs to be where there is heavy drive-by traffic. People should be able to see the merchandise and promotional signs from the roadway as they drive by.

When selecting a site, keep in mind that it's crucial to have ample parking space. The last thing you want is for potential buyers to be driven away in frustration because they can't park or fear being trapped in a traffic jam! Some sites to scout include schools, the parking lot of a local civic organization or a mini shopping mall.

Make a Date

The event itself can be held on a Friday afternoon, all day Saturday and again Sunday afternoon. While you can hold it at any time of the year, many groups opt for summer months. Right after loading up on "spring cleaning" donations, summer's good-weather days are ideal for leisurely garage sale shopping.

Keep three important points in mind when selecting a suitable date:

1. Schedule the event when the weather is likely to be favorable and reserve a rain date in case Mother Nature refuses to cooperate.

2. Pick a date when people aren't working, but are still in town. Most weekends are fine, but avoid holidays like the Fourth of July when your sales profits are likely to be less than explosive.

3. To avoid attendance competition, don't hold your fundraising sale at the same time as another major local event.

Create a Buzz Blitz

When it comes to promotions and publicity, go for it! Word-of-mouth is still a fantastic way of publicizing your event. Start creating positive hype for the event as early as possible through pre-event publicity and promotional activities—radio public service announcements, local newspaper coverage, an ad (donated, if possible) in local papers or penny-savers and announcements at prior community events. Then, on the actual day of the event, make lots of eye-catching posters and signs to attract the attention of passersby; also place them throughout the community, especially at popular business sites. Just don't stand in the middle of whizzing traffic—you want to raise funds and awareness, not increase talk about how you've upped the accident stats!

Final Pointers

Remember, this is not a junk yard sale. Sell only items that are clean and in good condition.

Generate extra profits by featuring concession stands of donated soft drinks, candy, cookies and hot dogs. Be sure to have sufficient cash on hand for ready change. Accept checks (with proper identification, of course).

Piggyback other fundraising projects with the sale. For example, offer to wash the customers' cars for a reasonable $2 to $3 and/or hold a raffle.

Always have adult supervisors present during the sale hours.

Store any unsold items until the following year; donate unwanted or excess items to local charitable organizations.

Realize that this fundraising project can easily become an annual event so you'll need the cooperation of those who helped this year in the future. It's a good idea to write thank-you notes to those who donated sale items and to other contributors, such as store owners, who allowed you to post signs.

Be sure to clean up the site where the sale was held to prove to your "landlord" that your group's a trustworthy renewal bet.

American Cheerleader
13–18 years
884 words

From the Author

I've written over 200 articles and 10 books, three on fundraising (an outgrowth of my 20 years experience in that field). I wrote "The Annual Garage Sale" at the request of *American Cheerleader*.

I write fundraising articles for different publications, so I created a template (a general outline of topics to cover) to use whenever I write an individual fundraising article such as this one. Armed with the template, all I have to do is provide distinctive factors for each particular fundraising strategy.

I always keep my intended audience in mind. The readers of *American Cheerleader* are different from readers of a scholarly book on the art and science of fundraising. My greatest challenge is in writing for a specific audience.

I find that revisions are almost always necessary, at least for me. Frequently, an editor will make small or large revisions; other times the manuscript is returned to me with a request to alter it to meet the publication's specifications and standards. Thank goodness I've been blessed with excellent editors. They make the task much, much easier.

Hostage to Her Habits

As told to Sandy Fertman

One out of 50 Americans suffers from a form of mental illness called obsessive-compulsive disorder (OCD). They may appear normal, but their minds are constantly invaded by disturbing fears that something bad is about to happen. To get rid of the anxiety caused by these obsessions, they develop compulsions—repetitive rituals used almost superstitiously to ward off the perceived harm. For example, a person with OCD may be afraid she'll pick up deadly germs just from touching a doorknob, so she'll wash her hands for 30 minutes afterward. While we all obsess over certain things, for people with OCD, compulsive behaviors consume hours each day, cutting into sleep and social time, eventually taking over their lives.

It started when I was six with that rhyme, "Step on a crack, break your mother's back."

Some experts believe OCD, which typically shows up between the ages of nine and 11, is caused by an imbalance of chemicals in the brain and is probably triggered by stress. "OCD is a genetic disorder," says Courtney Jacobs, Ph.D., a psychologist specializing in anxiety disorders at the University of California at Los Angeles. "Typically, you'll find someone else in the family who has it, like an aunt who hoarded things or a grandfather who constantly had to check the lights." The most effective treatment to date is a combination of drugs (often antidepressants like Prozac) and behavior therapy that teaches patients to confront their fears without resorting to their rituals. It's a painful, scary process. But, for people who've been trapped in an obsessive-compulsive mind, this is the key to freedom. Here is one girl's account.

I'd stay up late at night organizing my closet and jewelry box.

It started when I was six with that rhyme, "Step on a crack, break your mother's back." Not only did I believe it was true, but if I stepped on a crack or a bump in the pavement with one foot, I'd have to run back and touch it with my other foot. If I didn't, I was certain someone in my family would be hurt or even die.

When I was about eight, my fear of something terrible happening to the ones I loved came out in other ways. I began needing to balance out my body at all times. For example, if I touched my left leg, I had to touch my right leg. Or if I held something cold in one hand, I had to have something cold in the other hand. It even went so far that I would actually hurt myself to be balanced. In other words, if I ran past a branch that scratched me, I'd have to go back and scratch my other side. If I burned my right hand on the stove, I'd have to touch it with my left hand. I noticed people on TV didn't do these things, so I knew something was wrong with me. But I didn't know what.

By 10, I began having a problem with making certain my *things* were balanced and symmetrical or, again, someone would get hurt. All the clothes in my closet had to be hung on specific types of hangers, all the skirts together, pants together and shirts together, all facing one direction. Each group of clothes was organized by length, so everything hung in a very straight line, in perfect order.

My jewelry box also had to be just so—rings in one place, earrings in another, all facing the same way, colors in a certain order, never out of alignment. A silver ring had to be in this place and a gold ring in that place or it would drive me nuts. I'd stay up late at night organizing my closet and jewelry box, using a flashlight in the dark so my parents wouldn't know what I was doing. If I had extra time in the morning, I'd organize some more. It wasn't like I had a choice. If I didn't find the time, someone would get hurt.

I was about 13 when I began to have this need to remember every single number I saw.

My life became very unmanageable. Instead of doing my homework or sleeping, I felt compelled to count and recount, organize and reorganize. It was like there was an intruder in my mind. My head hurt all the time from thinking so much, and I constantly had this feeling of impending doom. I was always drained and exhausted. Often I'd stay up hours past my bedtime trying to make things just right with my homework. If there were just one little detail out of place, I had to do it all over again.

Checking the lights was another thing I began doing at about age 10. My routine was that I'd leave the room and then I'd think, Wait a second. Did I turn the light off? And I'd go back to check it. I was terrified that if I didn't, robbers or kidnappers would come into the house and hurt us. After checking the fifth time, I had a ritual of hitting the light extremely hard so I'd know it was off. I tried to stop at five because I didn't want anyone to know what I was doing. Most times, though, I'd recheck the lights at least 15 times.

I tried to hide my problem mostly because I was scared people would think I was nuts. I was also too embarrassed to tell anyone. The worst thing was not telling my mom. We were very close, and aside from worrying about her thinking I was crazy, I thought telling her about my problems would cause her harm or death.

When I was 12, I found a copy of *Good Housekeeping* which had an article about "the boy who had to touch the doorknob 250 times." After reading it, I thought, This is my story! The article explained what obsessive-compulsive disorder was and how to treat it. I was incredibly happy. I thought, Oh my God! There's a name for this! I still was afraid to tell my parents, but I decided to do what I could on my own, thinking maybe I could fix my problem so no one would ever have to know about it.

One thing the article stated was that OCD is the bad guy and you have to tell the bad guy "no." After that, whenever I had a compulsion, I'd say, "No, I'm not going to do this!" Some of my behaviors did disappear, but new and worse ones took their place.

I was about 13 when I began to have this need to remember every single number I saw. I must have had thousands of phone numbers and addresses stored in my head. Math homework turned into an absolute nightmare, taking hours every night. I'd tell my parents I was done in what seemed like a normal amount of time. Then, later, I'd go back and work on it another hour or so in secret.

It got more and more extreme. I had to memorize anything with a list of numbers—billboards, signs, license plates. To help me, I started adding them in strange combinations. First I'd add them until I got to a single digit, like 2916 is $2 + 9 + 1 + 6$, which is 18, and $1 + 8 = 9$. Next, I started grouping numbers—like I had to group them into 10s; then I started grouping them into nines . . . . For some reason, it was logical to me.

The worst was the license plates. I had to remember every plate I saw. If I missed one, I felt like it was the end of the world. That started when I heard stories on the radio about kidnappings and

I was 16 when everything reached the breaking point—if I didn't do something fast, I knew I'd fall apart.

how you should always memorize license plates. It got so bad that when my mom drove me home from private school on the weekends, I had to immediately fall asleep in the back seat because it became physically painful for me to see all the license plates. I'd tell her I was just really tired from the week, but it was so depressing to have to force myself to do that. I wanted to get my driver's license, but I was terrified that I wouldn't be able to concentrate on the road.

I was 16 when everything reached the breaking point—if I didn't do something fast, I knew I'd fall apart. That's when I got up the nerve to sit my par-

---

I hated telling people I'd never met what was going on inside my head.

---

ents down and tell them about the *Good Housekeeping* article. Once I started talking, I didn't stop. They were in complete and utter shock, and we all ended up crying. They kept asking, "How come we didn't see this? What did we do wrong?!" and I felt like I disappointed them tremendously. But they were incredibly loving and supportive.

Since they weren't sure what to do, they called our pediatrician, who sent me to some psychiatrists. That was awful. I hated telling people I'd never met what was going on inside my head. I hated talking to a shrink who just sat there with a little notepad. I didn't want to be there. It made me feel worse about myself. After going to three or four, I wasn't any better.

I can actually drive now, and I don't even look at license plates anymore.

Luckily, my parents happened to see a *20/20* story on television that was about OCD, and they called the doctor from the show for help. He referred us to Courtney Jacobs, a psychologist in our area.

I was so scared of doctors by then, it took me months to agree to see Dr. Jacobs. But I finally did. She sent me to another doctor who prescribed antidepressants. She also put me on a program of behavioral therapy, which included something called "exposures." For my compulsion to balance things, Dr. Jacobs took out a cold can of soda, rubbed it up and down my right arm and then put it away. The first time she did it, I was crying and actually couldn't breathe! I had to have it on my other arm to feel right. It was unbelievably hard. We also did exposures where I touched the stairs a certain way

with one foot only. But I still felt I had to it with my other foot. It was torture. At first I could only handle practicing about once or twice a week, but later, I practiced every day.

After a year of therapy, I am a lot better. Balancing hot and cold is still hard for me, but my problem with numbers has improved. Recently, I entered college as a psychology major so I can become a therapist for children with OCD.

I can actually drive now, and I don't even look at license plates anymore. For me, simple things like that are a tremendous accomplishment.

JUMP
14–19 years
1,739 words

Alternative Families

By Debi Martin-Morris

A pretty but modest house with a white picket fence and a manicured lawn. Mom's making dinner. Dad pulls his car into the garage. Little brother slides through the front door from baseball practice just as big sister finishes her homework, and everybody heads to the dinner table to eat and talk about the day.

> *"Over the last 15 years, the kinds of families we have in this country have changed dramatically."*

If this doesn't sound at all familiar, you could be wondering what planet these people live on. Maybe this is the sort of life you've seen only on TV, or maybe it's a fairly accurate description of your family. After all, there's really no such thing as a "typical" family these days. Sure, a "traditional" family is defined by Mom, Dad, siblings and pets all living (and coping) together under one roof. But there's room for all sorts of families on this planet, and just because they may not be conventional doesn't mean they're not cool.

Alternative Families Defined

Families today are of all shapes and sizes. Besides the "traditional" tribe, there are real-life Brady Bunches (divorced or widowed moms and dads who remarry others and start stepfamilies), joint-custody arrangements and single-parent homes. There are gay unions with children from previous (straight) relationships, parents who adopt children, kids being raised by grandparents or older siblings (think *Party of Five*) and all sorts of combinations of the above.

"Over the last 15 years, the kinds of families we have in this country have changed dramatically," says David S. Liederman, executive director of the Child Welfare League of America. "What has evolved is a wonderful concept of the blended family. What matters is whether the adults and the children feel supported and loved, and that the kids get good values and role models."

The average American teen today lives in one of three types of households: with the biological mother and father; with mom, a stepdad and his kids; or with just the biological mother. According to the Children's Defense Fund's 1996 data, of children under age 18:

71.6 percent live with two parents
24.2 percent live only with a mother
3.4 percent live only with a father
0.6 percent are foster children

While these statistics show that the two-parent home is still in the majority, data from the Stepfamily Association of America indicate that 35 percent of all children born in the 1980s will experience life in a single-parent family for a total of about five years before their eighteenth birthday.

Growing up—whether your family is traditional or alternative—is rarely easy. If you're having problems coping within your family structure, remember to take stock in yourself. "Do well in school, have something spiritual in your life, participate in activities you enjoy and have a support group of friends you can really talk to," says Child Welfare's Liederman.

Also, don't be afraid to reach out to others. Discussing family problems with a caring yet objective adult you trust (school counselors are pretty hip, and a good place to start) can really help. If your family is currently in a state of flux, bear in mind that change is often good—even if you don't understand why it's happening or you wish things would just "be normal." And it's important to remember that love and happiness can grow in any home. Check out the alternative family portraits we found.

Jessica Yager, 15

Divorced parents with joint custody
Situation: Jessica's parents divorced when she was 4 and have joint custody of her and her little brother.

I have a bedroom at my dad's but I stay at my mom's more—it's closer to everything. Some people see their dads only on weekends, but I see mine every day. He drives me to school each morning. He comes to my drill team performances. Although he doesn't live with me, he's there for me. Like recently I had a fight with my mom, and he cheered me up and calmed me down. He made me feel better and helped me realize I just need to talk to my mom when I get mad.

Everybody in my family is there for each other; we just don't live in the same house.

When it comes to the rules for my brother and me, my parents decide stuff together. Once, when I wanted to go to some parties and my mom didn't want me to, she called my dad and they talked about it. My dad agreed with my mom, and they both explained that they thought they should be able to talk to the parents of the kids giving the parties before making the decision to let me go or not. Personally, I think that's too strict—I'm still working on that one.

The adults in my life get to do whatever they want, but I accept and understand that. My mom has a boyfriend, and that doesn't bother or affect me. I like him, my mom's happy and they're going to get married in about a year. It's her life. Why should I put restrictions on her?

Everybody in my family is there for each other; we just don't live in the same house. I feel they are

the people who love me and care about me, and we can always turn to each other.

Avi Goldgraber, 14

Stepfamily
Situation: Avi's parents divorced when she was 2, then remarried other people when she was 5. On her mom's side, she now has a stepdad, a stepbrother (15) and a half-brother (7). On her father's side, she has a stepmom and two half-sisters (8 and 4). Both families live in the same town.

It's fun having so many siblings, but sometimes I get pulled in different directions. Both families will ask me to do something the same day. The holidays aren't that hard because my dad's family leaves town, so I stay with my mom. But I'm always worried about hurting someone's feelings. Like I don't go over to my dad's house as much. I don't have

---

It's really hard with grandparents. You don't want to call them step-grandparents because it might insult them.

---

my own room there, and it's hard to do homework with little sisters around.

Another hard thing about the situation is deciding what to call stuff or people. I say I'm at my mom's house or my dad's house, not my house. I don't call my stepdad "Dad"—I use his first name. If I'm with my mom's father, I call my dad's family "the other family." It's really hard with grandparents. You don't want to call them step-grandparents because it might insult them.

Sheana Wendorf, 15

Foster child; adopted at age 12
Situation: Her mom left Sheana, her sister and two brothers with their grandmother, who raised all four of them until Sheana and her older sister were preteens. The brothers stayed with the grandmother, and the sisters were placed in foster homes. Sheana's sister, 16, still lives in foster care. Sheana was adopted by a couple she now calls "Mom and Dad." The couple also have two biological sons (23 and 19).

I haven't seen my birth mom since I was 3. I don't even know who my dad is. My grandmother just couldn't handle all of us kids. I do get to see my sister once every two months, and we talk on the phone. She's happy that I got adopted, but I feel bad for her.

Being told I was a child no one wanted really hurt. But the majority of kids think it's really cool that I got a good home. People don't realize that if you're in a foster home and want to get adopted, you have to work for it. You have to work on your

Getting used to having a real family was hard.

self-esteem, and you can't be short-tempered. A family won't want a kid who's full of rage. You have to deal with your past; you have to forgive and say: "That was then and this is now."

Getting used to having a real family was hard. At first I thought I'd better not get too close—it might not last, and I'd have to move again. But a couple of weeks after I got here I was going through a problem, and Mom and Dad said they'd always be there for me. I think I knew for sure then that this is a permanent home. I also knew when my brothers teased me. One time during dinner I left the table for just a minute, and my brothers poured salt in my drink—everybody laughed when I drank it. When I figured out what happened, I laughed too. I guess I felt I was a part of a family. I feel I have a place in the world.

Joshua Stevens, 16

Half African-American, half Caucasian; adopted by an interracial couple
Situation: Joshua was adopted as an infant by an interracial couple who have one child of their own and three other non-biologically related children from interracial (African-American and Caucasian) backgrounds.

I'm half black and half white, but I look more black, and people consider me to be black. To me, I'm both. But I have to deal with that. I read about blacks and Martin Luther King and what he did for oppressed blacks in America, and then I think:

"Was it the white side of my family that oppressed the black side?" It just boils down to the fact that I'm not on any one side—I'm black and white.

What does still hurt is feeling rejected by my biological parents.

Being adopted into an interracial family was the best thing that could have happened to me. It gives me the history of both parts. In this family there are the typical arguments, like who gets to sit up front in the car, but no arguments about black or white. This is one big family that's colorblind.

The downside of being biracial? I hear rude comments when I play soccer. They call me "nigger" if they don't like what I'm doing on the field. I consider it their ignorance and just shrug it off. I'm biracial and proud of who and what I am.

What does still hurt is feeling rejected by my biological parents, feeling like I was an accident and that my parents didn't want me. That is still with me. But the fact that these people came looking for me and wanted me, that evens it out. I've been told that my biological mother said she wanted me in a good family with one black parent and one white parent. She cared about that. Maybe she feels she

made a mistake and tried to correct it. I'd like to meet her one day.

Teen
12–19 years
1,725 words

Lucky To Be Alive

By Carol Ann Moorhead

Despite Chicken Little's insistence that "the sky is falling, the sky is falling," I never believed him. When I was a young child, the sky was as secure above my head as the ground was beneath my feet. That was before I felt the Earth quake, and before I learned that Chicken Little is sometimes right.

My sky fell one summer evening in Massachusetts. It did not fall all at once nor without warning. It heaved and cracked with the roll of thunder of an ap-

---

I felt a sharp thrust upward, and then heard a muffled thump.

---

proaching storm. It shattered into pieces with cloud-to-cloud lightning as a few raindrops began to fall. My friend Bill and I hurried down a woodland path, making jokes about lightning and trying to remember tips about lightning safety. Not to worry, we assured ourselves. This isn't a bad storm. As if to prove us wrong, the winds picked up. Black clouds rolled in, releasing rains so heavy that we were soaked within seconds. Our clothes clung to our bodies, and our feet sloshed through instant puddles. We fell silent, fearful of the storm upon us.

Behind us bright bolts of lightning began probing the woodlands, lighting up the forest, and sparking our conversation. We made a plan: Exit the forest, skirt its edge, and re-enter on the other path. The other path, I knew from a previous hike, would quickly lead us to an abandoned car. It was the best option. The storm was gaining on us, and my own car was across an open meadow at least four football fields long.

The sky was so dark now that we could barely see. Carefully we made our way out of the forest and along its edge. Suddenly, BAM! There was an explosion of white light at my feet. I felt a sharp thrust upward, and then heard a muffled thump.

I landed on my back: Ears ringing and skin tingling, I struggled to roll onto my feet, but my legs couldn't lift me. I squatted in the darkness, trembling, and shouting, "Bill! Are you okay?! Bill!"

Bill didn't answer. I strained my eyes to see if I could see him lying near me. If I could only crawl to him I could help, I thought, but I could see nothing but darkness. Seconds ticked by, maybe minutes. Slowly I raised myself into a skier's crouch. I shouted again, and suddenly a wet hug answered my call.

"I couldn't answer," he said. "The muscles around my mouth wouldn't move. Come on. Let's go!"

Our legs trembled and tingled for over an hour as we waited out the storm.

By now, the storm was centered above us. A second bolt hit the forest, then a third. Like shell-shocked soldiers, we fell to our knees each time. A fourth bolt. I don't recall being afraid, only angry—angry at this deranged storm that seemed determined to find us. Luckily, on the fifth bolt I saw the silhouette of a small car. "Oh, please," I thought, "let it be unlocked."

Bill lifted the handle. To our relief, it unlatched. We piled inside the abandoned car and shut the door. Finally we were safe. We pinched ourselves and poked each other to make sure we were alive. Our legs trembled and tingled for over an hour as we waited out the storm. Bill complained of a sharp pain on the ball of his foot. My feet ached all over. Once the storm seemed safely past, we walked on wobbly legs back to my car and drove home to my sister's house. By the time we arrived, we felt less shaken. Despite her encouragement, we decided not to go to the emergency room.

The next day Bill and I walked back to the site where we had been struck. A mangled birch tree stood beside the path. Its trunk was split wide open, and a black streak blazed its otherwise yellow insides. Several broken limbs hung to the ground.

Suddenly my eyes settled on four dead grassy spots along the path, only 2 meters from the tree. Our footprints! We guessed that these were the points where the electricity entered and exited our bodies.

Bill and I knew that we'd been lucky, but just how lucky, we didn't know until later that week when we visited the Boston Museum of Science. The museum had just opened a lightning demonstration and we

The bolt had hit the tree, traveled through the ground, entered one foot and exited the other.

couldn't resist going. Using large *Van de Graaf generators*, scientists created electrical strikes that looked like lightning bolts, right inside the museum! Bill ducked at the first strike and I jumped. Despite knowing we were safe behind a shield of grounded wires, it was hard not to be scared.

After the demonstration, Bill and I approached one of the scientists. We told him our story, described the dead grassy spots, and showed him the burn marks on our sandled feet. "You're lucky to be alive," he said, shaking his head. "If you hadn't been walking, you might not be here today."

The scientist explained that we had survived an indirect lightning strike. The bolt had hit the tree, traveled through the ground, entered one foot and exited the other. Had we been standing with our legs together, instead of walking, the current might have struck our heart and other organs, perhaps killing us because we had been so close to the tree. He added that being soaking wet may also have helped. Much like the car's metal exterior, the thin film of water coating our skin may have allowed some of the current to pass around us, rather than through us.

Bill and I left the museum, once again pinching

ourselves and poking each other. It was a beautiful sunny day and we were grateful to be alive.

Some people are not as lucky as Bill and I after a lightning strike. In her book, *A Match to the Heart*, Gretel Ehrlich writes, "The pain in my chest intensified and every muscle in my body ached. I was quite sure I was dying." Gretel suffered from, and survived, a heart attack after receiving a direct hit from a lightning bolt on a Wyoming prairie.

According to Steve Marshburn, Sr., founder and president of Lightning Strike and Electric Shock Victims International (of which Gretel is a member), victims of direct strikes are either seriously injured or they don't make it. He adds, "With indirect hits, there is a better chance of survival, but the effects may be just as severe," He lists heart attacks, nerve damage, and certain types of cancers, such as *melanoma* (a fast-growing skin cancer), as some of the conditions members of his organization suffer from as a result of lightning strikes. After talking with Steve, I realized that Bill and I should have taken my sister's advice and visited a doctor. We recovered fully without medical attention, but we were simply lucky.

Sabrina, a 10-year-old who was indirectly struck by lightning when she was seven, says the worst thing about the experience is the fear she lives with today. Sabrina and her parents were struck while hiking in the Grand Canyon.

"When I go to the Grand Canyon now, I am nervous about going on the trails," she says. "Even seeing a small cloud makes me scared. Before I was struck, I was perfectly happy in thunderstorms, but now I'm really afraid of thunder," she adds.

Lightning can hit you.

To try to cope with her fear, Sabrina researched, wrote, and, with the help of her father, created an award-winning Web site called, "Kids' Lightning Information and Safety." "I created my Web page because I wanted to help other people learn about lightning so they would be safer," Sabrina says. "And I actually feel a little less scared since I did it."

Filled with personal tales, scientific information, safety tips, book references, and links to other Web sites, Sabrina's Web page is an excellent resource for both children and adults. Check it out at http://www.azstarnet.com/ ~ anubis/zaphome.htm.

When Henny Penny asked Chicken Little how he knew the sky was falling, he shouted, "Oh, I saw it with my eyes; I heard it with my ears; and part of it fell on my tail." Gretel, Sabrina, Bill, and I experienced a similar lesson about lightning. Take our word for it: Lightning can hit you. Learn the precautions and be safe.

Myths and Realities

Myth: A car's rubber tires will insulate and therefore protect a person from a lightning strike.

Reality: A lightning bolt has already pushed its way through air, another good insulator. It won't be stopped by a thin or even a thick layer of rubber. The reason a car is a safe place to be in a lightning storm is its bubble-like structure. If the abandoned car Bill and I sought refuge in had been struck, the electrical current would have traveled around us on the car's outermost layer of electrons.

Myth: The bright flash of a lightning bolt travels from cloud-to-ground.

Reality: The bright flashes we recognize as lightning actually travel from the ground upward. They roar up electrically-charged channels created by dim and difficult-to-see leader strokes, which travel from cloud-to-ground. Lightning flashes are so fast that it's difficult to detect which direction they travel.

Myth: Lightning always strikes the tallest objects around.

Reality: Although lightning usually strikes the tallest objects, there are many exceptions. Sometimes lightning will strike an open field even when trees are nearby. Other times, as in the case of Bill's and my experience, it will choose a tree shorter than others in a forest. Yet it is important to remember that one of the main causes of lightning-caused deaths is taking refuge under a lone tree.

Myth: If a person is hit by lightning, he or she will have burns to prove it.

Reality: Many lightning strike victims, even if badly injured, have no external burn marks.

Myth: Lightning never strikes the same person or the same place twice.

Reality: Gretel Ehrlich wishes it were so. She has been struck twice—once indirectly and once directly. Many other people have been struck more than once. The Empire State Building averages 23 strikes a year.

Myth: Buildings of any type are safe places to be in an electrical storm.

Reality: Unenclosed structures such as covered bus stops or rain shelters can be dangerous hideouts. Not only are they exposed to the air, they may be the tallest objects around.

Myth: Enclosed buildings offer complete protection from lightning strikes.

Reality: Lightning can enter buildings through pipes, telephone lines, electrical wires, windows, and open doors. Talking on the telephone is the leading source of indoor deaths from lightning.

Myth: You must be in the midst of a thunderstorm to be hit by lightning.

Reality: People have been struck by storms 16 or more kilometers away. These strikes are called bolts from the blue because the sky overhead can be sunny and blue. Sabrina and her parents had climbed out of a side branch of the Grand Canyon after some rain had stopped. The sky overhead was patchy blue. While holding hands, they were all hit by a lightning bolt from the storm that had just passed.

Odyssey
10–15 years
1,797 words

From the Author

I'm a nature and science writer and illustrator. In addition to magazine articles, I've written two books: *Wild Horses,* for upper elementary students, and *Colorado's Backyard Wildlife,* for young adults. (I wrote the latter as part of my thesis for a master's degree in wildlife biology.) Prior to my writing career, I held positions as a biologist, an environmental educator, and an exhibit artist.

Because I've published in *Odyssey* before, the editor sent me an annual theme list. The topic of lightning caught my eye because I am a lightning strike survivor. I knew telling my story would be important, but I didn't want my article to be purely anecdotal, so I settled on a combination of personal experience backed up by empirical studies. My query, including outline and bibliography (both required by *Odyssey*), was accepted, but the editor suggested I interview fewer people than I proposed.

I chose Sabrina, the 10-year-old lightning strike victim, who I initially learned about through her Web site. I contacted her father through the e-mail address listed there and asked for permission to interview his daughter by telephone, letting him know the kinds of questions I would ask her. I also decided to interview Steve Marshburn, who could provide an overview of other victims' experiences. I relied on current books, articles, and reliable Internet sources, such as *National Geographic* and *Nova,* for scientific information for the sidebar.

Once I'd researched the facts and conducted my interviews, I wrote a brief outline. To appeal to *Odyssey's* audience, I began and ended with a theme from *Chicken Little,* included the interview with Sabrina, and kept the article's language concise. I knew my biggest challenge would be describing my own and others' experiences without an abrupt change in narrative point of view. Luckily, the narrative was conversational enough to permit easy segues into other victims' experiences.

I did one revision before submitting my article to *Odyssey,* and one after. The editor made a few grammatical changes and content suggestions.

I believe that the most important point to keep in mind when writing nonfiction for children is that they deserve the same respect as adults. Use current sources of knowledge. Interview interesting, credible people. Most importantly, write *to*—but never *down to*—your audience.

Senioritis

By Kim Ratcliff

You're a senior and that means final. As in goodbye. Think you're on Easy Street, right? Then the day you've waited for turns into a bad case of senioritis.

Romy Segall of La Jolla, California, envisioned her senior year as *Romy & Michele Meet Club Med.* She and her friends would take trips to nearby Windansea Beach and Mexico, make roadside stops for fish tacos and dance till dawn at BabyRock, a club in Tijuana.

Two weeks after school started, Romy sat cross-legged in the middle of her bedroom staring at a mound of college catalogs. Her fingernails were covered with Liquid Paper from filling out applications to schools like UCLA, the University of Arizona and the University of Colorado–Boulder. Already exhausted, Romy hadn't even started visiting campuses yet.

Welcome to senior year. Never have you waited so long for something, only to realize, when it finally arrives, that it's not quite the slackfest you imagined. But don't despair. The key to surviving your final year of high school is to strike a balance between working hard and having fun. Along the way you'll be seesawing between conflicting emotions, too—excitement and bittersweet sadness; joy and high-octane energy; outright fearlessness and nervousness about striking out on your own. And like your moods, the pressures you face are also everchanging.

First Semester: Meltdown Time

Life may seem like a big test—you have to take the SATs, the ACTs—but you're also writing college essays and applying for scholarships. "Along with keeping on top of grades, there are a million other things to worry about," says Melissa Laue, a senior from Tucson, Arizona. "I feel like I've been tossed out to sea and have to navigate my own course."

The first thing to go, it seems, is the social life. "It's hard to put your friends on the back burner," says Melissa. "But you're not getting a grade for hanging out with them."

With a potential scholarship to Snow College in Utah hinging on one honors class, Lindsay Eaton of Idaho Falls, Idaho, can relate. While her friends cut classes to hit the ski slopes in Kelly Canyon in Ririe, Idaho, she stayed behind. "I was stuck in AP

"I've already pulled five all-nighters this semester."

English thinking to myself, Oh, man, the snow is deep, and I have to sit here and review Truman Capote's *In Cold Blood!"* When ultramotivated Ariel Dekovic, a senior at the private Lick-Wilmerding High School in San Francisco, decided to apply to 12 schools, including Vassar, Mount Holyoke and Brown, she totally missed out on Halloween. Instead of trick-or-treating with her pals, Ariel sat chained to her computer, she says, "typing the last words to my essay."

Ariel had expected that filling out college applications would be a pain, but she hadn't realized that homework would be so brutal. "I've killed five or six forests' worth of paper," she says. "I've already pulled five all-nighters this semester."

As if everything on the school front weren't stressful enough, you also have to sit down with your parents and decide if you're going away to college—and how *far* away. The thought of cutting the umbilical cord from Mom and Dad is huge—a nerve-racking prospect. "I'm so freaked. It's like all my life, I've been taken care of," says Lindsay Eaton. "Now they're telling me I'm going to have to go out on my own." Shelley Whitney picked Santa Barbara City, a college that wasn't too far from her family in La Jolla, California: "I figured I can't go to an East Coast school, because I might get too homesick for my brothers and sisters," she says.

Second Semester: The Temptation to Blow It All

"You've reached the home of a second-semester senior. I'm not here right now, and I don't know when I'm gonna be back, so leave a message." (Message on Ariel's answering machine.)

At the beginning of second semester, the tension seems to lift. You've mailed your applications, filled in those SAT bubbles and now you're in limbo, waiting for the envelope. Time to party, right? The countdown to graduation has begun, and you want to create as many lasting memories of your final months as you can. After seeing your classmates day in and day out for four (or more) years, you realize that you may never see them again. And what better way to forge those memories than by having a really spectacular prom, the last dance of your high school life?

"Prom is put on this pedestal. You know the buildup: You're going to marry the person you go with, or tell your kids about it someday," says Shelley.

Alexis Swain of Malibu, California, now a freshman at UCLA, confesses that she'll always remember her senior prom—"for all the wrong reasons." She scoured every boutique in Santa Monica until she found The Dress: a pomegranate-colored halter with matching satin opera gloves, something Sarah Michelle Gellar might wear to a Hollywood premiere. When the big day finally arrived, Alexis was so busy—and excited—she forgot to eat. As she and her posse passed the communal curling iron in a friend's bedroom, they sipped Moët champagne from plastic glasses. By the time the girls' dates arrived in a limo, Alexis was definitely buzzed. There were a few chilled bottles on ice in the car, too. Needless to say, Alexis was smashed when the limo pulled up in front of the posh Loews Santa Monica Hotel. She managed to make it through the front door but not to the table.

"I literally wasn't in the building for more than ten minutes before I got sick," she says. Sprawled out on the floor of the bathroom, Alexis moaned to her friends, "I can't believe I did this." The bathroom was shut down to keep out the other students. "It was major," she cringes. Her best friend, Kristy Michaud, recalls huddling in the stall with Alexis as school counselors passed cold compresses under the door. The vice principal carried Alexis out to her mother's car.

Alexis feared the worst and received it—expulsion, three weeks before graduation. "I wasn't a bad kid—I'd never even been to the principal's office," she explains. She was also a straight-A student. As part of her punishment, she didn't get to participate in the graduation ceremony. "I sat in the audience wearing my cap and watched my best friends walk across the stage." Alexis' advice to high school kids hoping to make their last few weeks unforgettable? "Don't ruin it by doing something dumb."

The desire to leave your mark with a stellar prank may be stronger than a quad mocha at Starbucks.

As graduation day nears, the desire to leave your mark with a stellar prank may be stronger than a quad mocha at Starbucks. After all, you're *almost* outta there. No matter what you do, you think, you will escape bodily harm or disciplinary action.

Think again. Streaking through campus had been a tradition at northern California's Saratoga High for "forever," says graduating senior Lindsay Smith. She'd wanted to take part in the ritual since her freshman year, when she'd watched "one girl who'd painted eyes on her chest" sprint across the quad.

What had started as a high-spirited stunt had evolved over the years into an embarrassing event for the school—especially after the class of '96 streaked through the high school, then treated nearby middle schoolers to a peep show. So administrators made some hard-and-fast rules for the class of '97: Absolutely no nudity on campus. Still, the urge to flash their tan lines proved irresistible to Jessica Jones* and her friends. She and 30 of her buddies masterminded a PG-rated prank that they believed was saucy enough to keep the 'Toga High tradition alive but tame enough not to offend administrators. The guys wore briefs and football helmets; the girls slipped into short-shorts and see-through bras. Then they all gathered for a body-painting party, followed by a campus run. "Technically we didn't streak," says Jessica. Unfortunately the administration saw it differently and gave them the choice of either not attending prom or not walking across the stage at graduation. They opted to go to prom.

"It was a long end of the year," says Jessica, who ended up graduating in a private ceremony in a classmate's backyard, which was also attended by TV news crews after the incident became a media cause célèbre.

Running through the quad in a mesh Victoria's Secret bra is nothing compared with one prank that ended in tragedy for some Napa Valley, California, seniors a year ago. Minutes before boarding a bus back to school during an annual senior class trip to Waterworld USA in northern California, students crammed onto the Bonzai Pipeline in an attempt to break a Napa High School record for the most students on a waterslide at one time. When the chute collapsed, dozens of students were injured and one girl died. Instead of celebrating their final days together, classmates and teachers went to her funeral.

Tales from Senioritis Survivors

Not all stunts backfire. Maggy Krell cured her senioritis with an ingenious scheme. As student-council president at the private Urban School in San Francisco, she and her fellow students devised a plan that was so original, future classes will have a hard time topping it: The scheme took months to plan, and the students cleared it with their respective deans beforehand. A month before graduation, kids at Urban and at Lick-Wilmerding arranged to trade places, identities and schedules for a single day.

Both senior classes made name tags for one another. They also printed and distributed school maps with classroom numbers. While a senior from Urban read Cervantes in AP Spanish Lit at Lick, a Lick senior did trig equations at Urban. The game lasted for two classes, with the teachers playing along. After it was all over, the seniors cut out early and headed for a day of fun at a friend's lakeside home. Maggy was thrilled at the success of her switcheroo: "We got compliments from teachers,

and that was cool," she says. "I didn't want to leave school with a bad taste after we'd worked so hard for the last four years."

Name has been changed.

Seventeen
13–18 years
1,708 words

Seen and Heard

Compiled by Mark Haverstock

Meals on Wheels

Why go to the drive-thru when your car can do the cooking? According to Bill Scheller and Chris Maynard, co-authors of a car cookbook titled *Manifold Destiny*, your engine makes a great oven and can cook meals by using the heat from the manifold.

No burgers or teaching old hot dogs new tricks— these guys are into gourmet cooking. Maynard's favorite is boned chicken thighs stuffed with leeks and oysters. Cooking time: 50 to 200 miles.

Sometimes accidents *do* happen. "From time to time, I've dropped a chicken on the road," says Scheller. "You just have to write it off as tenderized, pre-seasoned road kill."

Sword Fishing

When 13-year-old Christian Bell tossed his line into the Maury River near Buena Vista, Virginia, he didn't reel in a swordfish. Instead, he pulled up a real sword —one that belonged to an artillery officer in the Civil War.

According to experts, the sword was probably used by a Union officer who had been assigned to a unit that set fire to the Virginia Military Institute in 1864. "All I ever found before were pieces of cars and old washing machines," said Bell.

Or Is That Cheese and Macaroni?

According to Kraft Food Co., Bob Watkins of Odessa, Ontario, is the king of macaroni-and-cheese dinners. Thirty-five-year-old Watkins claims to have eaten 10,000 of the blue box meals over his lifetime—including many days where he ate them for all three meals.

"I don't consider it an addiction," he said. "I honestly don't get sick of it."

Most Say "No"

For the first time in this decade, more than half of America's high school students are saying no to sex. Fifty-two percent of those surveyed said they're still virgins, continuing a trend towards abstinence.

"It's an important milestone because students who have not engaged in intercourse can say they're in the majority," says Dr. Lloyd Kolbe of the Centers for Disease Control and Prevention.

How's the Weather up There?

Sixteen-year-old Travis Wolf of Wisconsin got a leg up on the world stilt-walking record. Wolf teetered 25 steps on a pair of 41-foot-high stilts at Orlando's Universal Studios, beating the 1988 record set by his dad, "Steady Eddie" Wolf.

How does Wolf keep from tilting when he's stilting? He practices in a silo, using a ladder to get on the stilts.

Give Me Your Tired, Your Poor, Your Beanie Babies

Put away those green cards and get out some greenbacks. Beanie Babies are no longer illegal immigrants. Ty Inc., maker of those popular pellet-filled critters, has agreed to allow international travelers to bring up to 30 Beanies into the U.S. The previous limit was one.

But what will Customs do with all the thousands of previously seized Beanie Babies? "We don't want to throw them away because people would be going through our garbage," said Pat Jones, a spokeswoman for the Customs Service in Washington. For now they're holding onto the seized Beanies in hopes of donating them to charity.

Pooch Pillow

Eleven-year-old Alfredo Iannone is alive and well today thanks to the heroic efforts of his watchful canine pal, Stella, a German Shepherd mix. The brave mutt watched her master with concern while he and his friends went climbing on a building under construction in Salerno, Italy. When Alfredo suddenly fell, Stella was ready—she raced under the boy and cushioned his fall. Amazingly, neither dog nor boy was seriously hurt.

Save Those Quarters

You'll only need 44,000 of them, or about $11,000 a year, for tuition at the nation's first four-year college of video game development. The DigiPen Institute of Technology opened in Redmond, Washington, last year with a class of 40 students.

The competition is tough—there are over ten applications for every space in the next freshman class. And it's not all fun and games. You have to study computer languages and graphics, in addition to more traditional subjects like math, physics, and marketing.

Air Pollution Solution

Does that kid sitting by you in class have morning breath that smells like ripe sweat socks? Do *you*? Forget the breath mints. Dental hygienist Carol Meyer of New York City has a better answer—a fresh-breath makeover.

For a mere $125, Meyer will diagnose halitosis (bad breath) using a Halimeter, a device that measures the amount of sulfur compounds or bacteria found in the mouth. Next, you'll get your teeth scrubbed and hear some advice on how to clean up your act. Take-home tools include a tongue comb and some sample gels and rinses to keep that breath minty fresh.

A Ride on the Flip Side

Katina Pride and her 13-year-old friend, Isha Leon, got the ride of their lives when they boarded The Demon, a roller coaster at Six Flags Great America Amusement Park in Gurnee, Illinois. As they were screaming their heads off, the coaster suddenly came to a complete stop—right in the middle of the second loop! They were suspended upside-down 60 feet above the ground. Luckily, their safety harnesses held them in place for the more than *two hours* it took rescuers to get them down. They were bruised and shaken, but otherwise all right. The ride has since been repaired and reopened, but Katina and Isha may think twice (or 3 times, or *20*) before they get on it again.

Pretty in Pink

With memories of destructive Hurricane Andrew (1992) still in their minds, workers at Miami's MetroZoo scrambled last September to shelter the animals from the approaching Hurricane Georges. But space was tight, and concrete buildings filled up fast.

Finally, zoo workers rounded up this flock of flamingos and herded then into the closest available shelter—the men's restroom. (No one's ever seen that much pink in a men's room!)

Guideposts for Teens
7–12 years
964 words

From the Author

I started writing for computer magazines and later entered the children's market. This wasn't much of a stretch since I'm a middle-school teacher and thoroughly versed in the culture of 10- to 14-year-olds.

I'd written trivia and fun-fact pieces for *Guideposts for Kids* for a number of years when the editor approached me about doing a trivia column for a proposed new publication, *Guideposts for Teens*. The idea was to assemble tidbits of interest to teens, focusing on news and fun facts. Research included reading a variety of local and national publications, as well as doing some extensive Internet research.

Teens are a notoriously tough audience who often respond by saying "...whatever," "Who cares?" or "So?" News pieces involving teens or featuring a universally weird or humorous slant seem to grab them best. The first column featured quick takes of unusual news items, accompanied by art and photos. Everything from "dead bear with tortilla found in its mouth" to virtual homework help sites to a museum exhibit entitled "Things People Gagged On" appeared in the first "Seen and Heard."

Title Index

Author Index

Magazine Index

This index lists articles and stories under the magazines in which they were published. The following key identifies reader age level: YF = Youngest Readers' Fiction; YN = Youngest Readers' Nonfiction; IF = Intermediate Fiction; IN = Intermediate Nonfiction; TF = Teen Fiction; TN = Teen Nonfiction.

Magazine Index (continued)

Acknowledgements

The publishers wish to thank the following authors and publishers who graciously gave permission for work to appear.

"Mary Ellen Had a Sheep" by Karen Troncale. Reprinted by permission of LADYBUG magazine, January 1999, Vol. 9, No. 5, © 1999 by Karen Troncale.

"The Bridge of Liars" by Bonnie Highsmith Taylor. Used by permission of Highlights for Children, Inc., Columbus, Ohio. Copyright © 1998.

"Late for Lunch" by Betty G. Birney. From *Humpty Dumpty's Magazine*, Copyright © 1992 and reprinted in 1998 by Children's Better Health Institute, Benjamin Franklin Literary & Medical Society, Inc., Indianapolis, Indiana. Used by permission.

"Zack and the Cornstalk" by Joanne Coughlin. Reprinted with permission of *The Good Apple Newspaper*, a Frank Schaffer publication, Copyright © 1998.

"The Night Before Thanksgiving" by Virginia Kroll. Copyright © 1991, Virginia Kroll. Published by *Primary Treasure*, November 16, 1991, and by *Story Friends*, October 1998.

"The Blue Demon" by William Groeneweg. Copyright © 1998 by William Groeneweg. Reprinted by permission of the author. From *Acorn; Early Years Storyteller*, March/April/May 1998.

"The Boomerang Smile" by Sara Murray-Plumer. Reprinted with permission of *Pockets*, a devotional magazine for children, April 1998. Copyright © The Upper Room, P. O. Box 189, Nashville, TN 37202.

"The Best Word of All" by Dawn Lamuth-Higgins, reprinted from *Story Friends*, February 1998, Copyright ©1998. Used by permission of the author.

"Aunt Millie's Handbag" by Eileen Spinelli. Used by permission of Highlights for Children, Inc., Columbus, Ohio. Copyright © 1998.

"Prairie Light" by Marcia S. Freeman. Reprinted by permission of LADYBUG magazine, June 1998, Vol. 8, No. 10, © 1998 by Marcia S. Freeman.

"Something Terrible" by Lisa Harkrader, reprinted from *Story Friends*, January 1998, Copyright © 1998, by permission of the author.

"Windows of Gold" by Marianne Mitchell. Used by permission of Highlights for Children, Inc., Columbus, Ohio. Copyright © 1998.

"A Fishy Story" by Linell Wohlers. From *Children's Playmate*, Copyright © 1992 and reprinted in 1998 by Children's Better Health Institute, Benjamin Franklin Literary & Medical Society, Inc., Indianapolis, Indiana. Used by permission.

"Zindy Lou and the Dark Place" by Judy Cox. Reprinted by permission of SPIDER magazine, September 1998, Vol. 5, No. 9, © 1998 by Judy Cox.

"Brrrr!" by Bonnie Compton Hanson. Published in *Radar* in March 1997 and in *Story Friends* in January 1998. Reprinted by permission of the author.

"Snackin' Snowmen" by Peggy Robbins Janousky. From *Children's Playmate*, Copyright © 1998 by Children's Better Health Institute, Benjamin Franklin Literary & Medical Society, Inc., Indianapolis, Indiana. Used by permission.

"I Only Have Beats For You" by Tamara Angier. From *Humpty Dumpty's Magazine*, Copyright © 1997 by Children's Better Health Institute, Benjamin Franklin Literary & Medical Society, Inc., Indianapolis, Indiana. Used by permission.

"Let's Celebrate" by Darlene Buechel. Reprinted from *Boys' Quest*, December 1997/January 1998. Used by permission of the author.

"An Eye For Ants" by Gretchen Noyes-Hull. From APPLESEEDS' Charter Issue: Learning with Animals, © 1998, Cobblestone Publishing Company, 30 Grove Street, Suite C, Peterborough, NH 03458. Reprinted by permission of the publisher.

"Dead Or Alive?" by Victoria Earle. From *Hopscotch*, © 1998. Used by permission of the author.

"Bird Alarm" by Cynthia J. Breedlove. Reprinted from *Nature Friend*, June 1998. Reprinted by permission of the author.

"The Black And Blue Ballet" by Amy Cooley. Reprinted with permission from *My Friend*, a Catholic Magazine for kids. Pauline Books & Media, January 1998.

"Soap It Up!" by Amy O. Barish. From *U.S. Kids*, A Weekly Reader *Magazine*, copyright © 1998 by Children's Better Health Institute, Benjamin Franklin Literary & Medical Society, Inc., Indianapolis, Indiana. Used by permission.

"Growing Up in Another Time, Another Place" by Peggy Wilgus Wymore. From APPLESEEDS' February 1999 issue: Children of Ancient Egypt, © 1999, Cobblestone Publishing Company, 30 Grove Street, Suite C, Peterborough, NH 03458. Reprinted by permission of the publisher.

"Watching A Beekeeper" by Joan Davis. Used by permission of Highlights for Children, Inc., Columbus, Ohio. Copyright © 1998.

"Scary Science" by Barbara A. Tyler. From *Jack And Jill*, copyright © 1998 by Children's Better Health Institute, Benjamin Franklin Literary & Medical Society, Inc., Indianapolis, Indiana. Used by permission.

"Knuckle Down That Taw!" by Beth Kennedy. Used by permission of Highlights for Children, Inc., Columbus, Ohio. Copyright © 1999.

"All In The Family" by Sandy Stiefer. Reprinted from the November 1998 issue of *Ranger Rick* magazine, with the permission of the publisher, the National Wildlife Federation. Copyright 1998 by the National Wildlife Federation.

"The Mysterious Yawn" by Lee Ann Howlett. Reprinted from *Hopscotch*, February/March 1998, by permission of the author.

"Teddy's Bear" by Janeen R. Adil. Reprinted by permission of SPIDER magazine, May 1998, Vol. 5, No. 5, © 1998 by Janeen R. Adil.

"Danger On The Canal." Reprinted by permission of SPIDER magazine, July 1998, VOL. 5, No. 7 SPIDER, © 1998 by Carol Ottolenghi-Barga.

"Cussing And Swearing" by Bob Hartman, reprinted from April 1998 *My Friend*: The Catholic Magazine for Kids; copyright © 1998 Daughters of St. Paul.

"The Flamelights of Oolumaree" by Bonnie Bisbee. Reprinted from the February 1998 issue of *Ranger Rick* magazine, with the permission of the publisher, the National Wildlife Federation. Copyright © 1998 by the National Wildlife Federation.

"Champs." By permission of James M. Janik and *Boys' Life*: April 1998, published by the Boy Scouts of America.

"Treasure in the Trash" by Jeannie McGinnis. First published April 1998 in *On The Line* magazine. Reprinted by permission of the author.

"The Problem With Georgina" by Debbie Levy. Used by permission of Highlights for Children, Inc., Columbus, Ohio. Copyright © 1998.

"Danger On The Red Planet" by Sigmund Brouwer. First appeared in *Clubhouse* Magazine, May 1998. Reprinted by permission of the author. Author's website: coolreading.com.

"Sapphire's Eyes" by E. M. Schumacher. First appeared in February/March 1998 *Horsepower* Magazine for Young Horse Lovers.

"A Place Of My Own" by Judith Montgomery Inman. Reprinted with permission of *Pockets*, a devotional magazine for children, May 1998. Copyright © The Upper Room, P. O. Box 189, Nashville, TN 37202.

"A Peruvian Christmas" by Diana Conway, reprinted from *Children's Writer*, November 1998, by permission of the author.

"The Grass Is Too Tall" by Nancy Lammers was first published in *On The Line*, April 1998. Copyright © 1998 by Nancy G. Lammers. Reprinted with author's permission.

"San Luis Rey" by Annette C. Deamond. Reprinted by permission of CRICKET magazine, July 1998, Vol. 25, No. 11 CRICKET, © 1998 by Annette C. Deamond.